79?
s shou e return

7

D1433305

IRISH THEATER
in America

Irish Studies

James MacKillop, *Series Editor*

Other titles in Irish Studies

Catholic Emancipations: Irish Fiction from Thomas Moore to James Joyce
Emer Nolan

Contemporary Irish Cinema: From The Quiet Man *to* Dancing at Lughnasa
James MacKillop, ed.

Grand Opportunity: The Gaelic Revival and Irish Society, 1893–1910
Timothy G. McMahon

An Irish Literature Reader: Poetry, Prose, Drama. 2d ed.
Maureen O'Rourke Murphy and James MacKillop, eds.

Joyce and Reality: The Empirical Strikes Back
John Gordon

Of Irish Descent: Origin Stories, Genealogy, and the Politics of Belonging
Catherine Nash

Party Pieces: Oral Storytelling and Social Performance in Joyce and Beckett
Alan W. Friedman

Two Irelands: Literary Feminisms North and South
Rebecca Pelan

Twentieth-Century Irish Drama: Mirror up to Nation
Christopher Murray

Women, Press, and Politics During the Irish Revival
Karen Steele

IRISH THEATER
in America

Essays on
IRISH THEATRICAL DIASPORA

Edited by
John P. Harrington

Syracuse University Press

Use of the following material in chapter 7 is gratefully acknowledged:
John Quinn Papers. Manuscripts and Archives Division. The New York
Public Library. Astor, Lenox and Tilden Foundations.

The paper used in this publication meets the minimum requirements
of American National Standard for Information Sciences—Permanence
of Paper for Printed Library Materials, ANSI Z39-1984.∞™

For a listing of books published and distributed by Syracuse University Press,
visit our Web site at SyracuseUniversityPress.syr.edu.

ISBN-13: 978-0-8156-3169-9
ISBN-10: 0-8156-3169-3

Library of Congress Cataloging-in-Publication Data
Irish theater in America : essays on Irish theatrical diaspora / edited by
John P. Harrington.
p. cm. — (Irish studies)
Includes bibliographical references and index.
ISBN 978-0-8156-3169-9 (alk. paper)
1. English drama—Irish authors—History and criticism.   2. English drama—
Irish authors—Appreciation—United States.   3. Theater—United States—History.
4. Irish—United States—History.   I. Harrington, John P.
PR8783.I75 2009
792.09415'0973—dc22
2008051656

Contents

Contributors

CHRISTOPHER BERCHILD is an assistant professor in the Department of Theater at Indiana State University, where he teaches theater history, play analysis, theater theory, and directing and serves as advisor for the graduate (MA) program. He has served as artistic director for the Claremont School of Theatre Arts at Pomona College in California for four years, edited *TheatreForum* (an international journal for theater studies), and has worked for DeafWest Theater for the Deaf in Los Angeles.

JOAN FITZPATRICK DEAN is Curators Distinguished Professor and professor of English, University of Missouri, Kansas City. Her books include *Dancing at Lughnasa* (Cork University Press) and *Riot and Great Anger: Stage Censorship in Twentieth-Century Ireland* (University of Wisconsin Press).

CLAIRE GLEITMAN is associate professor and chair in the Department of English at Ithaca College in New York, where she teaches dramatic literature. Most recently, her work has been included in *The Concise Companion to Contemporary British and Irish Drama* (Blackwell); *Out of History: Essays on the Writings of Sebastian Barry* (Catholic University of America Press); and *The Cambridge Companion to Twentieth-Century Irish Drama*.

NICHOLAS GRENE is professor of English literature at Trinity College Dublin and the founding chair of the Irish Theatrical Diaspora project. He has published widely on Irish drama and on Shakespeare, his recent books including *The Politics of Irish Drama* (Cambridge University Press), *Shakespeare's Serial History Plays* (Cambridge University Press) and (co-edited with Chris Morash) *Irish Theatre on Tour: Irish Theatrical Diaspora Series 1* (Carysfort Press).

JOHN P. HARRINGTON is dean of the School of Humanities, Arts, and Social Sciences at Rensselaer Polytechnic in Troy, New York. He is the author of *The Irish Beckett, The Irish Play on the New York Stage,* and *The Life of the Neighborhood Playhouse on Grand Street.* Harrington is also editor of the *Modern and Contemporary Irish Drama* anthology in the Norton Critical Editions series.

PETER KUCH is the inaugural Eamon Cleary Professor of Irish Studies at the University of Otago, Dunedin. Former convenor of Irish studies at the University of New South Wales, he has been a visiting fellow at Trinity College Dublin and at the Humanities Research Centre, Canberra.

PATRICK LONERGAN lectures in English at National University of Ireland, Galway. He writes about theater in the west of Ireland for the *Irish Times,* is reviews editor of *Irish Theatre Magazine,* and is an officer of the International Association for the Study of Irish Literatures. He has lectured on Irish drama at many venues, including the Royal Irish Academy, the Edinburgh International Festival, and the Notre Dame Irish Seminar.

LUCY McDIARMID, Marie Frazee-Baldassarre Professor of English at Montclair State, was a fellow of the Dorothy and Lewis B. Cullman Center for Scholars and Writers at the New York Public Library for the academic year 2005–6. While at the Cullman Center, she completed a study of "the peacock dinner" (18 January 1914), the dinner arranged by Yeats, Pound, and Lady Gregory in honor of the poet and anti-imperialist Wilfrid Scawen Blunt. Her essay on that topic, "A Box for Wilfrid Blunt," appeared in the January 2005 issue of *PMLA.* Her book *The Irish Art of Controversy* was published by Cornell University Press in 2006. Her other books include *Auden's Apologies for Poetry* (Princeton), *Saving Civilization: Yeats, Eliot, and Auden Between the Wars* (Cambridge), *Lady Gregory: Selected Writings,* edited with Maureen Waters (Penguin), and *High and Low Moderns: Literature and Culture 1889–1939,* edited with Maria DiBattista (Oxford).

DIERDRE McFEELY is completing a Ph.D. at Trinity College Dublin on the politics of Dion Boucicault's Irish plays.

CHRISTINA HUNT MAHONY is the director of the Center of Irish Studies at the Catholic University of America in Washington, D.C. She is the author of *Contemporary Irish Literature: Transforming Tradition* and the editor of *Out of History: Essays on the Writings of Sebastian Barry* and *The Future of Irish Studies: Report of the Irish Forum,* published in 2006.

MICK MOLONEY, New York University Global Distinguished Professor of Music, is the author of *Far From the Shamrock Shore: The Story of Irish American History Through Song,* released by Crown Publications in February 2002 with an accompanying compact disc on Shanachie Records. He holds a Ph.D. in folklore and folklife from the University of Pennsylvania and has taught ethnomusicology, folklore, and Irish studies courses at the University of Pennsylvania, Georgetown, and Villanova Universities, as well as NYU. Moloney has recorded and produced over forty albums of traditional music and acted as adviser for scores of festivals and concerts all over America. In 1999 he was awarded the National Heritage Award from the National Endowment for the Arts, which is the highest official honor a traditional artist can receive in the United States. His essay on Harrigan and Hart appears in different form in the liner notes to *McNally's Row of Flats* (Compass Records CO 6440).

MAUREEN MURPHY is interim dean, School of Education and Allied Human Services, and professor of curriculum and teaching at Hofstra University.

GWEN OREL writes for *Back Stage,* the *New York Times, American Theatre,* and other periodicals. From 1999 to 2004 she ran the Southern Writers' Project as literary manager of the Alabama Shakespeare Festival. Orel produces Celtic Music concerts for the Folk Project of New Jersey, where in 2005, she presented Mick Moloney. A graduate of Stanford University, she holds a Ph.D. in theater from the University of Pittsburgh.

Introduction

JOHN P. HARRINGTON

The third annual Irish Theatrical Diaspora conference was held at Glucks-
man Ireland House at New York University in April 2006 on the theme of
"Irish Theater in America." The previous meetings had been devoted to
"Irish Theatre on Tour" and to "Irish Theatre in Britain." Through a kind
of configuration like astronomical triangulations that are very likely but not
fully predictable, the 2006 meeting happened or happened because at the
same time there were Broadway openings of Conor McPherson's *Shining
City* and Martin MacDonagh's *The Lieutenant of Inishmore* and a Broadway
revival of Brian Friel's *Faith Healer*. Simultaneously, there were off-Broadway
vehicles at New York's Irish Repertory Theatre and the Irish Arts Center
as well as continuing discussions on the Great White Way about distinc-
tively Irish successes, such as Garry Hynes; failures, something that even
Friel has not been immune to in New York; a host of new Irish dramatists
recently produced in New York such as Enda Walsh or Mark O'Rowe; and
the even greater host of Irish playwrights who have not been prominently or
consistently produced in America, especially Tom Murphy or Marina Carr.
Disagreements about what was happening or what was not happening made
it clear that Irish theater in America was not the same as Irish theater in
Ireland and that this difference was at the same time a most obvious and
conspicuous and also an unarticulated dimension of cultural transaction in
the globalized context of the early twenty-first century.

One interesting discussion of the conference not memorialized here was
a panel intended to add the media press perspective to the academic one.
In one of the final sessions, Belinda McKeon, who writes about theater for
Irish Theatre Magazine and the *Irish Times,* and is also an Irish playwright

addition, the Irish Research Council for the Humanities and Social Sciences has funded an Irish Theatrical Diaspora Project on "The Internationalization of Irish Drama, 1975–2005." This research project "will locate the development of Irish theatrical culture during this period in a comparative international context, with a major focus on Ireland's changing relationships with the wider world."[6] The results of the project will have social science as well as scholarly impact and help assess interconnections between Ireland's cultural practices and its economic standing in the world marketplace.

The essays in this volume contribute to this evolving subject area on how Ireland's relationships with the world have been more complex than they are often represented and how the "wider world" is already developing new relationships with Ireland. Interactions, as these essays document, have been developing for some time, but at the end of the twentieth century, marked by a new leadership role for Ireland in the European Union, questions of national relationships and relations between large countries and small ones have taken on new urgency. The situation was memorably phrased by Fintan O'Toole, a public intellectual as familiar with spheres of international trade as with international theater. He noted that end of century brought a series of anniversaries of nationalist victories at the beginning of the century and that these events resonated differently now than then:

> This is the paradox of the Republic in the aftermath of the British Empire: its national independence is underwritten by transnational corporations and by a supra-national European Union. Its sovereignty is a power that can be exercised mostly by giving it up. . . . Its cultural distinctiveness lies not in any inherited tradition but in the particular way it reacts to an overload of global stimuli, taking possession of Anglo-American norms, putting its own stamp on them and exporting them back to England, America and the rest of the world.[7]

This is a new, undeniable, and underexamined dynamic. In terms of theater, for example, it provokes consideration of the formative experiences in America by Irish playwrights such as Brian Friel or Marina Carr or the stage director Garry Hynes, who were all U.S.-based for important early phases of their careers. In his essay in this volume on *Dancing at Lughnasa* in the United States and Ireland, Patrick Lonergan discusses an interrelationship of Ireland and America around Friel's work in which the extraordinarily positive America reception of the play had a retroactive effect on the previously understated reception of the play in Ireland. Lonergan has located a paradox similar to O'Toole's. The theatrical interaction is not one of America accepting gratefully dramatic gifts from Ireland. In this case, at least, it is one in which Irish reception is instead conditioned by international venues and international endorsement shapes Irish acceptance.

That international influence over national validation is merely a single force in a complex relation. Though there has been some eager reception in America of playwrights of work less familiar than Synge or Friel, there has also been conspicuous resistance to work that extends beyond predictable expectations. Memorable examples in recent years of vocal disappointment in America of new work from Ireland include Marina Carr's *On Raftery's Hill* in Washington, D.C., in 2000 and Tom MacIntyre's *The Great Hunger* in 1988. I have written previously about the latter and how New Yorkers appeared to be disappointed that what they were seeing was not what they thought of as the "real" Abbey Theatre and how once outside its nitch Irish theater risked duplicating New York theater strengths. The second of these perceptions is the "Coals-to-Newcastle" complaint: if the Irish National Theatre comes to New York with work inspired by Grotowski or Peter Brook instead of Synge or Friel, they are viewed as strangers from afar bearing nothing but what America already had.[8] What, then, is a national theater to do? Two of the contributors to this volume have explored this syndrome. Christopher Berchild, in "Ireland Rearranged: Contemporary Irish Drama and the Irish American Stage," has studied how Irish theater is presented to the specifically Irish American, diasporic audience. In this "community" and its theater producers, he defines a typology of Irish theater companies as conservative, moderate, or aggressive in degrees of change they present to their core audiences and how these programming alternatives represent company goals that are respectively nostalgic, educational, and artistically assertive. It is not a revelation to learn that art and commerce are frequently antithetical and coexisting in close quarters. However, in this context Berchild is able to infer from this box-office function new conclusions about Irish American identity. Christina Hunt Mahoney also defines a new typology, but of audiences rather than companies: the Irish American audience along with habitual theatergoers, social scene theatergoers, and "Big Night Outers." The expectations of all groups are defined around those forms of eloquence that Deane described as maladies for Brian Friel, and theater as a participatory, audience-driven art form consequently limits experimentation and what

Berchild calls artistic assertiveness. Both authors also discuss exceptions to this general syndrome of box-office pressure.

The expectations about Irish drama among theatergoers in America are well defined because they have been developed over a considerable span of time. It can even be said that Irish drama has a longer history in American than in Ireland. Irish dramatists had of course been producing work for London venues at least since the Restoration, and there were occasional works that chose Ireland as subject. But when, in New York, in the 1860s, Dion Boucicault defined himself as an Irish playwright writing Irish plays about Ireland, he was considerably in advance of late-century Irish historical melodramas or the famous declaration of Irish theater by Lady Gregory, W. B. Yeats, and Edward Martyn in the West of Ireland in 1897. Insofar as it is descended from Boucicault, even if in reaction to his "stage Irishman," Irish drama can be said to have originated on foreign soil and developed internationally. The fact that Boucicault's Irish dramas *performed* Ireland before a mixed and an Irish American audience heightened tensions deeply embedded in nineteenth-century American immigrant society. Among the complex dimensions of Irish theater in America is the tension created by performing it—Irishness—before an audience in part identified with Ireland and in part unrelated or actively hostile to it. Two of the contributors to this volume focus on the evidence of contemporary American print journalism to analyze the kind of provocation represented by what were in a period marked by race riots not at all merely light entertainments. In the record of the reaction to Boucicault's *The Shaughraun* in the *Irish World*, Deirdre McFeely finds that widespread reaction to Boucicault among Irish Americans was not pride but disappointment: not disappointment in caricature of manners, but disappointment in insufficiently Irish-nationalist politics. However, contemporary with that disappointment, Gwen Orel documents from a survey of source material from *Irish World* and other journals significant pride in the same community in Boucicault the successful playwright as role model and community-builder for them in a hostile environment. Both essays examine a Boucicault letter to the *Irish American* and find contradictory resonances: one set to the play and to Irish politics, and the other to the author and to American immigrant experience. In a broader historical survey, Maureen Murphy also studies the relation of Irish drama to Irish American communities and the manner in which this self-representation before mixed audiences evolved from Boucicault through and beyond John Patrick Shanley. The

Irish drama that originated with Boucicault in America was replaced by the Irish drama of the twentieth-century launched by Gregory, Yeats, and Martyn, which, for American audiences, had greater authenticity by originating in Ireland and more compelling exoticism than "Irish" plays that mirrored American experience.

Readers of this volume and attendees at the Irish Theatrical Diaspora conference in New York City were treated to another compelling account of mixed audiences, Irish American identities, and the tensions involved in, at the same time and place, "being Irish and being American," by Mick Moloney, the great folklorist, musician, scholar, and historian. In the opening essay of this volume, Moloney, who has received the National Heritage Award from the American National Endowment for the Arts for his studies of sung music as an instrument of cultural memory, provides a very spirited account of the career of Ned Harrigan. His new work adds two dimensions to our understanding of Harrigan. First, Moloney establishes the extent to which his work was a collaboration not only with the well-known partner Tony Hart but also with the little-known son-in-law David Braham. Second, he also traces how Harrigan's progress from song-skits to full-length musical plays provided a foundation for the development of the American musical: how, in other words, Harrigan and Hart led to Rodgers and Hart. As a musician, Moloney is able to add to historical information additional theatrical insight into how performance requirements would lead to performance design such as instrumentation or intermissions. Following Harrigan's journey from nineteenth- to twentieth-century musical entertainment, Moloney refers us to very performative cultures such as that of marches and parades as well as to isolated and intriguing instances such as transvestite blackface touring troupes in Midwest America. Like the other authors in this volume writing about the nineteenth century, Moloney finds in Irish theater in America a complicated and sometimes contradictory dynamic that, in a society in transition, helped create new neighbors and form new communities. A more musical version of the Mick Moloney performance of the Ned Harrigan story can be found in his popular CD *McNally's Row of Flats*.[9]

Not at all immune to box-office pressure, and in fact a quite ready and willing collaborator with it, Ned Harrigan's story also introduces the element of commercial influences that so often inform or contrast artistic ones. These interactions can be as different as the cases of St. John Ervine's *John Ferguson*, which in America provided the business plan and box-office opportunity for the Theatre Guild, or Michael Flatley's *Riverdance* and spinoffs, which were "Celtic" Broadway extravaganzas of spectacular American scale. Two authors in this volume present detailed case studies of Irish theater as intersections of arts with commerce. Peter Kuch examines records of the career of George Tallis—Irishman, Australian, and theater, radio, and cinema producer—to help define the material culture of theater. In this case, Irish theater in America (during Tallis's regular visits to New York) projects beyond itself to impact on Australian culture. In another case, as presented by Lucy McDiarmid, Irish theater in America (during Lady Gregory's visits to Chicago) fulfills some of the expectations for the cultural production of art as defined by Pierre Bourdieu. Using the case of the "guarantee fund dispute," a debate over where raised revenues for Hugh Lane's art gallery in Dublin would be redirected when government refused to support the planned initiative, McDiarmid studies the role of "helpers" embedded in production of Irish theater in America—the lawyers, bankers, society hostesses, and cultural committees hovering over productions of the Abbey Theatre on American tour. In archival papers housed in the New York Public Library, McDiarmid finds correspondence and other records of Lady Gregory's strategic "development" of cultural workers for her national theater enterprise and how, rather than seeking merely to please the Irish diaspora by representing its homeland, she very shrewdly managed and "developed" the diaspora for Irish cultural purposes. That is an early twentieth-century practice not unknown in the early twenty-first century.

If those two cases suggest exploitation of the American field by Irish theater producers, two other examples of reception studies suggest some of the provocative destabilizing influences Irish theater has brought to American culture. In the 1960s, Micheál Mac Liammóir toured America with his one-man show *The Importance of Being Oscar*. His representation of Wilde was simultaneous with and a provocation to a period of uncertainty in America over presentation of homosexuality. Joan FitzPatrick Dean studies the reception of this touring production. Though Mac Liammóir did not design his production around representation of homosexuality, he and his work certainly suggested that subject and by doing so represented to America a new dimension of being Irish. The reception was not warm, and Dean finds in archival evidence handwritten notes of Mac Liammóir's frustration with American "excretia." In a second essay of reception study, Clare Gleitman finds a more public destabilizing force grounded in international relations in her examination of the performance of Frank McGuinness's *Someone Who'll Watch Over Me* in New York in 1992. The dramatic situation in McGuinness's play about the Irish, British, and American prisoners had to evoke in American immediate memory the case of hostages taken in Lebanon in the 1980s, and its treatment of the situation made certainties of national identity at least problematic. Gleitman analyzes the critical reception and the timeliness of the play in 1992, and she is able to infer from that reception some of the forces that control reception of this Irish play in America and elsewhere post-9/11.

Dean and Gleitman have focused on the complex nature of production reception. Two other authors have made that subject diachronic by studying the complex nature of production history. Like Patrick Lonergan, Nicholas Grene compares theater receptions in New York and in Dublin: in Grene's case, the work is Brian Friel's *Faith Healer*. From unpublished drafts of the work and correspondence of the playwright now housed in the National Library of Ireland, Grene is able to hypothesize on the impact of venue on reception. Further, the nature of accounts of the receptions of *Faith Healer* in Dublin and in New York allows him to comment on the mythologies of retrospectively constructed production histories. I have taken a similar topic in my essay in this volume, "Beckett and America," where the examples of the mythologies of the history of *Waiting for Godot* in New York City contrast sharply with the successful artistic endeavors represented by Beckett's *Film*, which was shot in the 1960s in New York under his observation, and the American composer Morton Feldman's scoring of Beckett's *Words and Music* in the 1980s.

This volume, *Irish Theater in America*, provides a comprehensive dossier on how Irish theater in America is not the same as Irish theater, how Irish theater is fundamentally international in relations including American, how the transatlantic cultural transaction it represents is inherently complex, and how accounts of this intercultural phenomenon—including mythologized ones—must embrace informative, provocative, and counterintuitive nuances of old worlds meeting new ones in order fully represent and usefully forecast the nature of national performance in the contemporary international context.

IRISH THEATER
in America

1

Harrigan, Hart, and Braham

Irish America and the Birth of the American Musical

MICK MOLONEY

Most people are familiar with Tin Pan Alley, that kaleidoscopic outpouring of songwriting that crystallized in the first two decades of the twentieth century. Yet few are aware that many of the finest songs in the history of American popular music were already decades old by that time. Written in New York City from the early 1870s on by the famed songwriting team of Ed Harrigan and David Braham, they were published in sheet music, songsters, and. songbooks and sung from coast to coast. Harrigan and his stage partner Tony Hart became household names performing the songs in lavish theatrical productions that were the talk of the land. They were hugely successful figures who for decades enjoyed almost impossible fame and renown and lived life on a grand scale, making vast fortunes by the standards of the day.

They were the original men who owned Broadway. Yet their story ultimately ends in conflict and tragedy and, for one of the partners, destitution and madness. It is an epic tale that for drama and poignancy far exceeds the melodramatic plots and outcomes of the plays they starred in.

The songs were written as an integral component of stage sketches and later as full-length theatrical productions, which dominated the New York stage for over twenty years between the early 1870s and the mid-1890s. They were performed on the vaudeville and minstrel stage and in variety theaters big and small. They were sung in concert saloons and taverns and in people's homes wherever there was a piano or organ handy. The songs were beautifully constructed with Braham's gorgeous melodies and Harrigan's finely crafted lyrics painting vivid images of the realities of daily life in urban America at a time when millions of immigrants were flocking to the land of opportunity in search of a new life. Yet today these songs, their authors, and the remarkably talented men who performed them on the stage are largely forgotten.

Ed Harrigan's story begins with his grandfather, a fisherman from County Cork. Like many other men from the Southwest of Ireland he was drawn by the lure of riches in the cod fishing trade to emigrate to the eastern Canadian province of Newfoundland in the late eighteenth century. He settled there with his wife and raised a family. A son, William Harrigan, was born in Carbonier, Newfoundland, in 1799. Indications were that he had a troubled childhood. In his early teens he followed the seafaring trade and became alienated from his family in the process. He left home for good, shipped on board a Yankee clipper as a cabin boy, and worked his way over the next decade up to first mate. He renounced the Catholicism of his parents and became a Protestant. In the early 1830s he was staying at a boarding house in Norfolk, Virginia, and there he met and fell in love with Ellen Rogers, the daughter of the woman who owned and ran the boarding house. Ellen had been born in Charlestown, Massachusetts, in 1814, the daughter of a gunner on board the *Chesapeake,* a U.S. Navy ship. He was killed in the War of 1812 and her mother moved with her daughter to Norfolk.

When her mother died, Ellen married William Harrigan. They moved to New York City and settled in the Lower East Side of Manhattan in a heavily Irish area known as Corlear's Hook near where the Williamsburg Bridge now stands. They had thirteen children but only four survived infancy. One of those was Edward Harrigan, who was born on 26 October 1844, the year before the beginning of the Great Irish Famine. Corlear's Hook was to become even more Irish in the next decade as it accommodated floods of Irish immigrants fleeing starvation and misery in their ravaged homeland. By 1860 over 50 percent of the inhabitants of the Lower East Side of Manhattan were Irish born. Edward (or, as he became known to most of his friends, Ned) Harrigan grew up in this teeming Irish neighborhood on the perimeter of the notorious Five Points District.

Harrigan became interested in the stage through the influence of his mother, who used to do song and dance routines at home taken from the minstrel shows that swept the country in the 1840s and 50s. Harrigan took part in amateur hour, blackface performances in his mid-teens with a well-known minstrel troupe called Campbell's Minstrels, but it was an occasional pursuit—little more than a hobby. By this stage he was a full-time wage earner. He had been apprenticed by his father to the trade of ship's caulker—making ships waterproof. By the standards of the day this was a skilled, well-paid, secure, and prestigious job.

But his life was about to change dramatically. His father divorced his mother when Ned was eighteen. He didn't like his stepmother, a severe and very strict Methodist widow, and Ned hit the road and went to the South to Florida, Louisiana, and Alabama, and stayed there during the Civil War years. After the war he returned to New York briefly and then headed off again. He sailed to Central America, traveled across Panama and then up the West Coast, and arrived in San Francisco in 1866. He found it easy to get work as a caulker in this great port town, but he became increasingly fascinated by the popular stage, which was now flourishing in San Francisco. The city had enjoyed great prosperity and growth ever since the Gold Rush of 1849, and theaters and places of amusement flourished throughout the city. People had money to spend and they flocked to minstrel and variety shows.

Ed Harrigan started to appear at local theaters, including the Olympic, and he began to write songs and sketches. He left the caulking trade and took to the stage. He performed with minstrel groups and briefly toured Northern California as a solo artist before he teamed up with Alex O'Brien, a singer and comic. Alex was an alcoholic, however, and was unreliable, and the partnership did not last long. He acquired another partner named Sam Rickey, and they enjoyed some success in San Francisco and later in Chicago. They returned east and got an engagement in the Globe Theater in New York in 1870. By now Harrigan was starting to make a name as a very talented singer, banjo player, and songwriter. But Sam Rickey had the same problem with alcohol as O'Brien and that partnership also ended.

Harrigan then traveled as a member of Manning's Minstrels. In Chicago he met a young man who sang and danced named Tony Cannon. Tony was born 25 July 1855 in Hill Street just behind St. Anne's Church in Worcester, Massachusetts. His father, Anthony Cannon, and his mother, Mary Sweeney, were immigrants from Clare Island, County Mayo. Young Tony was the eldest of five children. He grew up in Worcester and appears to have been a problem child from the outset. He missed school and terrorized the neighborhood kids, but he loved to sing and dance. Unknown to his parents, he began to organize concerts in the basement of the family house when he was eleven. Boys were charged one cent—the girls got in for free! He nearly hanged himself accidentally in a sketch rehearsal and was rescued from near death by his father. Tony was sent at the age of twelve to a state reformatory—the Lyman School in Westbury. He hated it and before long escaped. He briefly joined a traveling circus as a cook, but then he left and started to make a living singing and dancing in saloons. He moved to Providence, Rhode Island, joined the Arlington Minstrels, and became known as Master Antonio. He left that company for Madame Rentz's Minstrels, a group of female impersonators in blackface, and ended up in Chicago with them at the same time as Ed Harrigan.

Harrigan and Cannon teamed up immediately. They needed a stage name. They didn't think that Cannon sounded right, so Tony changed his surname to Hart, and the duo became officially known as Harrigan and Hart. One of their first major engagements together was in Boston, in the Howard Athenaeum in 1871, where they were hired by impresario John Stetson. They were billed as the "Famed Californian Artists," though Tony had never been west of Chicago! According to Harrigan biographer Richard Moody, "No one could match their walkarounds, their jigs and clogs, Harrigan's trembling tenor and Hart's tender falsetto and above all their joyous and extravagant clowning."

They made a salary of $150 a week each, which was rich for the times. At the invitation of Tony Pastor, the charismatic entertainer who later was to achieve lasting fame as the man who invented vaudeville, they left Boston and took up an engagement in New York, first at the Union Square Theater and later, after a couple of East coast and Midwest tours, at Pastor's Theater. After a brief stint there they were hired by the impresario Josh Hart to appear in variety shows in his Theater Comique at 541 Broadway. Before Harrigan left Boston, John Braham, who was the leader of the orchestra at the Atheneum, had given him a letter of introduction to his Uncle David, who was leader of the pit orchestra at the Theater Comique. Born in England on 1 January 1834, David Braham came from a very musical family. He came to America with his brother Joe in 1856. By this time he was an accomplished violinist and had no trouble finding employment as a musician in New York.

Harrigan and Braham decided to write songs together. Harrigan visited Braham's house frequently to work on the songwriting. But he ended up being totally distracted by a beautiful young girl in the house, Annie

Braham, one of David's five daughters. And he kept coming back to the house even when he did not have to. The attention was reciprocated and a lifelong romance was under way. Within a few years they were married—she was seventeen and he was thirty-two. Annie had ten pregnancies. Three children died in childbirth but seven survived. And by all accounts Ed was a devoted husband and father for the whole of their marriage.

Harrigan and Hart settled into the Theater Comique at 541 Broadway. Before long they were the most popular artists on the bill and eventually produced the whole show. Originally they leased the building from Josh Hart on a show-by-show basis, but then they took it over themselves as a full-time partnership venture. It was at this time that Harrigan started to write thematic sketches, which began as afterpieces following a night of variety. He based these on life in the mostly Irish neighborhood of the Lower East Side of Manhattan. These afterpieces, including "Who Owns the Clothes Line," "The Gallant 69th," "The Day I Kem Over," and "The Day We Celebrate" were a success, and he started to expand them both in length and complexity. It was a sketch called "The Mulligan Guard" that was to become their first monster hit. "The Mulligan Guard" was a mythical Irish American target-shooting company located in the Lower East Side. Target companies were informal clubs organized in great numbers after the Civil War. They held excursions, picnics, and other social outings, which often turned into drunken revelries, and they conducted an inordinate number of marches through city streets. According to Moody:

> Every loyal patriotic able-bodied man who loved to march, shoot, and carouse could join the Cleveland Light Guards, The Garibaldi Guards, The Lafayette Battery, Oregon Blues, First Ward Magnetizers, Mustache Fusiliers. The Washington Market Chowder Guard, The Napper Tandy Light Artillery Company, The Liberty Guards, the Gotham Guards, The Kelly Guards, The Killarney Volunteers. On one Sunday alone over 127 companies comprising over 12,000 men paraded up Broadway.

"The Mulligan Guard" sketch was satire from the outset. The largely working-class audience who knew about and often were members of these target companies could relate directly to the characters and to the humor. There were only three members of the Mulligan Guard. There was Dan Mulligan, who was a tailor in the Seventh Ward, and Captain Jack Hussey, who was named after a baggage master at Castle Garden whose chest was covered with medals awarded for rescues from drowning along the East River. The third member was a young boy named Morgan Benson, an African American teenager who was barely able to carry a target that was almost as big as himself. Harrigan led the company as the captain, wearing an oversized Napoleonic hat and an ill-fitting military tunic. Strapped to his belt was a huge sword that dragged along the ground. Hart, the one-man army, wore undersized clothes, leaving an expanse of dirty white shirt showing between his tight fitting tunic and his shrunken pants. On his head he wore a moth-eaten giant shako, a plumed military hat.

The song Harrigan and Braham wrote with this name was a major commercial success. It was the signature tune of the Mulligan Guard series, and Harrigan would introduce it time and again into various productions decades after he and Braham wrote the original. It was by far their most popular song. Ironically, it was the only one that they signed away outright to William Pond and Company. It was sung on every New York City street corner by newsboys. It spread through sheet music and songsters across the United States and beyond. The catchy melody was adopted as a standard in the repertory of the United States brass bands of the day, including Patrick Sarsfield Gilmore's Band and John Philip Sousa's Band—the two most popular ensembles of late nineteenth-century America. It was also played further afield by military bands such as the Coldstream Guards in England. It is even featured in Kipling's novel *Kim* where it is performed by a British regimental band in India. Little did Kipling, that grand supporter of all things British and imperial, know that it was a satire on the military and written by an Irish American!

The lyrics for "The Mulligan Guard" are:

I crave your condescension I'll tell you what we know
From marching in the Mulligan Guard to the Sligo Ward below
Our captains's name was Hussey, a Tipperary man
He shouldered his sword like a Russian Duke whenever he took command.
We shouldered guns and marched and marched away
From Baxter Street we marched to Avenue A
Our fifes and drums so sweetly they did play
As we marched, marched, marched in the Mulligan Guard
When the band played Garryowen or the Connemara Pet
With a rub a dub dub we marched in the mud to the military step
With the green above the red boys to show where we come from

Our guns we'd lift with a right shoulder shift as we marched to the beat
   of the drum
When we got home at night boys the divil a bit we'd ate
We'd all and drink a sup of whiskey strong and nate
And we'd all march home together as slippery as lard
The solid men would all fall in and march to the Mulligan Guard

The song and the sketch were so popular that Harrigan made a daring move and considerably expanded a version of the sketch into a full-length play. It was an instant smash hit. A whole series of plays on the Mulligan Guard theme resulted over the next seven years, and a cast of central characters expanded as the series developed.

In the series, the main character is Dan Mulligan, an immigrant from County Tipperary who served in the Irish Brigade in the American Civil War. He works at various times as a sailor, garbage collector, and saloonkeeper, and eventually he becomes an alderman in the Irish-dominated Tammany political network. Dan is good-natured and garrulous but at times ill-tempered; he likes to have a few drinks, he is very proud to be American, and he is equally proud to be Irish. His wife Cordelia (played by Annie Yeamans, who was originally from the Isle of Man) is a practical, faithful, generally even-tempered, lifelong companion who is always looking for ways to improve the family circumstances. Rebecca Allop (played by Tony Hart in drag) is a much married and much widowed African American neighbor who at times was Cordelia's housekeeper. She is also a bookkeeper and takes bets on a variety of gambling ventures. Her consort is Captain Sam Primrose, a flamboyant African American (played by Johnny Wild) and very much an urban, Zip Coon dandy prototype. Another African American character of dubious character, Palestine Puter, was played by William Gray. Playing a prominent part in all the Mulligan Guard productions were the Skidmore Guards, an African American target company. In the tradition of minstrelsy, the members are represented by white actors in blackface, often including Harrigan and Hart.

There were many Irishmen in the plays, such as Walsingham McSwiney who ran "The Wee Drop" saloon, and there were Germans like Gustav Lochmuller the local butcher with an Irish American wife. A Chinese immigrant, Ah Wung, ran a laundry, flophouse, and opium den. In later productions Harrigan would introduce Italian and Jewish characters as those ethnic populations increased in the Lower East Side. Harrigan and Braham wrote scores of songs for these plays, and, like the dances, which often accompanied them, they were woven seamlessly into the plot and action of the theatrical productions in a fashion that anticipated the birth of the modern musical. Harrigan had a great eye for talent and assembled a brilliant and versatile cast that could play a variety of roles with ease. All were "no namers" that Harrigan discovered, but they went on to achieve stardom with him. They earned good salaries and were also paid for rehearsals—a major innovation in American theater at that time. They were a happy crew and almost all stayed with Harrigan for years.

Harrigan and Hart were not the first to depict lower-class American urban life on the stage. Dublin-born John Brougham had done it in the 1860s and so had Augustine Daly. The Dublin-born playwright Dion Boucicault had achieved a measure of popularity with *The Poor of New York*. But compared with Harrigan and Hart's productions their depictions of lower-class life were generic and superficial. It was the deep social insights in Harrigan's works that set them apart from anything that had taken place up to that point on the American stage, along with the extraordinary blend of theater, music, and dance and comedy that was to become the cornerstone of everything they produced. Harrigan and Hart began a series of full-length production runs. A three-month run was the norm for their shows, and this kind of longevity was unprecedented in the history of American theater.

Audiences certainly got value for money. The shows were at least three hours in length. The sets, many designed by people at the pinnacle of their profession, such as David Witham, were positively sumptuous. Master machinist Robert Cutler introduced special sound and lighting effects, often highly dramatic, that were far more adventurous and technically advanced than in any other New York theater. There were overtures and musical bridges between scenes and acts and musical introductions to characters entering the stage, and these were performed in magisterial style by David Braham and his pit orchestra with a lineup that could include up to three fiddles, viola, cello, bass, clarinet, flute, cornets, trombone, timpani, and piano. In each new show there was a combination of very singable original Harrigan and Braham songs and old favorites from previous productions. There was always great dancing, and Harrigan hired the top choreographers of the day to produce the routines.

There were highly entertaining, melodramatic, and often outrageous comic plots and also lots of humor and slapstick. There was interethnic rivalry in abundance, and perhaps this acted as a catharsis for audiences experiencing the day-to-day stress of adjusting to new neighbors in unfamiliar surroundings. There were wonderfully authentic costumes—in fact Harrigan and Hart often traveled around Manhattan buying clothes off the backs of newly arrived immigrants. The characters in the shows were highly realistic and accessible to the audiences, and they appeared in familiar social settings. Moody quotes Harrigan as saying: "I didn't have to hunt up characters, I had thoroughly familiarized myself with every existing type . . . commingling with these characters in their everyday life . . . Though I use types I try to be as realistic as possible. Not only the costuming and accessories must be correct, but the speech and dialect, the personal 'make up,' the vices and the virtues, habits and customs must all be accurate."

Urban America was seeing itself comprehensively represented on the popular stage for the first time. It was the ultimate theater of realism, and critics did not miss the opportunity to compare Harrigan to Dickens, Balzac, Zola, Molière, and even Euripides. The Harrigan/Braham composition "Babies on Our Block," written in 1879, is a good example of social panorama:

If you want for information or in need of merriment
Come over with me socially to Murphy's tenement
He owns a row of house by in the First Ward by the dock
Where Ireland's represented by the Babies on our Block
There the Whalens and the Phalens from sweet Donaghadee
They are sitting on the railings with their children on their knee
All gossiping and talking with their neighbors in a flock
Singing Little Sally Water with the Babies on our Block
Little Sally Waters sitting in the sun
Crying and weeping for her young man

Rise Sally rise wipe your eye out with your frock
That's sung by the babies a living on our block

Of a warm day in summer when the breeze blows off the sea
A hundred thousand children lay on the Battery
They come from Murphy's building oh their noise would stop a clock
There's no perambulatory with the babies on our block
There's the Clearys and the Learys from sweet Blackwater side
They are laying on the Battery and they're gazing at the tide
All royal blood and noble all of Dan O'Connell's stock

Singing Gravel Greeny Gravel with the Babies on our Block

Oh gravel greeny gravel how green the grasses grow
For all the young pretty fair maidens that I know
Green gravel green wipe your eye out with your frock
That's sung by the babies a living on our block

It's good morning to you landlord come how are you today
When Patrick Murphy Esquire comes up the alleyway
With his shiny silken beaver he's as solid as a rock
The envy of the neighbors boys a living off our block
There's the Bannons and the Gannons Far Downs and Connaughtmen
Quite easy with the shovel and so handy with the pen
All neighborly and friendly with relations by the flock
Singing little Sally Waters with the babies a living on our block

Little Sally Waters sitting in the sun
Crying and weeping for her young man
Rise Sally rise wipe your eye out with your frock
That's sung by the babies a living on our block

A later (1882) Harrigan/Braham song, "McNally's Row of Flats," written for the play *McSorley's Inflation,* offers a more gritty and humorous perspective on tenement living. This shows Harrigan at his best as a wordsmith painting the most evocative of pictures of life in teeming multicultural Lower East Side Manhattan at a time when Irish post-famine immigrants and their descendants were living side by side with their African American neighbors and newly arrived Asian and European immigrants:

Down in Bottle Alley lived Timothy McNally
A wealthy politician and a gentleman at that
Admired by the ladies, the garsoons and the babies
That occupy the building called McNally's Row of Flats.

Chorus–

Ireland and Italy, Jerusalem and Germany,
Chinese and Africans and a paradise for rats.
Jumbled up together in the snow and rainy weather
They constitute the tenants in McNally's Row of flats.

That great conglomeration of men from every nation
The tower of Babylonium couldn't equal that
Peculiar institution where the brogues without dilution
Rattled on together in McNally's Row of Flats.

Chorus

Bags of rags and papers, tramps and other sleepers,
Italian lazaronies and lots of other cats
Lyin' on the benches an dyin' there by inches
From the open ventilation of McNally's Row of Flats

Chorus

It never was expected that the rent would be collected
They levied on the furniture, the bedding, and the slats
It's then you'd see the rally as they battled down the alley
Evicted from the building called McNally's Row of Flats.

Harrigan's realism was of course selective. The popular theater was a place of escape for many mired in the drudgery of hand labor, and Harrigan steered clear of themes like infant mortality, disease, and violent crime. But he certainly did not shy away from provocative social themes such as interethnic and racial disputes and tensions. And the plays were suffused with all manner of personal animosities. Yet despite all the personal and interethnic conflicts in the shows happy, endings always rounded them out and audiences left the theater in good spirits.

The productions were particularly attractive to Irish American audiences that saw themselves represented with uncanny accuracy. The characters were sketched with great attention to detail, and Harrigan moved the image of the Irish on the American stage emphatically away from the simian depictions that had proliferated for decades in England and America.

Harrigan did retain some elements of this stage stereotype, particularly the drinking and fighting. But generally his Irish characters were positively sketched. In some productions they might be vagabonds, pugilists, rogues, or drunks, but never bums. As a whole, they were depicted as jovial, neighborly, talkative, witty, resilient, friendly, sentimental, patriotic, and loyal. And every other one of them seemed to be a singer, dancer, musician, or comic.

Harrigan's low-class Irish urban neighborhood was a warm supportive environment. The world represented was largely the home, saloon, places of work, places of recreation, and the all-important arena of ward politics. By the time Harrigan and Braham wrote the song "Old Boss Barry" for the full length 1888 theatrical production *Waddy Grogan,* the figure of the Irish American Tammany Ward Boss had become a stock figure in American urban politics. He was usually an alderman, the single most crucial grassroots figure in the Irish Tammany network. He provided food, clothing, housing, medicine, domestic guidance, and help with naturalization. He was on hand for weddings, christenings, and wakes. He controlled city jobs. He attended every christening, wake, and major social event in the community. He knew everybody and everybody knew him. He had an intimate knowledge of the lives and concerns of his constituents and presided through a complex system of reciprocal favors and obligations over a world of patronage that he often ruled through fear and intimidation. This figure was also a staple in Irish American popular song in vaudeville and popular theater, as in "Old Boss Barry":

There's a quiet little room at the back of the saloon
That stands on the tip of Cherry Hill
Where men from tenements hold lengthy arguments
On everything besides the liquor bills
The owner of the place has a Connemara face
A leader do you hear me through and through
When he comes in through the door we all bow to the floor
Saying Old Boss Barry how d'ye do

Then it's Old Boss Barry how d'ye do
Is there anything that we can do for you
Come tell us of your plan, we're with you to a man
For Old Boss Barry how d'ye do

He's a dude in the ward and he's perfectly adored
By those in the front and in the rear
And to his constituents he speaks with eloquence
So flowingly beside a keg of beer
For country and the state he's the maker of the slate
A leader do you hear me through and through
Sure the rank and the file they all greet him with a smile
Saying Old Boss Barry how d'ye do

Then his they fall in line around election time
Yes all from the top of Cherry Hill
Sure it's he could colonize and really paralyze
The party that would vote against his will
No office would be take but let him take a rake of boodle
Do you hear me though and through
Sure he's in never out and that's why the people shout
With Old Boss Barry how d'ye do

Religion was one very significant omission from Hannigan and Hart's Irish American world. The overwhelming majority of New York's Irish immigrants might have been Catholics and Democrats, but in Harrigan's plays there was never any mention of creed or faith and this helped set the tone for what became a very American tradition of secular popular entertainment.

It was hard to get a seat in the Theater Comique even though it held over one thousand people. There was plenty of competition. Harrigan and Hart were operating alongside the likes of Edwin Forrest and Edwin Booth in Shakespearean productions. Buffalo Bill was often in New York City with his Wild West show. P. T. Barnum's extravagant productions were taking place nightly in his huge Hippodrome. There were performances by Tony Pastor and Bryant's Minstrels and hundreds of other troupes. Luminaries such as Bret Harte and Mark Twain gave widely publicized public lectures. In the late 1870s Gilbert and Sullivan hit town, and over a decade later Victor Herbert arrived on the scene. All these were highly successful artists, but none could compete in popularity with Harrigan and Hart. They went from success to success and in 1881 moved triumphantly uptown to their New Theater Comique at 728 Broadway, which they designed specially as a permanent home for their productions. As quoted by Moody, the theater was described in the newspaper *Spirit of the Times*, as "the first thoroughly American Theater." There was comfortable seating for 1200 in a main floor, balcony, and gallery. There were nightly shows and matinees on Tuesdays and Fridays. Admission prices ranged from 25 cents to $1.00, and this was easily affordable to working-class audiences. Harrigan stated that wealthy people were welcome "as long as they did not inhibit the shirt sleeve brigade." When they took a break from the Mulligan Guard series, they put on plays such as *The Major, McSorley's Inflation,* and *Squatter Sovereignty,* where most of the action took place in the notorious Irish shantytown in what is now Central Park. All were huge successes and had record runs. In the 1880s Harrigan, Hart, and Braham were at the height of their powers.

But there was trouble on the horizon and it arrived in the form of a beautiful woman. Gertie Granville was an actress who was engaged by Harrigan to appear in *The Major,* the first production at the New Theater Comique. Tony Hart was thoroughly smitten, and after a brief romance they were married. Gertie expected to be part of the inner Harrigan company circle immediately and to get the best female parts, but that was not to be. Many in the company did not like her, especially the women. Annie Harrigan and Annie Yeamans were particularly wary of her motives and viewed her as an ambitious gold digger using Tony as a career stepping-stone. Tensions mounted.

Then the unthinkable happened. On 23 December 1884, the New Theater Comique burned to the ground. The building was uninsured. Offers of assistance poured in, with friends and colleagues offering space for their productions as they made plans for a new home. However, loss of the venue was financially crippling, especially to Hart, who unlike Harrigan and Braham had never earned royalties on composed work. Harrigan and Hart struggled on for a while but things went from bad to worse. The two could hardly have been more different in their personalities. Offstage, Harrigan, a man of sober, disciplined habits, spent his days writing, rehearsing, auditioning, and involving himself in the business aspects of running a theater. His life was devoted to work and family. Tony Hart was most diligent about his responsibilities as a performer, but when the show was over he would enjoy the recreations offered by a great city like New York. He was high-spirited and impetuous and loved the bright lights. Those personality differences never divided them before, but now, under new pressures, they helped widen the growing chasm between the two old friends. Five months after the fire Hart announced that he was leaving the partnership and striking out on his own. Their fans and indeed the general public were aghast, finding it almost impossible to believe that the most famous partnership in America was ending.

Tony's career went downhill very quickly. He was unable to find material of the quality of the Harrigan productions that provided such a perfect vehicle for his great talents. He also began behaving erratically, accentuating a pattern of behavior that had surfaced near the end of his relationship with Harrigan. Then the awful truth came out. Tony Hart was suffering from the advanced ravages of syphilis. Not only was that dreaded disease a death sentence at that time, but most cases declined into insanity in the final stages. Tony Hart was admitted to an asylum in his native Worcester shortly after his last stage performance, *Donnybrook,* at the Boston Athenaeum.

Gertie, too, started to behave oddly and fell mortally ill. She died in March 1890. As recounted by Moody, Hart came out of the asylum for the funeral and, according to the *Dramatic Mirror,* followed the coffin down the aisle of St. John's Roman Catholic Church in Worcester "sobbing like a baby" every yard of the journey. He went into a major decline after Gertie's death and died in Worcester on 4 November 1891, three months after his thirty-sixth birthday, leaving an estate of 80 cents. His friend Nate Goodwin wrote: "That boy caused more joy and sunshine by his delightful gifts than any artist of his time. To refer to him as talented was an insult. Genius was the only word that could be applied. He sang like a nightingale, danced like a fairy and acted like a master comedian. His magnetism was compelling, his personality charming." There was a big funeral in Worcester. Ed Harrigan did not come because he was in the middle of rehearsing for a new show. But he sent a bouquet of flowers with a centerpiece of red roses surrounded by a border of white chrysanthemums. The roses spelled out the one word: "partner."

Life went on. Ed Harrigan opened a new theater on Broadway and Herald Square and named it Harrigan's Theater, later to become known as the Garrick. With most of the Theater Comique cast members he produced popular shows such as *The O'Reagans* and then the hugely successful *Reilly and the 400,* which unveiled the great song hit "Maggie Murphy's Home." *Reilly and the 400* dramatizes themes of upward mobility in American urban ethnic life. Willy Reilly is a pawnbroker on the Lower East Side whose son is a lawyer engaged to be married to the daughter of an extremely prosperous upper-class businessman. Willy Reilly wants to conceal his occupation and masquerades as a baronet. A dastardly German threatens to reveal his true identity. All sorts of hilarity ensue as the drama plays out amid scenes of upper- and lower-class Manhattan neighborhoods. It has of course the usual Harrigan happy ending. The upper-class New York milieu is suggested by the use of the term "the 400"—coined by noted social commentator of the day, Ward McAllister, to denote the number of upper-class swells that could fit into the Delmonico Ballroom.

Emma Pollock, a fifteen-year-old actress from the Lower East Side, played Maggie Murphy. She appears on the stage surrounded by firemen, sailors, coachmen, chippies, seafaring men, vagrants, and fallen women. She dances an Irish jig and breaks into the song that became one of the biggest American hits of the early 1890s. The image of the organ in the parlor deftly denotes the genteel respectability sought by many in working-class life. That Maggie Murphy's mother was a single parent is again evidence of how well Harrigan knew his Irish American community. The life expectancy of postfamine Irish male immigrants was dramatically lower than their female counterparts. Brutally hard working conditions in occupations such as mining, canal, and railroad construction, tunneling and building trades, combined with rampant alcoholism, decimated the male Irish American population and created a whole generation of young widows bringing up their children alone.

Behind a grammar school house,
Near a double tenement
I live with my old mother
And always pay the rent
A bedroom and a parlor is all we call our own
And you're welcome every evening
At Maggie Murphy's Home

One Sunday night it's my delight and pleasure don't you see
Meeting all the girls and boys who work downtown with me
There's an organ in the parlor to give the house a tone
And you're welcome every evening
At Maggie Murphy's home

Such dancing in the parlor
There's a waltz for you and I
Such courting in the corner
And kisses on the sly
Oh bless those leisure hours
That working people know
And they're welcome every evening
At Maggie Murphy's Home

I walk by Hogan's Alley
At the closing of the day
To greet my dear old mother

And hear the neighbors say
Oh there's goes little Maggie
I wish she were my own
And may blessings ever linger
Round Maggie Murphy's Home

There were later shows afterward such as *The Last of the Hogans, The Woolen Stocking,* and *Marty Malone,* but *Reilly and the 400* was to be Harrigan's last major success. New York was changing rapidly. Immigrants from Russia, Ukraine, and Eastern and Southern Europe were replacing the Irish in the New York lower-class neighborhoods. Harrigan was not familiar with the new ethnic cultures in the old neighborhoods he knew so well, and he began to lose touch with his audience. Like other entrepreneurs, he was badly affected by the economic depression of the 1890s, which had a severe impact on the American entertainment business.

Harrigan suffered personal tragedy when his beloved son Eddie died of peritonitis at the age of seventeen. Eddie seemed destined for stage stardom even at such a young age, and Harrigan was devastated by his death. He closed the theater for the summer and went on his first trip ever to Europe. He went to London and from there to Ireland where he met members of his ancestral family. He brought back a tweed suit with extra large pockets where he could place the notes for new sketches on which he was working. However, his stage productions became fewer and fewer. He began to spend more and more time with Annie and the children. He still did stage performances, but mostly in other peoples' productions. He even compacted some of his own earlier works into short vaudeville sketches. His career was now ironically turning full circle. His last engagement was in 1909, blacked-up as a minstrel in a Lambs Society production. He collapsed during a rehearsal, probably of a mild heart attack or stroke, and never appeared on stage again.

David Braham had passed away four years earlier, and, with his halcyon years now well behind him, Harrigan, convinced that he was a forgotten man, grew increasingly melancholic and reclusive. One of his greatest admirers was George M. Cohan, who two years before had written a song in his praise of his hero as part of his musical *Fifty Miles From Boston.* He named the song "Harrigan." The last verse goes:

Where is the man never stood for a gadabout
Harrigan that's me
Who is the man that the town's nearly mad about

Harrigan that's me
The ladies and babies are fond of me
I'm fond of them too in return you see
Who is the gent that deserves his own monument
Harrigan that's me

Ed Harrigan himself attended the show a few weeks after it opened and sat in the front of the theater where he was applauded by the audience. Moody reports that inn later years George M. Cohan was to say: "Edward Harrigan was a fine artist, a great writer of human comedies and one of the grandest men it has ever been my pleasure to meet . . . Harrigan inspired me when I applauded him from a gallery seat. Harrigan encouraged me when I met him in after years and told him of my ambitions. I live in hopes that some day my name may mean half as much to the coming generation of American playwrights as Harrigan's name has made to me."

On 6 June 1911, Ed Harrigan passed away peacefully at home in New York surrounded by Annie and his whole family. He was sixty-six. In his *New York Times* obituary, Harrigan was described as "a man of kindly nature, well informed and thrifty and he will be remembered as one who served his era well and helped to lighten the cares of life. His death has ended an epoch, an era of good fellowship. . . . There was never a better man living than Ned Harrigan."

Today, apart from the Cohan song, the name of Ed Harrigan is largely forgotten, as is the enormous legacy of this most genial and remarkable man, his cohorts David Braham and Tony Hart, and all the other great actors and performers in his company. The collaborative genius of Harrigan, Hart, and Braham affords us a unique window not just into the evolution of Irish America but into America itself—its times of turbulent conflict and also the process of resolution that made day-to-day life possible in the teeming cities of the new Western world. Harrigan has been compared with Dickens, but he might also be compared with Chaucer, recognizing the foibles and eccentricities of his fellow travelers in life but rarely becoming judgmental. Ed Harrigan's theater always promoted the kind of accommodation that is the essence of true tolerance in any multicultural society.

2

From Scapegrace to Grásta

Popular Attitudes and Stereotypes in Irish American Drama

MAUREEN MURPHY

In *The Politics of Irish Drama,* Nicholas Grene argues that Irish drama is outward directed, a commodity for export that is valued for its Irish "otherness," an "otherness" that creates its dramatic energy. He observes that the Irish "otherness" reflects an anxious obsession with self-representation that originated with the colonial and postcolonial condition of the country.[1] Grene's thesis prompts the consideration of how Irish American drama represents itself. Is there an Irish American otherness? What is its relationship to the mainstream of American drama, and how does it interact with other ethnic American drama?

Grene also considers the representation of life, the gap in social milieu between characters and between characters and audience, observing that Irish playwrights have looked to social margins for settings among the deprived and impoverished from Sean O'Casey's tenement dwellers to Marina Carr's Hester Swayne in *By the Bog of Cats.* Where do Irish American playwrights find their characters and themes for their dramas of Irish American public and private life?

While the Irish characters live at the margins of Irish society and, in the course of the drama, usually lose their fragile hold on the margin, Irish American characters may be marginalized by religion or ethnicity, but they have a relationship with the American mainstream through the world of work, the defining force in the Irish American experience that offered the chance for immigrants to redefine themselves.[2] Want of work in Ireland was part of the legacy of colonialism. Jonathan Swift's *The Drapier Letters* and

19

"A Modest Proposal" are the eighteenth-century indictments of the colonial suppression of native industry. Nineteenth-century prefamine travelers' accounts provide anecdotal impressions not only of the want of work among those barely surviving but also of the negative stereotypes that had developed about the under or unemployed. In *Ireland's Welcome to the Stranger* (1847), Asenath Nicholson described the cycle of poverty and hopelessness.

> Taking a walk far out of town [Bandon, Co. Cork], I went into a miserable cabin where two women and their two daughters were at their wheels and a third old woman carding. This was an unusual sight, for seldom had I seen, in Ireland, a whole family employed among the peasantry. Ages of poverty have taken everything out of their hands but preparing and eating the potato; and they sit listlessly upon a stool, lie upon their straw or saunter upon the street because nobody hires them.[3]

Those coming to America had the possibility to remake themselves through work. In addition to looking at work as the transforming experience, particularly in the earlier drama, I will also look at the themes and characters that are unique to Irish American drama: the urban political play and the treatment of second generation Irish caught between the claims of family, particularly parents, and their opportunity to develop their own lives.

First, some history. The Irish who came to America, even those who arrived before the Great Irish Famine of 1845–52, came without a highly developed native drama. There are dramatic elements in early and medieval Irish literature like the dialogues between Oisin and Patrick in the Fenian cycle. Speaking of these early dialogues, Máire Mhac an tSaoi once made the intriguing suggestion that if there were an early dramatist who, like Aeschylus, could add a third voice, that drama could have developed from dialogues.

Instead, drama in the conventional sense developed in Ireland as the result of English influence, a cultural colonialism that came with the spread of the English language and with the growth of towns. There was almost no theatrical activity outside of Dublin in the seventeenth and early eighteen century, and in Dublin, even the Smock Alley Theater who produced its first play, William Philip's *St. Stephen's Green; or, the Generous Lover* in 1699 or 1700, did not encourage the development of native drama but instead offered traveling productions from the London stage to their Ascendancy audiences.[4]

During the nineteenth century, the Irish living in larger country towns were introduced to theater through visits of companies of traveling players. In his journal *Cín Lae Amhlaoibh,* Amhlaoibh Ó Súilleabháin mentions three such visits to Callan, Co. Kilkenny in 1829, 1831, and 1832. It is likely, however, that most Irish country people did not see even those rural performances. For those living in the northern and eastern counties, there were mummers' plays introduced by British settlers, acted by boys and young men, that involved a combatant's death and his revival. While they were traditionally performed at Christmas, some aspects of the play—costumes and processions—were features of other Irish calendar festivals.[5]

While the nineteenth-century Irish, especially the rural Irish, may have been unfamiliar with the theater, they were well acquainted with the popular pastimes of the countryside: music, dance, storytelling, and recitations, and they looked forward to the visits of itinerant fiddlers, pipers, poets, prophecymen, and storytellers. Prefamine fiction such as the novels and stories of William Carleton and the articles in such periodicals as the *Irish Penny Journal* featured these figures. When the Irish came to America, they brought these traditional forms of entertainment; therefore, Irish theater on the American stage from an early time became associated with music and dance.

Irish weddings and wakes also frequently featured dramatic activities. Folklorist Seán Ó Súilleabháin describes such music, dance, storytelling, and games in *Irish Wake Amusements.* Two of the more innovative imitative games, "Sir Soipín or The Knight of Straw," and "Nuala and Dáithí" even included improvisational dialogue and costumes.[6] Ó Súilleabháin suggests that these wake traditions were survivals of the customs associated with the great fairs of Ancient Ireland which originated at the funeral games of the high kings. Máire MacNeill's *The Festival of Luchnasa* suggested that ritual dance plays may have been part of the celebration of the Celtic harvest festival, and readers will recall Brian Friel's appropriation of that Lughnasa dance custom for his play *Dancing at Lughnasa.* Many survivals of these dramatic folk forms reappear in Irish American drama.

The development of Irish drama in America can be divided into six stages: the period before 1830, 1830–60, 1860–90, 1890–1918, 1918–65, and 1965 to the present. The Irish who emigrated before the famine were generally better prepared for American life than those who emigrated at mid-century. They usually had some education and some financial means and were emigrating to improve opportunity rather than to escape starvation. For the most part, these Irish were quickly assimilated into eighteenth- and nineteenth-century American life. Indeed, when the stage Irishman made his first appearance in farces by English and Irish playwrights, he was an amusing caricature who bore little or no resemblance to the reality of the Irish in America. His type was best described by Maurice Bourgeois in *John Millington Synge and the Irish Theater:*

> The stage Irishman habitually bears the generic name of Pat, Paddy or Teague. He has an atrocious Irish brogue, makes perpetual jokes, blunders and bulls in speaking, and never fails to utter, by way of Hibernian seasoning, some screech or oath of Gaelic origin at every third word; he has an unsurpassable gift of "blarney" and cadges for tips and free drinks. His hair is of a fiery red; he is rosy-cheeked, massive and whiskey loving. His face is one of simian bestiality, with an expression of diabolical archness written all over it. He wears a tall felt hat (billicock or wide awake) with a clay pipe stuck in front, an open shirt-collar, a three-caped coat, knee-breeches, worsted stocking and cockaded brogue shoes. In his right hand he brandishes a stout blackthorn or a sprig of shillelagh, and threatens to belabor therewith the darling person who will "tread on the tail of his coat." For his main characteristic (if there is any such thing as psychology in the stage Irishman) are his swagger, his boisterousness and his pugnacity. He is always ready with a challenge, always anxious to pick a quarrel, and peerless for cracking skulls at Donnybrook fair.[7]

The stage Irishman appeared in a number of plays in the 1820s. *The Poor Soldier,* popular in New Orleans in 1820, was played in Brooklyn by "a respectable company" in 1826. *The Irishman in London;* Sheridan's *St. Patrick's Day, or The Scheming Lieutenant; Love in a Camp, or Patrick in Prussia; Sons of Erin;* and *The Irish Widow* were also performed during the 1820s. The Earl of Glengall Richard Butler's English farce *The Irish Tutor,* which made its American debut at the Park Theater at New York in 1823, also had a New Orleans run. In addition to the plays featuring the stage Irishman, James McHenry's dramatization of early Irish history *The Usurper* appeared in New York in 1827; the following year there were productions of James

Sheridan Knowles's *Brian Boroimhe, or The Maid of Erin;* of Richard Butler's *Brian the Brave* and of George Pepper's *Ireland Redeemed.*

The early success of the stage Irishman in America prompted drama historian Margaret G. Maryoga to remark: "The stage Irishman is as old as American drama itself."[8] This figure, which appeared in plays set in Ireland, was one of a trio of Irish types that developed between 1830 and 1860; the others were the stage Irish immigrant and an American folk hero based on Irish immigrant antecedents who shared many traits with the stage Irishman but who appeared in an American settings and whose humor, like much ethnic humor, depended on the contrast between the speech and culture of the immigrant Irish and earlier American settlers like the stage Yankee.

Stage Irishmen continued to thrive in the second period of Irish American theater, 1830–60. Samuel Lover's *Rory O'More;* Tyrone Power's *St. Patrick's Eve, or The Order of the Day;* and J. Buckstone's *The Irish Lion* continued to be in demand not only in the eastern United States but also along the frontier and in San Francisco, where twenty-eight such plays were performed between 1851 and 1859.[9] In part, the success of such plays was based on their association with famous actors or actor-managers, such as Tyrone Power, John Brougham, Dion Boucicault, and Barney Williams, who made Irish comic characters their specialty.

The first of the actor-manager-dramatists was Dublin-born John Brougham (1810–1880), a Trinity medical student turned actor who debuted in 1830 in the Tottenham Street Theater production of *Tom and Jerry,* where he played six different characters. He joined the theater company of Madame Vestris and Charles Mathews in 1831, the year he wrote what would be the first of his some seventy-five plays, musicals, burlesques, and dramatic sketches. He added the role of theater manager when he took over the Lyceum Theater in 1840.

Brougham made his American debut at the Park Theater in New York. When he played Thomas Moore in *The Irish Lion* on 4 October 1842, he was proclaimed the successor to Tyrone Power. It was the beginning of a seventeen-year run as an actor and playwright in the American theater. He became known especially for his Irish American plays *The Irish Yankee, or The Birthday of Freedom* (1840). He wrote *Temptation; or, the Price of Happiness* in 1849 and played the part of O'Bryan, the Irish emigrant who appears seeking work and is hired by the carter Tom Bobalink. O'Bryan's unswerving honestly is a foil to Tom when Tom is faced with a moral crisis over whether to return a wallet of money to its rightful owner. Brougham's portrayal of O'Bryan made the play such a success that he retitled the play *Temptation, or the Irish Emigrant* in 1856. Eventually the play was billed simply as *The Irish Emigrant.*

Brougham himself played O'Bryan till he saw his fellow Dubliner John Drew play the role with dignity and not merely for comedic effect. Moved by Drew's O'Bryan, Brougham and said he would not play O'Bryan again. In his autobiography, Joseph Jefferson has left an account of Drew's O'Bryan in Richmond in 1856:

> I saw him in *Handy Andy, O'Flanaghan* and the *Emigrant* and his entrance in the latter character was one of those simple, bold, and unconventional effects that invariably command recognition from an audience, be they high or low, rich or poor, intelligent or ignorant. A figure passes an open window and pauses for an instant to look into the room; then a timid knock. "Come in!" The door slowly opens, and upon the threshold stands a half-starved man, hunger in his gaunt form and hollow cheeks, but kindness and honesty in his gentle eyes. What pathetic sight is this! As the character is developed through the incidents surrounding it, you see always the same man, changed only as he would by the circumstances which he passes. There is sincerity in this kind of artistic treatment that wins for it a lasting remembrance in the minds of those who have witnessed it.[10]

Mid-century attitudes toward the Irish are reflected in the way characters in *The Irish Emigrant* speak to and about O'Bryan. While he is sympathetic to O'Bryan, Tom calls him by the generic name "Paddy," he is marginalized as "only an Irishman," and dismissed with explicit and implicit ethnic stereotypes. The skinflint landlady Mrs. Grimgriskin calls O'Bryan an "ignorant Irishman" and "an Irish savage." Even Tom Bobalink assumes the Irishman is an idler. When O'Bryan appears at his door he says, "A big lump of a fellow like you! Wouldn't it be better for you to be at work than lounging about in idleness?" But he emerges as the honest working man and the image of O'Bryan looking in through an open window is the trope of the Irish in America in the nineteenth century.

Another of Brougham's Irish immigrant types, the social-climbing Murphy's of *The Game of Love* (1855) demonstrated that Irish immigrants were working and moving into the middle class. Maggie Murphy changes her name from Murphy to De Merfie when her husband makes his fortune.

Brougham's Murphys anticipate the Mulligans in the comedies of Ned Harrigan and Tony Hart later in the century and still later in the cartoon characters of Jiggs and Maggie.

Brougham brought the Irish into other theater venues. His burlesque *An Original Aboriginal Erratic Operatic Semi-Civilized and Demi-Savage Extravaganza Being a Per-version of Ye Treue and Wonderfulle Hystorie if Ye Rennowed Princesse Po-ca-hon-tas or, the Gentle Savage* (1855) ran for thirty years, toured Union Army camps during the Civil War, and was performed in the opening night of the Gaiety Theater in Dublin in 1872.[11] Brougham played H. J. Pow-Ha-Tan the King of Tuscaroras with a Hiberno-English dialect. After the opening chorus of "Tobacco is the solace of man," Pow-Ha-Tan sings his own introduction:

> I'll volunteer and sing a song about it
> To me 'twas by a wily Paddy whack sent
> Who had an axe to grind,
> Hence the broad accent.
> Then, to the air of "Widow Machree," he sings:
> Oh wid a dhudeen I can blow away care
> O hone wid a dhudeen.
> Black thoughts and blue devils will melt in the air.

Brougham changed the script to treat, with broad humor, topics of the day such as immigration and abolitionism. When the king asks whether he hears a band of minstrels, his sergeant says : "No, of foreigners, just cast on Castle Garden." In act 2, Pocohontas says:

> The king who would enslave his daughter so,
> Deserves a hint from Mrs. Beecher Stowe.[12]

While the stage Irishman and stage immigrant flourished on the stage between 1830 and 1860, the portrayal of the Irish began to change in those antebellum decades. They continued to enjoy great general popularity on the American stage. On the other hand, some of the characters were cruel and crude caricatures, meant to represent, at some level of reality, poor Irish immigrants, particularly those fleeing the Great Irish Famine. In his study of the Irish in New Orleans, Earl Niehaus cites examples from the *New Orleans Picayune,* including several court reports where writers compared the behavior of Irish immigrants in New Orleans with that of Irish stage characters.[13]

Some began to object to this image of the Irish. J. C. Prendergast of the *Orleanian* wrote in 1853 that he had never met any Irish as poor or debased as the Irish immigrant characters in the Irish Yankee sketches of Barney Williams and his wife Maria Pray. In New York, in 1847, two Irishmen were ejected from the theater for hissing during a revival of Tyrone Power's *O'Flannigan and the Fairies* (1837). That year, the worst of the Great Irish Famine, New Yorkers began to appreciate the generosity and self-sacrifice of the hard-working Irish immigrants. The American Quaker Jacob Harvey, who helped organize famine relief in New York, praised the generous support of the Irish working poor for those suffering from the Great Irish Famine at home.

While the stage Irishman and the stage immigrant flourished in the American theater, an original comic character, based on an Irish immigrant type, swaggered onto the stage in Benjamin Baker's *A Glance at New York* (1848). He was Mose the Bowery B'hoy-boaster and brawler, heroic fire fighter, and guardian angel of the greenhorns and of Linda the Cigar Girl. Whether or not Mose was based on Mose Humphrey, a printer for the *New York Sun* and a volunteer fireman with Lady Washington Engine No. 40, the character owes its origin to Irishmen in the city's volunteer fire companies.[14] The Irish were drawn to the fire companies by the excitement, the camaraderie, the horseplay, and the prestige associated with company uniforms, horse-drawn fire engines and fire-fighting equipment. The companies, which maintained fierce rivalries, were known to race one another to fires and fight over control of the water supply. The fire company was the start of many a local politician, including Tammany Boss William Tweed, and there is an engraving of him dressed in the uniform of a fire company officer.

Walt Whitman celebrated the Bowery B'hoy, whom he called "the boy I love," in section 47 of *Song of Myself*:

> Fond of his sweetheart, relishing well his steak,
> Unrequited love or a slight cutting him worse than sharp steel cuts
> First-rate to ride, to fight, to hit the bull's eye
> To sail a skiff, to sing a song or play on the banjo.[15]

One critic of the first edition of *Leaves of Grass* called Whitman himself "the Bowery B'hoy of literature."[16] Since the fireman was a well-known city figure, Mose was a great success in the decade between 1848 and 1858. *A Glance at New York* was followed by a number of Mose adventures, notably

A Glance at Philadelphia! (1848), *The Mysteries and Miseries of New York* (1850), *New York as It Is* (1851), *Linda the Cigar Girl,* or *Mose Among the Conspirators* (1856), and *Mose in California* (1857). In addition, Mose inspired other firemen plays including D. Johnson's *The Fireman* (1849) and John Brougham's *Life in New York, or Tom and Jerry on a Visit* (1856). Dion Boucicault adapted E. Brisebarre and Eugene Nus's *Les Pauvres de Paris* for his play *The Poor of New York* (1857). It featured Dan Puffy battling a blaze in a tenement and a fire truck arriving on stage. Fires were the great spectacle of the theater of mid-century. When municipal fire companies replaced the colorful volunteer companies and the steam engine came into service, the Mose figure vanished from the stage, but a heroic Irish fireman archetype lived on in Finley Peter Dunne's account of Chicago fireman Mike Clancy's last fire.[17]

By the mid-nineteenth century, the Irish immigrants were beginning to fulfill the prophecy of Thomas D'Arcy McGee and others that, given the opportunity, they would take their places in American life among leading citizens. The Civil War was the crucible for that integration; Irish volunteers on both sides helped destroy the anti-Irish, anti-Catholic nativism that manifested itself in the Know Nothing party and in the signs "No Irish Need Apply." Irish drama between 1860 and 1890 reflected this change in its two major aspects, both comic: in the romantic nationalism of Dion Boucicault's Irish melodramas, particularly *The Colleen Bawn* (1860), *Arrah-na-Pogue* (1864) and *The Shaughraun* (1874), and in the realistic sketches of Edward Harrigan's urban immigrants in the Mulligan cycle (1878–84).

Boucicault made his stage debut under the name Lee Moreton, as Teddy Rodent, an Irish rat catcher in *A Legend of the Devil Dyke* (1838). When he arrived in New York in 1853, Boucicault was known as an actor for his roles as rogue heroes and as a prolific playwright for a series of translations, adaptations, and original comedies and melodramas. Aware that contemporary Irish plays such as *Brian Boroimhe,* or *The Maid of Erin, Brian the Brave, Ireland Redeemed,* and *The Red Branch Knight* or *Ireland Triumphant* romanticized Irish history for the Irish immigrant, he wrote *The Raparee, or The Treaty of Limerick* (1870) and *Robert Emmet* (1884), but his best-known plays written in Irish historical setting were the Irish comedies. In writing them, Boucicault followed the practice he established in *The Octoroon,* his play about slavery that opened on December 6, 1859, five days after John Brown was hanged for his raid. (As usual, it was a Boucicault adaptation. The source was Mayne Reid's novel *The Octoroon*.) In his biography, Richard Fawkes quotes Boucicault's letter to the *Times* after *The Octoroon* opened in London. Boucicault said he had never personally witnessed any slaves ill-treated, but "behind all this there are features in slavery far more objectionable than any hitherto held up to human execration, by the side of which physical suffering appears as a vulgar detail."[18] Joseph Jefferson played the role of Salem Scudder the Yankee overseer. In his *Autobiography*, he described acting in the play at a time when feelings in New York were divided about slavery and what would become a civil war. "Then there were various opinions as to which way the play leaned—whether it was northern or southern in its sympathy. The truth of the matter is, it was non-committal."[19] Boucicault was also the consummate theater manager. When the audience objected to the death of Zoe (the octoroon) at the end of the play, the box office suffered. Boucicault simply offered a new ending, the one the audience wanted and the one that violated the moral sensibility of the drama. The new ending did not help, but Boucicault had worked out his strategy for dealing with plays on controversial themes. By both recognizing the injustice of slavery and, at the same time, sympathizing with the end of the way of life its loss threatened, he offended neither North nor South.

Boucicault treated Fenianism in much the same way in *The Shaughraun* and as a result the play was received with equal appreciation in Dublin, in London, and in the United States.[20] In both *The Shaughraun* and *Arrah-na-Pogue*, Boucicault relied on melodramatic structure with its convention of the restoration of order in order to maintain a light hand in dealing with the English policy of treating Irish political activists as criminals. He shared this theme with writers of nineteenth-century Irish fiction who made it the basis for serious social comment.

Boucicault's played the emigrant as well as the nationalist card in *Arrah-na-Pogue*. As Beamish MacCoul thinks of leaving Ireland for the last time, his speech is full of emigrant ballad clichés, which nevertheless reflect the anguish of separation.

> See, the morning beginning to tip the heights of Mullacor; we must part. In a few hours I shall be on the sea, bound for a foreign land; perhaps never again shall I hear your voices nor see my native hills. Oh, my own land! Bless every blade of grass upon your cheeks. The clouds that hang over ye are the sighs of your exiled children and your face is always wet with their

tears. Eire meelish, schlawn loth! Fare ye well! And you, dear Abbey of St. Kevin, around which the bones of forefathers are laid.[21]

Much of the success of these three Boucicault plays can be attributed to the clever peasant characters of Myles na gCopaleen in *The Colleen Bawn*, Shaun the Post in *Arraugh-na-Pogue*, and Conn the Shaughraun. Some critics such as David Krause suggest their origin in the parasite/slave relationship of Roman comedy; however, it is more likely that Boucicault found the model for his Irish heroes in native American dramatic figures like Mose and the Yankee.[21] Neither rogues nor romantic heroes, these characters are distinguished by their inherent kindness and loyalty, which make them protector but not the suitor of the heroine, by their knowledge of traditional lore, and by their instinctive courtesy and nobility.[23]

Influenced by Boucicault, the early Irish plays of Edward Harrigan (1845–1911) were the derivative *Arrah-na-Brogue* (1873) and the melodramas *Iascaire* (1876) and *The Logaire* (1878). At the same time, Harrigan began work on a comic series based on Dan Mulligan, an Irish immigrant grocer. Harrigan's affectionate portrayal of Mulligan was an improvement over the earlier stage Irish characters. Although Mulligan is impulsive and drinks and fights with little provocation, he is honest, generous, and loyal. Starting with *The Mulligan Guard* (1873), Harrigan's sketches differed from the plays of Brougham and Boucicault in that they did not portray the Irish in opposition to Yankee or English authority, but focused instead on those Irish who achieved some local status in the ward politics of their own community.

Unlike Irish drama with its otherness expressed in the difference between received standard English and Hiberno-English, the Mulligan plays demonstrate that in Irish American drama, the Irish American dialect is set not only against standard English but also against other Englishes: African American and German American. Irish and black fraternal orders compete in *The Mulligan Guards and the Skidmores* (1875); further rivalry is introduced with the German butcher Gustave Lochmuller in *The Mulligan Guard Picnic* in 1878. (The play was revised in 1880.) *The Mulligan Guard Ball* (1879) ends with the marriage of Tom Mulligan to Katrina Lochmuller, showing that ethnic intermarriage—albeit among Catholics—had come to the Irish immigrant community.[24] The success of Harrigan's Mulligan plays were based on the actors—Harrigan himself and his partner Tony Hart (Anthony Cannon)—

and the humorous, sentimental songs written by Harrigan's father-in-law David Braham.[25]

The last two Mulligan plays, *Cordelia's Aspirations* (1883) and *Dan's Tribulations* (1884), follow the rise and fall of the Mulligans from Mulligan's Alley uptown to Madison Avenue where Cordelia tries to be accepted by New York society. When their fortunes are reversed, they return to their old neighborhood, and Harrigan portrays them as loyal and devoted as they start over and work to rebuild their lives. While the Mulligans's qualities are attractive in themselves, they also reinforce the image of the Irish in America as not only high-spirited but also responsible and trustworthy. Large numbers of Irish were moving into the middle class and social mobility brought a concern for respectability.

Irish drama between the years 1880 and 1918 reflected the growth of Irish political power starting with William R. Grace's victories in the New York mayoral election in 1881 and again in 1885.[26] As nineteenth-century Irish appeared in plays as urban workers, later nineteenth-century Irish Americans appeared in plays about urban politics. There was a connection. Irish American politicians controlled patronage, which meant access to jobs. They also began to exert influence on national politics and, in their concern for Irish home rule, on international politics. Harrigan's *The Mulligan Guard Nominee,* a satire on the then current electioneering that set Mulligan against Gustave Lochmuller for alderman, can be considered a forerunner of political drama in America.[27] Local elections are also featured in other political plays of the 1890s. The rival candidates in Henry Grattan Donnelly's *A Tammany Tiger* (1896) compete not only for the same office but also for the same woman.[28] E. W. Townsend's *McFadden's Row of Flats* (1897) and the anonymous *McSorley's Twins* (1897), two Harrigan knockoffs, use alderman contests to frame Irish American songs, dances, and jokes.

While it was written in mid-twentieth century, William Alfred's play *Hogan's Goat* (1965) is set in Brooklyn's Sixth Ward (roughly Brooklyn Heights) during the 1890 mayoral election when Matt Stanton tries to unseat the corrupt Ned Quinn for the party's nomination and in doing so betrays the loyalty of the two women who love him.[29] To win the election and destroy his challenger, Quinn reveals that Stanton was Ag Hogan's "goat," a kept man, that he in fact had married Ag and was, therefore, a bigamist. When his secret is revealed and Quinn gets the nomination, Stanton's "second wife" Kathleen packs her truck and prepares to leave his house. She tells him that while he has "killed" Ag Hogan, who died without the sacraments because she was afraid she would betray Stanton, he will not kill her.

> You had to be the mayor of this city
> And she was in the way. You married me
> To make yourself respectable again.
> That's the only reason.[30]

As she goes out to the head of the stairs, Stanton grabs her shouting, "You'll not leave me! I'll see to that!" The stage goes dark. Kathleen screams and falls down the stairs. As she dies, Kathleen takes the blame for the fall, but Matt confesses to Father Coyne as he gives her absolution, "I flung her down the stairs to keep her here."[31]

Plays of the next decade focused on political leadership. In George H. Broadhurst's *The Man of the Hour* (1907, rev. 1916), financier Charles Wainwright and ward boss Richard Horigan recruit Alwyn Bennett to run for mayor.[32] He agrees but warns them that if elected, he will keep his oath of office. Bennett refuse to sign the bill for a railroad franchise that will benefit his backers.[33] He is saved by Boss Horigan's foil, the honest cop turned alderman James Phelan. The play is based on the story of New York mayor George McClellan (1904–9), who sacrificed his political career in 1906 when he repudiated his backer, Tammany boss Charles Francis Murphy. Murphy was also the model for Boss Haggerty in James S. Barcus's *The Governor's Boss* (1914), a dramatization of the impeachment of New York Governor William Sulzer in 1913.[34]

These were the years of Irish American support of Home Rule which, like Irish American support of the Land League in the 1880s, made the nationalist movement in Ireland far stronger that it would otherwise have been. At no time in the history of Irish drama in the United States were drama and politics so closely involved. An example of theater broadly used in the service of Irish nationalism was Anna Throop Craig's pageant of five hundred participants produced by the American Committee of the Gaelic League of Ireland in May 1913 at the Sixty-ninth Regiment Armory in New York to present Ireland's past in the context of its aspirations for Home Rule.

Given the strong Irish American involvement in Home Rule and the concern about the image of the Irishman in America, the 1911 tour by the Irish Abbey Theater was the cause of anxiety and hostility among Irish Americans who believed that some of their plays, particularly John Millington Synge's

The Playboy of the Western World, would jeopardize their hard-won respectability and political gains. The text of the *Gaelic American* for 14 October 1911 carried the resolution from the United Irish-American Societies of New York:

> RESOLVED: That we, the United Irish-American Societies of New York, make every effort, through a committee, to induce those responsible for the presentation of *The Playboy* to withdraw it, and failing in this we pledge ourselves to drive the vile thing from the stage as we drove *McFadden's Row of Flats* and the abomination produced by the Russell Brothers, and we ask the aid in this work of every decent Irish man and woman and the Catholic Church whose doctrines and devotional practices are held up to scorn and ridicule in Synge's monstrosity.[35]

While the *Playboy* reception dominates the history of the Abbey tour, it is important to mention the role that the Irish players and playwrights had on the development of the little theater movement in America.[36] The most significant Irish American connection with the little theater movement was its association with the work of Eugene O'Neill (1888–1953) with the Provincetown Players that began with the production of *Bound East for Cardiff* in 1916, a play that reflected the influence of Synge's *Riders to the Sea.*

Another theme unique to Irish American drama is the legacy of emigration: its effect on the emigrating generation and on their children who are often caught between the claims of family loyalty and the those of individual freedom. This tension is focused most intensely in O'Neill's finest play, perhaps America's finest play, *Long Day's Journey into Night.* John Henry Raleigh's analysis of the autobiographical and cultural contexts of the play argues that New England Irish Catholicism provides "the folkways and mores, the character types, the interrelationships between characters, the whole attitude that informs *Long Day's Journey* and gives it meaning."[37]

The characters of James and Mary Tyrone were based on O'Neill's Irishborn parents James O'Neill and Ellen Quinlan, who emigrated to American after the Great Irish Famine. The playwright gave the family the surname Tyrone, the Anglicization of Tír Eoghan, the land of the O'Neills. In naming his character Tyrone, O'Neill not only honored his O'Neill ancestors, but he also alluded to their shared history of dispossession, for Hugh O'Neill, the Second Earl of Tyrone, fled to the continent in 1607 after losing to the English at Kinsale in 1601. Born in 1847, the worst year of the great Irish

Famine, James O'Neill's family emigrated from Ireland early in 1856 at a time when the Irish poor continued to face eviction and the poorhouse.[38] Even after they emigrated to America, the O'Neills' life was perilous. While James O'Neill's optimism tended to romanticize the family's immigrant experience, Eugene O'Neill's James Tyrone is scarred by those memories. In act 4 of *Long Day's Journey*, Tyrone tells his son Edmund how his family suffered after his father returned to Ireland:

> My mother was left, a stranger in a strange land, with four small children, me and a sister a little older and two younger than me. My two older brothers had moved to other parts. They couldn't help. They were hard put to keep themselves alive. There was no damned romance in our poverty. Twice we were evicted from the miserable hovel we called home, with my mother's few sticks of furniture thrown out on the street and my mother and sisters crying. I cried too, though I tried hard not to, because I was the man of the family. At ten years old! There was no more school for me. I worked twelve hours a day in a machine shop, learning to make files.[39]

As a reaction to his early poverty and the shame of eviction, Tyrone impoverishes his own family by speculation in corrupt land deals.

Like James Tyrone, John Cleary, the father in Frank Gilroy's autobiographical *The Subject Was Roses* (1964), harbors a history of poverty and humiliation. In language close to O'Neill's, Cleary says in act 2, scene 2, "I'll tell you what rough is—being so hungry you begged. Being thrown out in the street with your few sticks of furniture for all the neighbors to enjoy. Never sleeping in a bed with less than two other people. Always hiding from collectors. Having to leave school at the age of ten because your father was crippled for life and it was your job to support the house."[40] About the same time as Gilroy, William Alfred wrote in *Hogan's Goat* Matt Stanton's monologue in verse of the shame and humiliation of immigration:

> Defiled with my own waste like a dying cat,
> And a lousy red beard on me like a tinker's,
> While a bitch of a doctor, with his nails too long,
> Dared tell me: "In Amurrica, we bathe!"[41]

Increase in Irish American prosperity and respectability, combined with the religious piety that characterized postfamine Irish Catholicism, produced an idealization of family obligations and responsibilities that encouraged the young to sacrifice themselves for their families and the old to maintain control over their families to ensure their own status and security in old age. Family pressure was reinforced by the church. These obligations played out differently in Ireland and among the Irish in America. In the first three decades of the twentieth century in rural Ireland, the transfer of land to a single inheriting son who was customarily married to a dowered woman brought with it the responsibility for caring for the son's parents not by their daughters but by the daughter-in-law of the inheriting son. In America, the matter of loyalty to and care for elderly parents often fell to the birth daughters who were married and mothers of their own families. Sacrificing daughters are usually portrayed realistically if ironically in Irish American fiction and drama as compared with the caregiving daughter in Martin MacDonagh's black comedy *The Beauty Queen of Lenane* (1995).

Nettie, the mother in Frank Gilroy's *The Subject Was Roses*, shares the competing claims of the roles of daughter and wife/mother with heroines of Irish American novels written or set at roughly the same time as Gilroy's play: Elizabeth Cullinan's *House of Gold* (1959) and Alice McDermott's *Wakes and Weddings* (1998). Nettie is attracted to John Cleary's drive to succeed, but his career is shaken by 1929 and stalled when she refuses to go with him when his work as a coffee broker offers an opportunity in Brazil. Her world is stunted by her sense of obligation to her mother and to her disabled cousin Willis. Like Nora in *A Doll's House*, Nettie walks out of the house in act 2, but no doors slam and she is back within the day. Why does she come back? Because, she tells her son Tim, she is a coward. She says her twelve hours away was the only freedom she has ever had, but her freedom was less from John and Tim and more from her mother and Willis, the freedom from being a daughter. When critics faulted Gilroy for violating an axiom of in the playwriting that characters must show progression, they failed to see Nettie's progress, however short-lived. She comes back but she refuses, at least for the night, to phone her mother as if to underscore the Irish American strategy for dealing with conflict—silence. (Another strategy is to use music or dance to express things unsaid. Gilroy uses music and dance in *The Subject Was Roses*, as does Philip Barry in *The Joyous Season* and William Alfred in *The Curse of an Aching Heart*.[42]

A new theme in Irish and Irish American literature is the undocumented Irish immigrants in America who arrived after the naturalization laws changed from a system of national quotas to one of family reunification.

Perhaps as many as 100,000 such immigrants arrived in the 1980s. While there were immigrants who arrived with financial, legal, and technological skills, the 1980s and 1990s brought unskilled Irish immigrants, those young people who were not the beneficiaries of the Celtic Tiger economy and who believed that there was no place for them in Ireland. These are the Irish emigrants of Greg Delanty's poem "To President Mary Robinson," his response to Robinson's promise in her inaugural address to put a light in the window of her executive residence Áras an Uachtaráin in an appropriation of the rural custom of putting a light in the window on Christmas Eve as a sign of welcome to the holy family.[43] Acknowledging the intention, Delanty's poem registers disappointment: "we're still turned away/To settle in the unfamiliar, cold hay."[44]

The trip of Sean and Finbarr, two young undocumented immigrants in Antoine Ó Flatharta's play *Grásta I Meiriceá* (1990) is a journey by Greyhound to Graceland, a post-Catholic Irish pilgrimage to a shrine of American popular culture. Grace is also saving grace: amnesty for the undocumented, grace of God that will help them avoid detection, spiritual grace conferred by visiting the home of the king and finally, in the play's last lines, Sean's father's message to his son that "he is praying for God's grace over me."[45] The play provides an insight into the life of the New Irish and it demonstrates that there is a not only an Irish and an Irish American drama but also an Irish language drama. *Grásta* opens as Sean and Finbarr prepare to leave for Graceland to see Elvis's guns and guitars; they are unsettled by the news that one of men on Sean's painting job was apprehended by Immigration Officers, taken to Kennedy Airport, and put on a plane for Shannon. Finbarr, who had been on the same job a month earlier, suspects the inevitable informer, and both know it could happen to them. Finbarr tries to dismiss the concern by saying that there is talk of amnesty and that they'd be legal within the year, but the deportation haunts them. Finbarr's fantasy is: "Ten years from today I'll be a millionaire—big house, swimming pool and Cadillac. You don't believe me? You'll see. Maybe. I'll buy Elvis's house in ten years. Graceland, home of the King."[46] While the ghost of Elvis Presley is the major presence, echoes of Elvis Costello's "boulevard of broken dreams" line from "Brilliant Mistake" provides an ironic counterpoint.

As they leave for Graceland, Finbarr begins to sing "Heartbreak Hotel," substituting "I've found a new place in hell" for the line "I've found a new place to dwell." Sean becomes annoyed not just because it is irritating to hear Finbarr sing the wrong words, but also because life with immigration closing in has, in fact, become a hell. When Finbarr and Sean get to Nashville a busker is singing "This Land Is Your Land," an ironic comment on their undocumented status. When they arrive in Graceland, they find there is violence at the end of the American dream in an "*áit lán le Sherriffs is cops craiceáilte*"[47] (a place full of sheriffs and crazy cops), where a run in with them could mean deportation. Sean thinks he has witnessed the murder of a waitress. Ultimately, the American dream disappoints. Sean and Finbarr visit Elvis's grave, but, in a parody of the resurrection, a woman there says the grave is empty, and Elvis is living in Nashville. They see the guns, the guitars, and the Vegas clothes—but ultimately they are afraid of getting locked in not just in Graceland but in America. Finbarr says, "*Ba cheart dúinn sheansáil abhaile faoi Nollaig a Sheáin*"[48] (We should chance it and go home for Christmas, Sean).

For Irish Americans, the most significant contemporary playwright is John Patrick Shanley, a 1977 graduate of New York University's Steinhardt School whose play *Doubt: A Parable,* the first of a trilogy of plays about hierarchies, in 2005 won the Pulitzer Prize for drama and Tony Awards for the best play, the best performance by a leading actress, the best performance by a featured actress, and the best director.[49] Set in a Catholic school in the Bronx in 1964 and based on his own memories of St. Anthony's School and his teacher Sister James, *Doubt* moves from an initial comedic scene (will this be more *Nunsense?*) to a meditation about doubt and certainty that applies to current political issues as well as to the issue of clerical abuse. In an interview with *Theater News,* Shanley said, "Whenever I write a play, I always start from where the audience is and bring them where I want them to go. In this case the audience starts with the idea that nuns are funny; so you might as well let them laugh, then calm down and walk them into the serious issues of the play." Shanley's concerns with hierarchy and moral certainty are far removed from dark comedies with jolts of on-stage gratuitous violence in the work of Marina Carr and Martin MacDonagh. Shanley describes the last act of *Doubt* as the one that "takes place when people leave the theater and begin to talk about it."[50]

The larger role of drama in transmitting Irish culture that has been demonstrated by these Irish American groups is a measure of the vitality of Irish drama in America today. Amateur and professional companies regularly offer plays by Irish and Irish American writers; playwrights continue to write about the Irish and Irish American experience, and both Irish American and non-Irish American audiences support this theater. Irish drama in the United States in its growth in characterization from caricature and farce to the sympathetic hero of a realistic play has informed American understanding of the Irish identity and of the Irish American experience. In doing so, Irish drama in the United States has enlarged the ideal of the founders of the Abbey Theater—to work for the dignity of Ireland—to include fostering Irish American pride in Irish heritage.

3

Ireland Rearranged

Contemporary Irish Drama and the Irish American Stage

CHRISTOPHER L. BERCHILD

At the beginning of the twenty-first century—when so much extraordinary social, political, economic, and cultural change is occurring in the Republic of Ireland—it is imperative that a critical eye be leveled on contemporary Irish drama and performance in an attempt to assess this change through what many feel is society's most effective reflection. While many studies have been launched over the last few decades analyzing and revising the "version" of Ireland that is being presented on the contemporary Irish stage, there has been surprisingly little scrutiny of the Ireland that is being presented within Irish diasporic communities around the world—including what is arguably the largest and most influential Irish diasporic community, the Irish American community. It is imperative for the study of the contemporary Irish identity to examine what this community is presented with onstage as "authentically" Irish.

In this chapter, I discuss the state of contemporary Irish theater being produced today, specifically on Irish American stages, through a brief examination of selected Irish American theater companies, their company missions, and their production choices over the past two decades. I briefly address the specific contemporary Irish works that are most often selected to present contemporary "Irishness" to American audiences, especially the culturally engaged audiences of the aforementioned Irish American theater companies, and the version of Ireland that is offered to these audiences through these plays.

In approaching this work, I chose to take my own research interests—the representation of contemporary Ireland on the Irish stage—and examine this same trend but through a different lens—the Irish American experience.

However, when I began to examine the works that were most often produced on a nationwide level, certain patterns began to emerge. Upon further narrowing the scope of my research, I found that Irish drama that challenges nostalgic notions of "the auld sod" fight a predominantly uphill battle that mirrors the recent trends in native Irish drama along the same lines. But in the United States, especially among the aforementioned hyphenated community, nostalgia concerning the contemporary state of Ireland takes on a new level of complexity—that of nostalgic exile, which often creates a nearly absolute insistence within Irish American communities of a unified and often romanticized (problems and all) image of Ireland that is central to their diasporic identity.

In the current trends section of the journal *Éire-Ireland*, Irish theater scholar Anthony Roche noted that 1989 was a transitional year for Irish drama that was decidedly antinostalgic in nature.[1] Even though many scholars claim that the shift occurred many years earlier—1964 to be precise—with the premiere of Friel's *Philadelphia, Here I Come!,* Roche seems to indicate that it was in 1989 that theater had truly begun to present a new version of Irishness that began to evade the specter of the past and to forge new roads into the future that exist independently of the traditional tropes of land, religion, language, and nationalism. Fintan O'Toole, in his "Irish Theatre: The State of the Art," even goes so far as to say that there is no longer a dramatic conflict in terms of these traditional tropes as they no longer exist in contemporary Ireland.[2]

Even in Ireland, this trend was painfully slow in its effective development. Declan Hughes, in his 2000 diatribe "Who the Hell Do We Still Think We Are," asks "why does contemporary Irish literature ignore contemporary Ireland?" and notes that "too often when I go to the theatre, I feel like I've stepped into a time capsule: even plays supposedly set in the present seem burdened by the compulsion to . . . well, in the narrowest sense, be Irish."[3] Though Hughes has admitted that he had somewhat slipped into hyperbole with this article, he did succeed in identifying a significant trend in Irish drama—that "nostalgia is in many ways the Irish disease"—which I will extend to the Irish American reception of the selfsame drama. But more recent trends in Irish drama have revealed a new way of presenting the island nation onstage that has moved in tandem with many of the economic and social changes that have effected Ireland during, and especially following, the now-legendary Celtic Tiger.

But this same criticism that Hughes felt needed to be leveled on Irish dramatists and theater companies can be quite easily and justifiably turned on many Irish-American approaches to this drama, though the "Irish disease" that Hughes mentions takes on a new meaning when confronting the largely Irish American spectators that make up the backbone of the audiences I will be discussing. Today, unfortunately, due to the social effects of the aforementioned nostalgic exile, this Irish "disease" becomes somewhat epidemic, especially when reinforced by international perceptions of Ireland and the ever-present cultural semiotics of Bord Failte and the like.

It is safe to say that a great deal of what we consider to be the tenets of Irish identity have been written for and performed on the stages of the twentieth century, not just in Ireland, but around the world. But for the diaspora, especially those of us in the United States, the construction of Irish American identity is most often based on a cultural memory of displacement and exile from an inhospitable homeland, whether from the famine exodus of the 1820s or from the economic stagnancy and joblessness of the 60s, 70s, and 80s. However, the mythology of "the auld sod," reinforced by a long history of strong diasporic community building among the Irish Americans, has stood the test of time and has been romanticized and made legend within our American communities, relying on the image of the ruralized and Celticized family unit to define who we are and to differentiate us from the rest of the "hyphenated" American populations.

Without going into the various levels of cultural investment in their own communities, it is worth noting that Irish American theater companies serve a distinct purpose for Irish Americans: to not only allow a window to the world across the Atlantic but also to represent an image and a vision of this site of displacement. But recent years have introduced these companies to the difficulties of what happens when an altered and alienating view of a fundamentally unrecognizable Ireland begins to appear on their stages, examining Ireland through an ever more Europeanized, globalized, and media-saturated lens. The questions that then arise are: do our Irish American theater companies have a responsibility to present this "Ireland rearranged" to their audiences and, if so, how does this responsibility manifest itself alongside the need for these audiences to maintain a more traditional view of Ireland—a view that is both culturally reinforcing and preferable to a large percentage of their audiences—and the need to uphold a unique and powerful dramatic legacy that is arguably unequaled in the English language in the twentieth century?

Having established the context for this survey of Irish American theater companies, I would like to now turn to the specific theater companies and their approaches to contemporary Irish dramatic work. For the purpose of this study, I have decided to limit my examination of American companies to theater companies that have prioritized the production of Irish drama and the perpetuation of "Irishness" for its audiences, henceforth referred to as Irish American theater companies. I say this with full awareness of the great commercial success of certain Irish plays in major regional professional theaters—including the majority of Martin McDonagh's works and many of Conor McPherson's works. These works, as I will discuss later, are cut from a different cultural cloth and therefore are intended to inspire different reactions for international audiences than those plays that are specifically aimed at expressions of Irish identity.

In the United States today, there are approximately a dozen theater companies that are principally dedicated to the production of Irish and Irish American drama, mainly (but adamantly *not* exclusively) for the benefit of local and regional Irish American audiences. Of these dozen or so theater companies, many are in a constant state of operational instability, no doubt due to the somewhat lethal combination of the state of the performing arts in the United States today and the limitations of appealing to a specific (and slowly shrinking) audience. A handful of companies that existed when I began my research are now defunct or are barely operational due to financial constraints. Another few companies are running at limited capacity while attempting to reestablish or resurrect their audience base. The remaining companies, which I largely focus on in this study, are moderately successful—at least in relation to the theater industry as a whole.

Before analyzing these companies in detail, I would first like to address an issue that is by no means an issue specific to the Irish American theater world, but rather to the nonprofit world as a whole, though it has extraordinary bearing on the ideas addressed below. Each Irish American company that I will address faces the extraordinary challenge of what I will call the functional and expressive imperatives of these companies. These ideas, usually at odds with one another, describe the relationship between the specific company's mission or goals and their basic ability to operate or stay in business. In theater, these two poles usually work in opposition, especially when presenting material that challenges, frustrates, or confounds their audience and/or community. An Irish American theater company must make difficult decisions to strike the delicate balance between these two objectives, and it is the unsuccessful company that is unable to do so. The influence of these ideas helps to divine the actual purpose of these companies and causes a significant reevaluation of mission, purpose, and overall goals. If a company tends to defer to their functional imperative, and essentially shift into survival mode, they tend to present their audiences with safer and more popular productions while running the risk of specializing in cultural artifacts or dramatic museum pieces. However, if a company is too brazen in their artistic goals, embracing their expressive imperative too strongly, they may present their audiences with new and challenging approaches to drama while running the risk of alienating their audiences, especially if those audiences directly associate tradition and convention with their own identities. The line between these objectives is a tightrope, and few companies have been able to negotiate it without falling victim to it.

In preparation for this work, I have contacted and conducted interviews with many of these most significant and successful companies concerning their missions, their season selection process, and the success—both critical and commercial—of their productions of contemporary Irish drama. After much deliberation, the companies that I chose to concentrate on and feature in this study are the Irish Repertory Theatre of New York, Súgán of Boston, and Solas Nua of Washington, D.C. I chose to feature these companies not only due to their cooperation but also due to the fact that these companies create and illustrate a spectrum of ideologies concerning the production and performance of contemporary Irish drama. Each of these companies represents an approach to the contemporary Irish experience as well as their own places as decidedly American companies. These three approaches I would like to identify as conservative, moderate, and aggressive. I would like to note that I do not use these terms to suggest value judgments concerning these companies—these are merely helpful terms to illuminate each company's core values.

I would like to define conservative companies as those that attempt to bring forth a balanced approach to the representation of contemporary Irish society onstage, but who, despite their mission, are often forced to indulge in more traditional and nostalgic views of Ireland to serve their more culturally conservative audiences. Productions from the more conservative companies tend to introduce one new contemporary work per season in order to fulfill their duty to their mission of presenting a view of the Irish identity—though they often tend to rely on works that feature more traditional Irish themes and tropes (land, religion, language). These companies tend more toward the functional side of the spectrum, realizing that their long-term success lies within their ability to both maintain long-time audiences as well as foster new audience members, and in doing so are hesitant to challenge them too often.

Moderate companies intentionally introduce challenging contemporary Irish works to their audiences with the attempt to both educate and inform their audiences while not ignoring the needs of their audiences to be reminded of the dramatic and literary history of the Irish nation. Productions are usually balanced in an attempt to give audiences the full spectrum of the twentieth-century Irish dramatic experience while still maintaining the significance of viewing the "new" Ireland. These companies attempt to strike a functional and expressive balance, attempting to provide for both traditional and innovative audiences without playing predominantly to either.

Aggressive companies, relatively new to the Irish American scene, actively ignore the more traditional works of Ireland's dramatic past in favor of a wholly contemporary and completely Celtic Tiger and post-Celtic Tiger view of the nation for American audiences. These companies actively seek out challenging new voices direct from Irish stages to present a new sense of Ireland, especially to a younger theater crowd that has grown largely unsatisfied with traditional representations and dramaturgies. Productions are usually quite new and selected not to create a dialogue between the old and the new (as the two aforementioned types strive to do at various levels) but also seem to disregard the significance of nostalgia and attempt to create a new relationship with Ireland and its American diaspora. Concerned principally with their expressive imperative, these companies attempt to cultivate smaller and more artistically assertive audiences who are more concerned with innovation than tradition.

In examining these companies' mission statements and self-articulated identities, they all, on some level, are dedicated to the presentation of Irish drama, and by extension Ireland, to American audiences. Statements such as "to provide a context for understanding the Irish (and Irish American) experience" and "to promote an awareness of contemporary Irish culture" are ubiquitous in these companies' missions—as they should be as cultural institutions—to be purveyors of Irish cultural awareness. This is a seemingly obvious, yet significant, point concerning these companies as it forces us to ask "what version of Ireland are these audiences being offered on these stages?"

But the cultural and artistic vision of the artistic director (and sometimes the board of directors) comes into question here and the major differences between these companies begin to become apparent. In a very significant way, season selection identifies each company's approach to and definition of both Ireland and contemporary Irish drama. For each company, I asked a number of questions in order to get a sense of their mission and specific goals in presenting a representation of Ireland to their audiences. These questions included:

• How does your company view contemporary Irish work? Do you feel that a new sense of Ireland fits into your company's vision/mission?

• How do you feel your audiences view contemporary Irish plays (as opposed to more traditional Irish plays or those that promote more traditional Irish themes)? Do audiences find more contemporary works less "authentically Irish" or problematic, or are these plays received with equal interest?

• Have your contemporary Irish productions been critical successes? Commercial successes (especially relative to the more traditional works)?

• What is the rough percentage of contemporary to modern (or more traditional) Irish works in your average season? Do you feel that this proportion is appropriate for your audiences?

• Which of your contemporary productions have been the most successful (in your view)? Is there a certain play (or playwright) that you would like to see your company tackle in the future?

From these questions I was able to posit the aforementioned models for the contemporary Irish American theater company.

My example of a more conservative company, the Irish Repertory Theatre in New York, has one of the most clearly articulated approaches to Ireland (and especially contemporary Ireland), listing that they have "presented major works by O'Casey, Synge, Shaw, Wilde, Dion Boucicault, Brendan Behan, Dylan Thomas, and Samuel Beckett, as well as the contemporary artistry of Hugh Leonard, Frank McCourt, Tom Murphy, Brian Friel, Peter Sheridan, Patricia Burke Brogan, Pat McCabe, Geraldine Aron, Jennifer Johnston, Tommy Makem, Shivaun O'Casey, Enda Walsh and Harold Prince."[4] An impressive theatrical pedigree to be sure, but in looking through this list of names, there seems to be a notable deficiency of those

Irish playwrights that have been aggressively and radically redefining the face of Irish drama in Ireland in the past two decades.

In discussion with producing director Ciarán O'Reilly, certain truths (and difficulties) concerning the operation of culturally centered companies such as the Irish Rep come into focus. O'Reilly notes that, when addressing this issue:

> We view new works by the same standard we hold to a play from the canon of classic and popular Irish plays: i.e. does the play have the legs to travel? Is the play accessible and/or relevant to an American audience? Does it merit a production? Our mission from the get-go has been "to present Irish and Irish American Drama performed professionally with a native understanding."[5]

Here, O'Reilly introduces us to an important idea, as it exposes the financial and cultural realities behind presenting a theatrical vision of a fundamentally altered nation to a traditionally nostalgic diaspora. The first question he asks is highly significant—as the "legs to travel" really introduces the question of appropriateness for an inherently Irish work that may be performed for an audience that may only have a limited understanding of everyday life in the Republic of Ireland, no matter how many times that audience may have visited or stayed in direct contact with the country. O'Reilly continues, "I would say there may be a resistance to new plays from our main constituency. Our audiences, comparable to those of many theaters, tend to be of an older generation and crave perhaps more sentimental fare." He does admit that:

> We have acquired a certain trust from our patrons and they are willing to go along with whatever we present. There is a resistance to plays with foul language—even though anyone that has ever stood in a pub in Ireland will attest that that attribute is very authentic. We do tend to present plays that are character driven and strong on plot. This is what our audience likes regardless whether it is a contemporary or classic play.[6]

Though less articulated by other Irish American theater companies, these concerns are real when presenting work to a community that is approaching their theatrical experience as a reinforcement of their imagined Ireland—once again, an Ireland reinforced by nostalgia. Whether we are willing to draw comparisons to early reactions to Synge and O'Casey in Dublin remains to be seen (and, of course, the stakes are much different), but it is significant to note that the Irish Rep acknowledges the important balancing act between artistic and cultural rigor and audience satisfaction.

O'Reilly's comment also identifies another concern for the reception of contemporary Irish drama in America—a dramaturgical issue regarding the dramatic structure of contemporary Irish drama. Irish theater, and the theater of its diaspora, has always been strongly text-driven—telling the story through strongly defined characters and straightforward (and usually highly realistic) Aristotelian plots. O'Reilly's statement seems to point toward trends in contemporary Irish drama that create works that confront, challenge, and confound traditional dramaturgy and present works that intend to subvert the past in various ways. This is not to say that the Irish Rep has completely ignored these trends in Irish drama, but rather that the more challenging works from the new Irish canon must be couched within seasons that feature more traditional visions of Ireland coupled with more traditional dramaturgies. One has only to look at a recent season to identify the problems that a company like this has with the aforementioned balancing act: Shaw's *Mrs Warren's Profession*, a rock opera version of *Beowulf*, Malachy McCourt's one-man performance of *You Don't Have to Be Irish*, and Keane's *The Field*.

My example of a moderate company, Súgán Theater in Boston, has a much more broad-based approach to presenting Irish work to their audiences, stating that their mission is to introduce to Boston audiences contemporary Irish and Celtic plays that present diverse perspectives of modern Ireland. In contrast to the writers that the Irish Rep has featured, Súgán's list engages with many of the voices that are featured on more progressive and experimental Irish stages, such as "Samuel Beckett, Brian Friel, Frank McGuinness, Tom Murphy, and W. B. Yeats, as well as Dermot Bolger, Marina Carr, Paul Durcan, Tony Kavanagh, Owen McCafferty, Martin McDonagh, Conor McPherson, Gary Mitchell, Rona Munro, Johnny Murphy, Janet Noble, Ronan Noone, Joseph O'Connor, Donal O'Kelly, Mark O'Rowe and Vincent Woods." Again, an impressive dramatic pedigree, but this time with a significant bent toward contemporary work that often challenges audiences to reconsider their definition of Ireland.[7]

Though I was unable to receive responses from the artistic staff of the company—I would assume due to a reported hiatus after a difficult 2005–6 season—it has been articulated in Súgán's own promotional material that they are a company that is completely grounded in the concern for direct connections between Ireland and the United States. Even their name, which translates to "a rope made of straw," was reportedly chosen to represent three separate approaches to their seasons and their audiences—the name calls forth the "twisting rope that represents the link between Ireland and America"; refers to the component rope from the traditional chair of Irish storytellers; and finally indicates cultural and social change by calling forth the first play (written in Irish) of the Irish literary revival at the beginning of the twentieth century, Douglas Hyde's *Casadh an tSúgáin* (translated as *The Twisting of the Rope*).

I mention these elements as they seem to disclose a different view of Irish drama than more traditional Irish American companies (such as the Irish Reps of both New York and Chicago, the Pittsburgh Irish and Classical Theater, and others of that ilk), though they still acknowledge the significance of earlier playwrights to the identity of both the Irish and Irish American communities. One of the great significances of this philosophy, championed by company directors Carmen and Peter O'Reilly, is the opportunity for audiences to find common links between the drama of the past and of the present in order to not think of contemporary Ireland as a separate entity altogether from the Ireland of Yeats, Synge, and O'Casey, but to see these works as intimately connected over time and create a greater Irish cultural narrative for its American audiences.

Additionally, Súgán opens its field of dramatic representation beyond merely Ireland and also engages with other contemporary Celtic cultures. Though their focus is on Irish works, this wider approach to their diasporic audiences tells the tale of a company that wishes to examine the connections between these communities and how we all, in this late twentieth-century construction of identity, can find that our communities, while fundamentally Irish American, have grown less than entirely homogenous over the years (especially the famine era diaspora) and should open their field of vision beyond the Irish stage to examine the Irish American identity.

It should be noted, however, that an attempt to strike a balance between a company's functional and expressive imperatives is not without peril. As reported by numerous sources, Súgán, in 2005–6 seemed to have fallen victim to an attempt to appeal to their audience too much, thereby lessening their more rigorous stance toward contemporary Irish drama. Though their last season was decidedly contemporary, it was made up of a solo performance *(Tom Crean: Antarctic Explorer)*, an over-the-top comedy (*Women on the Verge of HRT* by Marie Jones of *Stones in His Pockets* fame), and a philosophical political play *(Talking to Terrorists)*. Though each of these plays independently would strike a significant chord with the average Irish American audience, the season fell short of the mark, and seemingly the lack of truly challenging contemporary Irish drama—and recognizable contemporary Irish drama, upon which Súgán made its reputation—created a problem for audiences for which the company would have to regroup.

The final company I would like to discuss, Solas Nua of Washington, D.C., is my example of an aggressive Irish American company that is far less interested in any traditional view of Ireland and is instead focused upon dramatic images of a rapidly changing Ireland to express identity for their audiences. By their own mission, they display a new approach to the Irish stage: "Solas Nua seeks out both feted and obscure work by contemporary artists in Ireland, to promote awareness of modern Irish culture in Washington D.C."[8]

Artistic director Linda Murray, a young native of the Irish theater scene, moved from Ireland approximately three years ago and was vexed by the representations of Ireland that she found on American stages: "I don't know that I'm trying to create a new sense of Ireland [for American audiences], but rather am trying to portray the Ireland I know and belong to."[9] She notes that, despite the fact that she cannot truly call herself an Irish American (at least not yet), she cannot be naturally empathetic with the nostalgic leanings of her potential audiences, and therefore she put very strict criteria forward in order to form her company:

> I draw the line at work older than 15 years. I chose this date, because the early 1990s marked the change in economic climate which has resulted in the other modern manifestations of Ireland today—e.g. immigration, decline of the role of family and religion in society. So to produce work from that time of transition raises, for me at least, the very question of Irish identity itself which I find extremely interesting.[10]

I find this statement extremely telling about the company, as the company seeks to exist within this liminal space of transition in Irish culture and attempts to destabilize the familiar tropes of Irish and, indeed, Irish American cultural identity.

Her commentary on her audiences has, however, also been very telling about this approach to contemporary Irish drama: she notes that "that some of the more traditional Irish Americans (third or fourth generation, whose last Irish relative lived in Ireland more than a hundred years ago) have problems with some of our programming. . . . However, Irish ex-pats are very supportive of the company, as are regular theater-goers which I take as a good benchmark of the quality of the work itself, regardless of the nationality of the writer."[11] Additionally, Murray notes that she has noticed in her audiences that Irish Americans do tend to find some of the modern work less "authentically" Irish. This trend seems to go along with certain movements in contemporary Irish drama and theater itself, which concerns itself less with the reflection of Irish society for the benefit of its own national audiences—as was the case with Synge, Yeats, and most of Ireland's twentieth-century playwrights—but rather an attempt to present a new sense of Irishness for a decidedly international audience. These plays are meant to play in London or New York (and are often commissioned to do so) as much as on the Abbey stage. This drama, therefore, works in an opposite direction from more traditional Irish fare in that instead of existing to define and establish a community—Irish, Irish American, or otherwise—it attempts to eliminate cultural boundaries to show how American, European, or international—read "universal"—today's Ireland has become.

So why create an "Irish" theater company in the United States with a view toward a seeming "alienation" of traditional audiences? This seems to be wrapped up in another comment of Murray's, in which she states that while producing in the United States, she has a morbid fear of losing touch with what is going on dramatically and theatrically in Ireland, and therefore she must regularly travel back to attend theater in Ireland. This somewhat alters the frame of her company, however, creating less of a company that challenges more traditional tropes and themes and champions their replacements. Rather, it creates a direct bridge between the two cultures that is in constant negotiation and that is entirely based on the work that is creating a cultural buzz in Ireland.

I have presented these companies in this order very intentionally, ranging from the conservative to the aggressive as this, as you may expect, is how many of the Irish American companies arrange themselves. The more established and long-running theaters found that they had to make significant concessions to the tastes of their audiences, essentially becoming conservative in their work as a mechanism of survival. Many of the more aggressive and even moderate companies have faced extinction over the years, and many have attributed that to a failure to understand the target community at large. Contention with prevailing public tastes, especially when serving such close-knit and culturally defined communities as Irish America, has been one of the deciding factors in the success or indeed even the survival of a company that hopes to transcend the already difficult lot of producing artistically sound work today in the United States.

Having examined the nature of these companies, I would like to briefly stop and discuss the specific contemporary works that are coming out of these companies in order to come to an idea of the image of Ireland that is being presented to contemporary Irish American audiences. I do not intend for this to be a study of the critical response to these works but rather to decipher the intent behind the choices that lead to these seasons of shows.

For the purpose of this study, I have placed the following restrictions on the term "contemporary Irish drama": the work must have been written in the past two decades; the work must stage an Ireland (or an Irish sensibility) that is not inherently nostalgic, nor bound by the old tenets of land, religion, language, or nationalism; and the work must examine Ireland within the context of a nation that anticipates, is benefiting from, or has been profoundly altered by globalization and economic change—most significantly in the guise of the Celtic Tiger.

In examining the annual seasons for the history of many of the theater companies that I have considered, including but not limited to the three that I have previously discussed, there are distinct patterns that emerge concerning both the plays and the playwrights that are included within these seasons. Of these patterns, I would like to discuss two in detail.

First, there is a distinct proclivity for these companies to stage works that are reevaluative of traditional Irish themes and tropes, that take a world that is easily accessible and familiar to Irish American audiences, and that slowly (though often radically) deconstruct these themes in order to present a new Irish sensibility within the guise of "the auld sod." This group of plays was identified by a number of companies and directors as significant for their audiences and it is these plays, with very little exception, that can be considered the commercial successes—if there is such as thing in nonprofit theater—or the critical successes of these theaters. In many of the following examples, Irish American theater companies are allowed to have their cake and eat it as they are able to satisfy their more traditional audiences with comfortable settings and plot structures, while also delighting more contemporary or artistically savvy audiences with their often vicious commentaries.

Among the most produced plays of this group are the works of Marina Carr. As Linda Murray noted:

The Mai is a quite accessible play, set in the past (1979 and 1980), which gives the audience a more traditional view of Ireland. Of course, anyone who knows Marina's writing understands that she subverts traditional Ireland through her plays, but on the surface it seemed to be a simple love story set in rural Ireland and I think that this helped to sell it to the D.C. public.[12]

I think that this is true of almost every Irish American theater company's productions of Carr's work, due to her use of the Irish midlands as a significant point of transition between the new and the old, the east and the west, and the romantic and the ugly. Carr's plays epitomize the harsh and often violent contrast between the nostalgic Ireland of DeValera and the reality of today's complex social and political landscape.

Another popular choice among Irish American theater companies are Martin McDonagh's Lenane and Aran plays, frequently due to the popular (and critical) appeal of his work that has landed his plays on Broadway and in many major regional theaters throughout the United States. The appeal is also due to McDonagh's use of more traditional tropes of land, religion, and language, which he deftly perverts, while still presenting a superficial world worthy of an any of Synge's works. Many directors of Irish American theaters note that McDonagh slyly subverts all of the old indicators of Ireland in a way that by the time you realize that you are watching a savage critique or satire of traditional and contemporary Irish culture that you are already laughing too hard to care.

Conor McPherson's The Weir is a notable work that has been produced at almost every major Irish American theater since its premiere in the United States in 1999. From that point forward, McPherson's name became synonymous with the liminal space between the past and present of Irish drama. People flocked to this production, set in the traditional setting of a rural Irish pub, and may have never realized that this play had extraordinary commentary concerning the "new Ireland" and believed that they were having a great time listening to Irish ghost stories. Though many of McPherson's plays followed the same urge toward Irish storytelling, none were able to enchant Irish American audiences as effectively as The Weir, presumably due to their general lack of this aforementioned liminality.

Finally, although I must break my own definition of contemporary Irish drama to do so, I want to address the popularity of the works of both Tom Murphy and Brian Friel for contemporary Irish American companies. Murphy's deft manipulation of these two Irelands into a single work has appealed to Irish American audiences for years, and Murphy's name alone is enough to fill a house for the majority of a run. Plays such as *Famine, The Gigli Concert, The Sanctuary Lamp,* and *Conversations on a Homecoming* challenge traditional views of Ireland, its history, and the Irish psyche, even though most of his plays, as I noted, predate the "contemporary" parameters set by this study. The works of Brian Friel also find a place within this contemporary movement, but are almost exclusive to the more conservative theaters, except for some of Friel's more experimental work. All of Friel's Baile Beag/ Ballybeg plays share the dual qualities of the aforementioned plays, but more often than not, Friel's work seems to be conflated with more traditional plays, possibly due to his chronological and historical position, but more likely due to his association with the Field Day Company, which many feel makes his works artistic remnants of an earlier version of Irishness.

The second trend that seems to have found a place within many of these companies is what I would like to call the media-savvy trend in contemporary work. This trend, which explores Irish culture alongside global pop culture and more experimental forms of dramaturgy, tends to be evident mainly in the more aggressive Irish American companies, but also as experiments in even the most conservative of companies. I would suggest that this is largely due to economic factors that influence the programming of any theater company's production season. Many of the plays that fall into this group, such as the works of Enda Walsh (particularly *Disco Pigs* and *Bedbound*) and the recently popular monologic works of Friel and McPherson, are small-cast productions that also require little in terms of technical requirements. These plays allow for even the most conservative of companies to explore contemporary dramatic trends without significant investment in either talent or technology. Though this type of play does not dominate the Irish American theatrical landscape, it becomes a critical element in terms of the image of Ireland presented to American audiences.

As a final note, I feel it necessary to mention the works that are nearly unknown to the average theatergoer who supports Irish American theater companies. Many companies over the past two decades have largely ignored plays that have strong social and political messages and that illuminate many

of Ireland's growing pains in the periods preceding and immediately following the onset of the Celtic Tiger. A near complete absence of writers such as
Dermot Bolger, whose works have actively changed the way plays have been
written in Dublin; Declan Hughes, who created some of the most aggressive dramatic commentaries of the nineties; and Thomas Kilroy (save for a
recent collaboration with the Pittsburgh Irish and Classical Theater), whose
works define what we now consider to be the early period of contemporary
Irish drama. These names, along with others such as Mark O'Rowe, Ken
Harmon, and Paula Meehan, seem to fall through the cracks of many company's repertoires, creating a very narrow view of the contemporary Irish
theater scene.

At the end of my research, I have found that the majority of contemporary Irish theater as produced by Irish American theater companies provides
audiences with perfectly acceptable, albeit limited, representations of contemporary Ireland. But these audiences, usually approaching these theaters
and productions with preconceived notions of Irish life, are often confronted
by two Irelands—or what Fintan O'Toole called "a double world, a slippery
state in which the traditional and the modern jostled for the status of reality,
in which every truth was equally untrue, in which past, present, and future
seemed to melt into each other."[13] If the information that I received from
the Irish American theater companies included in this study is completely
accurate, it seems as though this double world is a comfortable place for
most audiences. However, due to the seemingly great differences between
approaches to what may even constitute and define "contemporary Irish
drama," I posit that, until American audiences truly allow a multifaceted
approach to what constitutes the Irish experience, contemporary Irish drama
will continue to be split along lines of the nostalgic and the progressive, giving a fragmented vision of Ireland for the foreseeable future.

4

Between Two Worlds

Boucicault's *The Shaughraun* and Its New York Audience

DEIRDRE McFEELY

Although he was born in Dublin in 1820, Dion Boucicault was a naturalized American citizen living in New York City when he wrote what many consider to be his finest Irish play, *The Shaughraun*. The play premiered on 14 September 1874 at Wallack's, then one of the city's most fashionable theaters, located at the corner of Broadway and 13th Street, and it ran until the following March, the playwright himself assuming the title role. It was an outstanding popular and commercial success, the longest running show at Wallack's that decade: the 118 evening performances and twenty-five matinees grossed just under a quarter of a million dollars, and receipts for the Thanksgiving Day matinee at $2,250 were the highest ever recorded in New York.[1] *The Shaughraun* has also come to be regarded as Boucicault's most political work: set in the immediate aftermath of the Fenian atrocities in England in 1867, the events at Manchester and Clerkenwell are referred to as recent happenings, and the action commences with the return home to Ireland from Australia of an escaped Fenian prisoner, Robert Ffolliott. Described by Elizabeth Butler Cullingford as Boucicault's "most subversively Fenian play," the nationalist content may suggest itself as an important factor in its American success, particularly among the Irish American community.[2] However, the main element in the play's popularity among that particular audience was Boucicault's stage portrayal of Irishmen of whom they highly approved. In fact, in February 1875, a group of "Irish-American gentlemen" organized a testimonial "in the name of the Irish people in America, to Mr. Dion Boucicault, the eminent dramatist, in recognition of the services he had rendered in elevating the stage

54

representation of Irish character."[3] At the presentation, made toward the end of the run of *The Shaughraun*, it was declared to Boucicault that the event was held "to express a thankful consciousness that you have elevated the Irish drama by a just appreciation and portraiture of the attributes and peculiarities to which it relates. In the character of the Shaughraun, for example, you have given us a true type of a class of the Irish peasantry."[4]

The mainstream, or Anglo-American, audience equally approved of Boucicault's representation of the Irish. The theater critics of the mainstream New York daily newspapers welcomed Boucicault's portrayal of what they considered to be the real Irish of Ireland, particularly as a relief from the reality of the Irish immigrant community with whom they were confronted on a daily basis. For Anglo-Americans, the Irish people they encountered in New York, or viewed as their entertainment on stage, differed greatly from their idealized image of the Irish race in its native Ireland. According to the *New York Times*, Boucicault had replaced the traditional stage Irishman with the real thing, and a tangible sense of regret was expressed that the New York Irish community could not be so easily replaced:

> He has created an Irish drama, and almost driven the old-fashioned rough-and-tumble Irishman from the stage. The caricature has gone. The portrait from nature has been substituted in its stead. . . . All Irishmen are not like the Shaughraun, but we hope some of them are, although we do not happen to meet with them in New York. Here we chiefly know the Irish through the medium of very bad domestic servants and political followers of "Boss Kelly." From neither point of view are they attractive.[5]

It might be expected that *The Shaughraun*'s New York audience would fall naturally into these two distinct groups—the mainstream or Anglo-American audience, and the Irish and Irish American audience—and that some reaction to the Fenian subject matter, positive or negative, would be evident. However, coverage in the five best-selling New York daily newspapers and the most popular Irish American newspaper of the time reveals that, contrary to such expectations, the play's nationalist content did not prove to be a factor in its reception at all, for any section of the audience.[6] However, in addition to those who welcomed *The Shaughraun* as an important contribution to Irish American culture, there was another Irish audience who rejected it as an utter insult to their understanding of the Irish race. The reception by this latter group is the subject of this essay.

Irish American journalism flourished from the mid-nineteenth century onward, and the most famous and influential publication was the *Irish World*, a weekly newspaper founded in 1870 by Patrick Ford. Ford was a Galway man who had come to America with his parents to escape the famine. During his forty-three years as editor, Ford was to prove to be a prominent and controversial journalist, and he came to hold a position of some importance within the Irish community. He exhibited a strong objection to anti-Irish prejudice and founded the newspaper during a period of intense anti-Irish prejudice which had resulted from the Orange and Green sectarian riots in New York City during July 1870. Throughout his career, Ford identified with his Irish readers, who were increasingly self-conscious about their ethnic origins. He condemned what he considered to be the Anglo-Saxon ascendancy over the Irish in America, which resulted in their alienation from the established American community. He blamed British rule in Ireland for the plight of all Irishmen, those who had emigrated as much as those actually living in Ireland. The newspaper's stated principle was that "the *Irish World* is Catholic, it is American, it is Irish and it is democratic," and, while being highly nationalistic and patriotic, it was mainly concerned with the interests of the urban New York Irish. However, its readership extended well beyond New York. Published on Saturdays in Brooklyn and costing 5 cents, its circulation had risen to 35,000 by 1876 and would peak in the early 1890s at 125,000.[7]

The *Irish World* did not, in the main, review drama or any other form of the arts. However, the opening of *The Shaughraun* prompted a debate in its letter column about the general issue of the stage portrayal of the Irishman, and the correspondence ran until the play itself closed the following March. The debate did not concern itself with any of the conventions of theatrical reviewing, nor was it concerned with any aspect of the drama as a form of art or entertainment. Its focus was instead on race: that of the portrayal of the Irish race on the American stage. While there was no strong criticism leveled at Boucicault in the early stages, there was equally a lack of any pride in their fellow countryman's achievement on the New York stage. It was generally acknowledged that Boucicault had done something to improve the lot of the stage Irishman, but the newspaper's correspondents called for more work to be done:

> You have done a great deal towards "reforming" the Irish drama, Mr. Boucicault, but you haven't reached the ideal yet, and please don't stop

half way. Why can't you give us a character and drama with the rags and the whiskey left out, and the chivalry, the patriotism, and the generous impulses brought in to set off the unmistakable humor of your native land, of which you possess so much. If we can't have an American drama, won't John Brougham or Boucicault, or someone else, give us the representative Irish drama?[8]

A great part of Conn the Shaughraun's appeal lies in the fact that his true qualities are hidden underneath a vagabond exterior, and at the end of every performance, the audience is called upon to overlook his faults, secure in the knowledge that he is a good person at heart. However, given Ford's support of the temperance movement, it is not surprising that a recurring criticism expressed by the correspondents of the *Irish World* about the stage Irishman, including Conn, is his permanent attachment to a whiskey bottle.

The Irish World's crusade to encourage temperance within the Irish community should not be regarded as a religious mission in itself, but as a tool that was used to promote the cause of that community and to portray the Irish as model citizens. Father Theobald Mathew had preached that "Ireland sober is Ireland free" when he visited the United States in 1851, and nationalists linked temperance to Ireland's national cause. However, observance of temperance by the Irish carried greater significance in terms of their social ambitions in their new homeland than in terms of their interest in Irish politics. "'The Irish people should never touch liquor or beer in America . . . if they are desirous of becoming good Citizens,' declared the Limerick born temperance crusader William Downes, 'total abstinence . . . is the golden lever which will guide our weak machinery to a successful goal.'"[9] Rather than confining its members to a subgroup of the Catholic church, the temperance movement was actually promoting their assimilation into a wider American society.

Given their renunciation of Conn the Shaughraun, it might be expected that the *Irish World* correspondents would have found Robert Ffolliott, the Fenian hero of the play, to be a more acceptable form of stage Irishman. Though he does imbibe a moderate amount of American whiskey, he is not portrayed as permanently attached to a bottle, and he can certainly be considered to be chivalrous, patriotic, and generous. However, he does not elicit any comment from any of the correspondents, either positive or negative. This may be because Ffolliott's character undoubtedly lacks Conn's dramatic appeal, or it may be due to his class. Although Ffolliott is a Catholic and a nationalist, he is representative of the nineteenth-century Anglo-Irish gentry for whom the *Irish World* displayed little tolerance.

It is clear that the letters were written by educated and well-informed people, and initially the tone of the letters was reasonable. But beneath this surface lay an acute distress about the representation of Irishmen on the American stage and the broader implication of the representation of Ireland in the United States. The representation of Ireland and the Irish is rejected as false, and the assignment of responsibility for this falsehood is an important element of the debate. Although it is acknowledged that every race is caricatured to some extent in society, the correspondents believe that the Irish caricature is the most debasing, and they claim that in America such false caricature is actually accepted as the real thing. For example, J. B. from Staten Island wrote to complain that:

> Our grumbling is not that Irish villains are put upon the stage, but because such villain [*sic*] is made the type of our race, the rule, not the exception. History, past and present, abundantly proves that Irishmen, with equal advantages, can hold their own, in every sphere, against any competition; and to-day, instead of painting exaggerations of what tyranny and misrule have made our lowest classes, and calling them "types" of our race, our representative should be chosen from the respectable classes, who against unparalleled oppression have kept themselves at their true level.[10]

The correspondence is intensely political and demonstrates a deep-seated hatred and resentment of England and of British rule in Ireland. The Irishman on the American stage is regarded as a representation of Britain's political oppression of Ireland, and this is expressed in angry terms over and over again. According to a correspondent from Brooklyn:

> It was England who first went systematically to work to debase the Irish character on the stage. Not content with robbing and oppressing us, she employed every contrivance that human ingenuity could suggest to brutalize and degrade us. She also found it to her interest to propagate the notion that the average Irishman was what she would like to see him be, and what she tried to make him—a semi-civilized buffoon. . . . Now, mark the purpose this caricature was made to serve: by pointing at this embodiment of her own ideal, England sought to justify the infamies of her rule in Ireland, saying: "How can I be expected to deal rationally with the wild hordes of which this fellow is a sample and representative?"[11]

It is an indication of the power and influence of the drama at that time that so much political intent was read into the representation of the stage Irishman. That the readers of the *Irish World* did so perhaps resulted from their distance from the front line of Irish nationalist politics in Ireland. Expression of their opposition to British rule, and to their perceived debasement at the hands of the ruling Anglo-Americans, through the subject of the stage Irishman, must be considered a form of cultural nationalism. They wanted Irish drama to register dissent against Britain and to establish the Irish race as culturally different from both the British and the Anglo-Americans. Catholicism, abstinence from alcohol, and nationalism were central to this cultural identity.

The *Irish World* strove to establish a particular cultural identity for the Irish community in America, yet the sense of existing between two worlds, old and new, is a striking facet of the newspaper overall and is central to the debate. In his discussion of *The Shaughraun* on the New York stage, Gary Richardson rightly points out that such an existence is demonstrated in the final verse of the rebel song, "The Wearing of the Green," from Boucicault's 1864 play *Arrah-na-Pogue*:

> But if at last our colour should be torn from Ireland's heart,
> Her sons with shame and sorrow from the dear old isle will part;
> I've heard a whisper of a country that lies beyond the sea
> Where rich and poor stand equal in the light of freedom's day.
> O Erin, must we leave you, driven by a tyrant's hand?
> Must we ask a mother's blessing from a strange and distant land?
> Where the cruel cross of England shall nevermore be seen,
> And where, please God, we'll live and die still wearing of the green.[12]

The up-and-coming educated Irish in America who were forming a growing middle class were trapped between the Catholic Ireland they (or their parents or grandparents) had left and the American Protestant society to which they had little or no access. Even the small professional class that constituted the Irish elite could not compete socially with the upper levels of New York society. Removed from Ireland, they were disenfranchised from Irish politics except to express trenchant nationalist views. In New York, they distanced themselves from the poor working-class Irish and from the established, corrupt Irish American political machine that thrived on the working-class vote.

As editor of the *Irish World*, Patrick Ford encouraged a veneration for the Ireland left behind while simultaneously pointing out the contribution made by Irishmen to American history. The concept of race, as opposed to the more limited idea of nationality, allowed for a broad interpretation of Irish character that extended beyond the island of Ireland. Thus, the Irish race could be disassociated from the poverty and destitution that drove the Irish from their homeland to America. The letter writers in the *Irish World* demonstrate an acute consciousness of belonging to a unique Irish or Celtic race, and their expression of a dogged nationalism appears to be more acutely the result of the alienation they suffer in America rather than their desire for self-determination for Ireland. In order to promote their own social cause in a society dominated by Anglo-American culture, they needed to convince others of the illegitimacy of British rule in Ireland. By so doing, they could demonstrate that the growing community of impoverished Irish in America did not exist as a result of a national Irish weakness or character flaw, but due to the external forces of an oppressive power. To this end, they believed that American society must be shown that the stage Irishman does not represent the real Irish; rather, it is of English construction and a direct product of British rule.

In the early stages of the debate, Ford had written to the leading theater managers in New York and beyond, inviting them to contribute. The general thrust of the in-depth and balanced response was that the theater is not responsible for setting trends but for following them and that theater managers must aim to provide entertainment for a broad spectrum of people. If they were to abide by the sensitivities of one particular group, theaters would quickly lose financial viability. Irishmen, they held, were far too sensitive about the dramatic portrayal of their race, and in fact they suffered no more on the stage than any other ethnic group. This response was rejected out of hand by the correspondents, who, if anything, regarded it as a further attack on the Irish race. The sense of being American society's underdog is carried to such an extreme that tolerance for external criticism, no matter how reasonable, is nonexistent, coupled with a complete absence of any faculty for self-criticism.

One particular response indicates the sense of alienation and deep injustice felt by the Irish American community. As with many of the other

correspondents, this response is rooted in the ideology of Ireland as a uto-
pia that produced a super race. The contribution made by the Irish in the
Civil War and in the rapidly developing modern American society apparently outweighed that made by any other ethnic group, to the extent that
the achievements of other races were ignored or denied. A correspondent
declared:

> Now, I do not think the average Irishman is *sensitive enough*! Suppose a
> man receives a kick, is he too sensitive if he resents it? Now, the Irishman
> claims a country that Nature has made the most beautiful on earth—"a
> miniature continent"—whose sons and daughters have won laurels in every
> age and clime. The orators, lawyers, missioners, soldiers, sculptors, mer-
> chants, sailors, mechanics, and laborers sprung from this stock, have all
> forwarded the interests of mankind more than any other distinct people.
> Their blood has flowed for freedom on every battlefield. . . . And what vic-
> tory on this side of the Atlantic was won without an Irishman? From the
> plan of the Erie Canal to the grading of the Union Pacific Railroad . . . his
> footmark may always be found.[13]

Ford turned next to Boucicault himself for his opinion, but if he had
hoped for a recantation, he was disappointed. In a stinging reply, Boucicault
explained why he felt unable to comment:

> As I commenced and am "the head and front" of the question you are dis-
> cussing—as, indeed, I am the subject of it—I am not at liberty to argue the
> matter. It is not a question for settlement in a newspaper. It is for the great
> English-speaking public to decide, and the Irish people sitting in judgment
> at the Theater Royal, Dublin, to render the final verdict. Whether my Irish
> Drama is or is not to supersede the dramatic pictures of Irish life that have
> heretofore occupied the stage, neither you nor I nor your correspondents
> nor your readers can say.
>
> My terms for an article in the *Irish World* are $1,000 a column. No
> charge for this letter.[14]

By referring the matter to a Dublin audience, Boucicault had selected a city
that held him as one of its greatest sons, and an audience for whom he could
do no wrong. Irish people in Dublin had long welcomed Boucicault as the
creator of such an Irish drama as the *Irish World* was now proposing. Boucicault was denying this Irish community in New York the right to comment

on matters relating to Ireland and, in so doing, added fuel to the fire. In considering why Boucicault took such an action, it is not impossible, given his temperament, that he wrote the letter out of pique because he was not lauded by the readers of the *Irish World*. However, given the mainstream reception and the financial success of *The Shaughraun*, this would seem unlikely. Whatever the reason, his dismissive, mocking, and arrogant method of refusing to enter into the debate does indicate an underlying anger.[15]

Ford erupted in a barely controlled fury, displaying his own prejudices, particularly anti-Englishness, and a distinct lack of editorial objectivity:

> The buffoons are very glib on the stage, when speaking through the Irishman of English conception and manufacture; but when asked to give their private opinion on that semi-barbarous character, they reply with a grunt. Well, it isn't surprising. If the thing is a libel, *they* are its publishers, and, of course, *they* share in the odium attached to the libel. . . . Mr. Boucicault says that an Anglo-Irish audience sitting in "Theater Royal," Dublin, is the only competent judge of the burlesque Irish Drama. Why select "*Theater Royal?*" Why look for a verdict under the shadow of the Castle? Is not an American theater a fit court? New York is the greatest Irish city in the world. It has a larger Irish element even than Dublin. Why, then, fear it? Mr. Boucicault contends that "it is for the great English-speaking public to decide." It is not English-speaking people merely, but people who like to think after the English style, that Mr. Boucicault prefers. He is one of the most respectable dramatists, but still his creations are a libel on Irish character. On this account he feels obliged to use the Lion and Unicorn as the trade-mark of his manufactures, and to look to the great public who talk after the English fashion for a verdict.[16]

That Ford considered Boucicault, and indeed all Dubliners, to be Anglo-Irish is evidence that the urban rural divide of Ireland, the area within and beyond the Pale, was an issue among Irish American immigrants, most of whom would have had rural backgrounds. He is insulted by the royal endorsement of a Dublin theater and dismisses the opinion of the Dublin audience. The emphasis laid on the actual physical proximity to Dublin Castle is important: the idea of an Irish drama in a theater enjoying royal patronage is unacceptable to Ford. The Irish in New York are, in a sense, nationless, yet in dismissing Dublin due to its British rule, Ford seeks to establish New York as the greatest Irish city in the world, and the New York Irish as more Irish than those people actually living in Dublin. The implication is, therefore, that a national Irish drama can find a true home only in America.

Ford's editorial reply to Boucicault was the opening shot of an enraged response from the *Irish World*'s readers. A key issue raised was their utter contempt for Dublin's Theater Royal, or any other institution, such as the Royal Irish Constabulary, that demonstrated a nominal connection with the British Crown. They decried Boucicault's "foul caricature on our religion and our race," and denied him any claim to be an Irish dramatist. One of the key enemies of the *Irish World* at that time was the satirical illustrator Thomas Nast, whose work appeared in the often anti-Irish and anti-Catholic publication, *Harper's Weekly*. A correspondent from Philadelphia now likened Boucicault to Nast as an enemy of Ireland:

> From his words, Dion Boucicault shows that he has a small heart and a greedy palm—ready to work for the British Government, the devil, or anybody who pays him—a counterpart of Tom Nast in New York, who would picture his dead father in the most hideous shape for money. If Boucicault has not been paid by the British Government for the work he has done, he is the most willing slave yet heard of.[17]

In this perspective, Boucicault's work was rejected completely, and any hope that may have originally been held that he would eventually produce the sort of Irish drama required was abandoned. Moreover, the *Irish World* readers were quick to suggest their own remedies for what a correspondent from St. Louis, Missouri, described as "this cancer, which is eating into our national life, and holding up to view before American audiences characters un-Irish in look, action, and manners":

> In every city and town in the United States let a society be formed composed of earnest, temperate, thinking Irish nationalists. Such societies to be called "The Irish Drama Protective Associations". . . . It will be the duty of the I.D.P.As. to visit the theater and see how they like it.[18]

The proposed title suggests a highly controlled, and controlling, organization that would do more to restrict creativity and entertainment than to encourage it. However, mere entertainment or financial considerations were not factors in the discussion. The key issues were the education of the audience as to the true nature of Irishmen and the promotion of self-determination for Ireland. By liberating Irish drama from caricature, they would actually be assisting in the liberation of Ireland itself, as outlined by Thomas M. Derrick, of Providence, Rhode Island, who imagined a Utopian Ireland akin to that envisioned in Eamon de Valera's famous Saint Patrick's Day speech:

> There are thousands of Irish societies scattered throughout America. We have plenty of talent and intelligence to organize a dramatic club in connection with every one of those societies. By a judicious selection of elevating, when possible, Irish national productions, we can foster a growing taste, and so exercise an influence that must eventually result in banishing from our midst the evils we complain of. . . . Before we acknowledge a dramatic work as being truly Irish, we must have the educated and refined Irish gentleman, the intrepid and intelligent patriot, and the virtuous and polished Irish maiden faithfully delineate. . . . Although thoroughly devoted to our adopted country, we yet aspire to work out the liberation of our native Erin across the Atlantic. As an auxiliary to this undertaking we have a right to emancipate the Irish drama from the grasp of a lot of buffoons who have control of it. Indeed, it may seriously be doubted whether a *free* country can exist without the aid of the drama.[19]

By calling for the stage Irishman to portray the virtues that they believed they possessed or to which they aspired, the correspondents were actually attempting to promote their own social acceptance within the Anglo-American community. While demanding that the drama hold a mirror up to nature, they certainly did not want it to reflect the contemporary social reality of immigrant life from which they strove to distance themselves.

What the correspondents really wanted was to hold a mirror up to nation, but a nation of their own construction. They wanted to dramatize Ireland's mythical and historical past in a manner to suit their own political and social agenda—to demonstrate English oppression and the superior characteristics of the Irish race in the face of such a greater power:

> Can we not have a drama—a hundred of them, in fact—based on the unapproachable Irish devotion to God, native land, and family? Is there not splendid material for dramas or tragedies in the lives and services of Hugh O'Neill, Robert Emmet, Wolf Tone, or Lord Edward Fitzgerald?[20]

> Could not a drama be composed on the fate of the children of Usna, the treachery of the English commander, Corby, at Mullaghmast, the last days

of Dunboy, the death of King Connor MacNessa, and Dathi—the battle of Clontarf and murder of King Brian in his tent?[21]

In drawing on Ireland's past, the correspondents ignore current Irish politics, including the fact that *The Shaughraun* drew on recent events in Ireland's political struggle with England and that it made many direct references to Fenianism. Although it might be expected that the play would have appealed for those very reasons, this certainly did not prove to be the case. Current criticism has commented on the politics of reconciliation in Boucicault's Irish plays that enabled them to be accepted and enjoyed by both English and Irish audiences. Yet, it would seem that the reconciliatory ending of *The Shaughraun* caused offense to the correspondents of the *Irish World,* and this was one of the reasons why they found Boucicault's work so objectionable. They advocated a "no surrender" approach, and thus rejected Boucicault's depiction of the British as inherently decent and sympathetic people. So rather than responding to the Fenian context of *The Shaughraun* in terms of contemporary Irish nationalism, the debate actually centered on the politics of class and race. Not only among the community of readers of the *Irish World* but also among the Anglo-American audience and the rest of the Irish American community. For all groups the authenticity of representation was of central importance.

This debate in the *Irish World* in the 1870s anticipated the evolution of a cultural nationalism in Ireland in the last decade of the nineteenth century. In New York it was demanded that Irish drama carry out functions of both resistance and education—resistance to English political and cultural oppression and education as to the true nature of the Irish. Such demands anticipate the formation of the Gaelic League and the Irish Literary Theater, and indeed, when reading the *Irish World,* Lady Gregory's 1897 manifesto certainly comes to mind: "We will show that Ireland is not the home of buffoonery and of easy sentiment, as it has been represented, but the home of an ancient idealism."[22] However, it must also be considered that the *Irish World* readers, while anticipating the later cultural debate in Ireland, would appear, somewhat paradoxically, to have been more aligned with those Dublin middle-class nationalist Catholics who objected to the Abbey's *Playboy* more than thirty years later.

5

Reporting the Stage Irishman

Dion Boucicault in the Irish Press

GWEN OREL

Playwright Dion Boucicault always claimed to have the heart of a patriot. Yet he ended his life not in Ireland, but as an American citizen, part of the Irish immigrant community in New York. Here his popular Irish plays— *The Colleen Bawn, The Shaughraun,* and *Arrah-Na-Pogue*—not only presented an amusing stage Irishman to confound the English but an idealized stage Ireland to console the homesick. Histories of nineteenth-century theater note Boucicault's prolixity, his enforcement of the copyright, and the technical innovations of his popular melodramas (such as the camera, first used onstage in the 1859 play *The Octoroon*). Although it is not possible to determine whether patriotism or profit drove Boucicault, it is possible to determine whether the community he claimed could claim any benefit from him. Ethnic communities used institutions such as newspapers and theaters to create their identity and sphere of influence in the New World, and Boucicault was highly visible in the ethnic press. The *Irish World,* the *Irish-American,* and the *New York Freeman's Journal and Catholic Register* demonstrate that Boucicault was indeed an important personality to that community—not only as a playwright but also as a successful native son.

For many non-English speaking immigrants in nineteenth-century America, ethnic papers were the only conduit of information. Irish American immigrants, like those in the twenty-first century, could read the *New York Times* for general news (they could also read the *Herald* and other now-defunct New York dailies). For them, the ethnic press primarily served to provide news specific to their community. It was the source for news from back home, lessons on social customs in America, information on relatives expected or missing, political rallying points, and instruction from Catholic clergymen.[1]

Today's *Irish Echo* and *Irish Voice* continue to serve these needs, minus the plaintive notices for missing relatives and overt religious instruction. The 26 April–2 May 2006 issue of the *Irish Echo,* in addition to its coverage of news from Ireland, includes "Irish Connections: Website Provides Links for Irish Expats in NYC" by Ailbhe Jordan, "Malachy's Run: Republicans, Democrats, All the Same, says McCourt" by the same writer (on his bid for governor); Elaiane Ni Bhraonain's column "An Tiogar Ceilteach/A Single Girl's Adventures in Manhattan" printed in Irish and in English; entertainment listings; and articles in editor Eileen Murphy's "The Buzz" that point out plays, performances, and readings with Irish themes or performers. The *Irish Voice* from the same week has as its cover story the headline "Family Torn Apart" about a pair of siblings who fear not being allowed back into America if they go to Ireland for a funeral and a banner for a story on "vital immigration meeting on Long Island."

The Irish American press also provided relief from the relentless stereotyping of Irish Americans that had grown increasingly virulent from midcentury on. The cartoons of Thomas Nast and John Tenniel portrayed the Irishman as the missing link between human and ape. From 1845 to 1855 over a million Irish immigrants arrived in America; the quick influx exacerbated religious prejudice and xenophobia. Fear of job shortages and stereotyping of the Irish as shifty drunks prompted newspaper job advertisements to add the line "no Irish need apply," a phrase immortalized in the 1862 song by John F. Poole. Although they spoke English, Irish Americans were as alienated as any immigrants in nineteenth-century America.

In its ability to draw disparate peoples together, theater was very like the ethnic press. Irish theater was more important in America than it had been at home, since it provided a place where Irish people otherwise separated by class, gender, and religion could gather to celebrate the home they had in common. The theater served to build community while representing it. And just as nationalism and the great dream of Irish independence ran through both religious and secular Irish papers, a coded call to arms or at least proud self-esteem for the Irish diaspora ran through the Irish plays of Dion Boucicault.

Boucicault's early acting roles were all of comic Irishmen, and his brogue was so thick (it remained with him for life) that at least one critic praised him for its remarkable accuracy.[2] Boucicault arrived in New York in 1853, at the age of thirty-two, following his actress girlfriend and later wife, Agnes Robertson (she appeared in a play he had adapted from Edward Lancaster first in Montreal and then New York, called by Boucicault *The Young Actress* and by Lancaster *The Manager's Daughter*). He made his American acting debut playing a comic Irish character called Sir Patrick O'Plenipo in 1854 in *Irish Artist*. By 1860, when *The Colleen Bawn* debuted, Boucicault was already a well-known figure in Manhattan through such now-forgotten plays as *Apollo in New York* (1854) and *Blue Belle* (1856) as well as more canonical *The Poor of New York* (1857). He was also known through his 1859 establishment of the Winter Garden Theater (although he abandoned his partnership with Wallack's manager William Stuart early on after a falling-out). After *The Colleen Bawn*'s success—it played for six weeks at capacity—Boucicault congratulated himself for "writing a play from material gathered from my native country,"[3] expressing surprise that such a rich history had not been dramatically explored before. Actually, the idea to write the play had not been Boucicault's but actor-manager Barney Williams, who commissioned him to write it the year before.[4] Boucicault and Robinson preferred to recount a fiction of how she happened to reread Gerald Griffin's novel *The Collegians,* which prompted Boucicault to consider adapting it.[5]

Boucicault derived the title for the play from the Irish ballad "Willy Reilly and the Colleen Bawn," (Colleen Bawn means a fair-haired girl), and the name for his second heroine Anne Chute (who does not appear in Griffin's novel) may be derived from another ballad, "the Colleen Rua" (the use of Irish ballads to stir national feeling was a technique Boucicault would return to in 1865's *Arrah-na-Pogue*).[6] Griffin's 1829 novel about a soldier who murders his peasant bride was based on a true incident; as a reporter Griffin had attended the trials ten years earlier of the soldier and boatmen who conspired to murder a beautiful peasant girl tricked into believing in a false marriage.[7] Boucicault transformed the story into a thrilling adventure with a happy ending, introducing the comic hero Myles-na-Coppaleen, whom he played himself, and making the attempted murderer the boatman, rather than the lover. Myles saves the day during a "sensational" head-first dive into a lake onstage (represented by yards of gauze). How far Boucicault departed from Griffin's novel, itself based upon a true crime story from

1819, may be seen in the response from the *New York Freeman's Journal and Catholic Register*. This paper, a weekly published from 1841 to 1918, had a wide national circulation, and with the Boston *Pilot* it was one of the most successful Irish Catholic papers:

> To put it on the stage, in its truth, is to confer the highest gratification; to put it on the stage, maimed and patched, clipped and altered, is to inflict insult and pain. This is what Mr. Bourcicault [*sic*] has done. Under his hands, the perfect conception of Griffin has shriveled into a thing misnamed a play, without consistency or form. The plot of the novel is altered, new characters introduced, and most of those which are not omitted are spoiled almost to disgust.

The *Freeman* objected to Boucicault's diminishment of Griffin's moralism, and particularly to his portrayal of the priest, Father Tom:

> It is the worse, because the real priest of the story, who is what a priest ought to be, and quite available too for representation, is exchanged for a whisky-drinker of the Friar Tuck school—one who smokes his pipe by the cabin fire while some one is fetching him a jar of whisky from the still; and afterwards talks of so-and-so who came to him the day before for absolution for such a sin, mentioning at the same time the sin.[8]

On the same day this review came out, the *Irish-American* pronounced a quite different verdict. The *Irish-American* was clearly a very different paper from the *Freeman's Journal*. Sympathetic to the intellectual and artistic movement known as Young Ireland in the 1840s and inclined to blame Catholic fatalism for the failure of the Young Irelander's revolt, it attempted to reconcile Catholicism and nationalism, particularly the Young Ireland brand of nationalism that emphasized a romantic past.[9] Under the heading "The New Irish Drama" the review in the *Irish-American* began:

> Mr. Dion Bourcicault [*sic*] deserves the credit of inaugurating a new era in the history of the Irish Drama by the production of his latest, and probably his most effective, piece, "The Colleen Bawn; or the Brides of Garryowen," now performing with such distinguished success at Laura Keene's Theater.

The review acknowledges Boucicault's changes from the original story, but approves of them, reserving sharp remarks for Laura Keene's Anne Chute and variations on Irish melodies. Overall, they found the piece to be a welcome foray into pleasant nostalgia: "The scenery irresistibly carries back the heart and mind of the Irish-born spectator to the loved scenes of his childhood home."[10]

One week later the *Irish-American* published a second review of the Colleen Bawn, praising Laura Keene for improving her performance and encouraging readers to see the show before it closed. On 19 May, the *Irish-American* covered Laura Keene's benefit performance, printing Keene's speech and also Boucicault's. Boucicault charmed the audience by invoking his Irish manners: "I hope I am too much of an Irishman not to know that a lady should always have the last word."[11] The play itself reflects the same conciliatory hope that the *Irish-American* had for nationalism and Catholicism, so it is not surprising that the paper's reviewer so enthusiastically promoted the play.

In all of Boucicault's plays, the oppressor is not so much the villain as the one who conspires with him. By lessening the moral turpitude of Hardress, who loves Eily more than he loves rich Anne Chute, and making the murderer not a faithless lover but a hired killer working for a greedy businessman, Boucicault dramatizes the hope of reform and reintegration. *The Freeman's Journal*, in contrast, specifically decried this plot invention. While the play presents class issues, specifically when Hardress attempts to tutor Eily out of her native brogue, they are ultimately elided in compromise. It is Corrigan, the evil rent collector, who hires the boatman to kill Eily. Rent collectors were often the villains in Irish political cartoons. Significantly, the English are not present in the play. The play's success was so great that Boucicault toured it to London, where Queen Victoria saw it four times. The play then went to Dublin, where it was ecstatically received. Boucicault did not return to New York for twelve years, during which he made and lost a fortune.

In the interval, Boucicault wrote his second Irish play *Arrah-na-Pogue*, which premiered in Dublin in 1865. The title, like *The Colleen Bawn*, refers to a girl, Arrah of the kiss, and its plot mirrors the earlier play in other respects. Boucicault played Shaun the post, a character not very different from Myles-na-coppeleen (though less amusing overall), in a drama set in the 1798 Fenian uprising led by Wolfe Tone and the United Irishmen. Boucicault wrote new anti-English lyrics to the ballad "The Wearing of the Green" that banned the song throughout the British Empire.[12] Again, the primary villains are not so much British officers, but the greedy Irishmen who collaborate with them. This play was so well received in New York that when the Boucicaults returned there in 1873, Boucicault decided to become an American citizen. Not surprisingly, it was after his naturalization that his intent and actions became most significant for the Irish American community.

Boucicault followed up this success with *The Shaughraun,* set against the Fenian uprisings of 1867. The title means "the vagabond," and the play again involves pairs of sweethearts and a priest. Conn is the shaughraun of the title, a wandering prankster and fiddle player. Boucicault himself played the role. The play was produced in autumn 1874. It was not the first time Boucicault lionized the Irish rebel, but setting the play in such a recent period was a risk. The Fenian movement was a sacred subject to Irish Americans.[13] The Irish American community was very concerned with the fate of its homeland; three out of four of the originators of the Fenian movement of the sixties were Irish expatriates in America. The Fenian Brotherhood itself was established by John Mahoney in Chicago in 1859. The American origins of Fenianism were lampooned in the humor magazine *Judy*:

Tis a treacherous baste, with never a taste

of honour, love, or pity

From Fenian name of old it came,

But was hatched in New York City![14]

A play about the uprising might flatter expatriate rebels, but it could also provoke anxiety, as some feared exacerbation of xenophobic prejudice. L. Perry Curtis Jr., in *Apes and Angels: The Irishman in Victorian Caricature,* suggests that the progression in stereotype from mildly brutish to irretrievably ape-like is connected to the perceived Fenian threat.

The reception of *The Shaughraun* in the Irish press demonstrates the varieties of reception the expatriate Irish community felt toward the Fenian movement. The Catholic clergy disapproved of the Fenians, and in 1870 excommunicated many of them. *The Shaughraun* received little mention in Catholic-Irish papers.

In late 1874, toward the end of the play's premier run, the New York weekly the *Irish World* began running a series of letters debating the nature of the stage Irishman and its reflection on the Irish. For several weeks the paper printed five or six of these letters at a time, including anonymous letters signed "Democrat" or "Gael," signed letters from readers, and considered responses from theater professionals—including one from Dion Boucicault.

The *Irish World* was primarily a working class paper that endorsed trade unions, opposed monopolies, and supported socialist doctrine.[15] It was a paper more interested in assimilation than heritage. Letters were printed with such headings as "Theatrical Misrepresentation of Ireland," "Where the Blame Lies," and "Wanted—An Irish drama." Today this kind of public commentary seems familiar, from the Internet, chat groups, e-mail lists, and blogs. On such groups, "threads" are sustained, primarily, through debate, with articles that are quoted and rebutted, point by point. People who make frequent posts are quickly viewed as recognizable personalities in this community, and occasionally a famous person tied to the group will "lurk" (i.e., read but seldom post). However, despite the infrequent responses, many posts acknowledge the celebrity and address him or her, and the "community" is that much more vital for the idea of that presence. There is a group for every rare medical condition, every interest, every hobby. Within such a group, one is suddenly no longer alone, no longer an outsider.

The *Irish-American,* a paper interested in the glorious Irish past, whose editor Patrick Lynch blamed Catholic fatalism for the failure of the 1848 revolt, avoided the political issues by printing a review of the manuscript by a Dublin critic (who had had no opportunity to see the play) and evaluating the play only as an evening of theater. Part of the anxiety about the image of the Irish movement was its popularity: receipts for the Thanksgiving Day matinee were the highest ever in New York.[16] How seriously the accuracy of the representation of a typical Irishman was taken can be seen by this criticism in one letter in *The Irish World:*

> Boucicault is said to have done more to elevate the tone of this school than any other author known to us. Well, perhaps on the whole, we might allow the claim; I have no time to enter upon any lengthy analysis, but, just think of it, in his latest play *(The Shaughraun)* he introduces *Two Fiddles* among the accompaniments at an Irish wake![17]

One letter suggests the Irish were "too sensitive," and a rebuttal found the caricatures anything but harmless: "It may, indeed, be that dramas which burlesque the Irish character draw better houses, but the motives of the persons thus attracted are as patent as the religious views of Thomas Nast, or the political animus of the *Times.*"[18] Theater manager Henry D. Palmer defended the stage Irishman by citing Boucicault's plays as examples. On 6 February, Boucicault himself jumped in:

Dear Sir—As I commenced and am "the head and front" of the question
you are discussing—as indeed, I am the subject of it—I am not at liberty
to argue the matter. It is not a question for settlement in a newspaper. It
is for the great English-speaking public to decide, and the Irish people sitting in judgment at the Theater Royal, Dublin, to render the final verdict.
Whether my Irish Drama is or is not to supersede the dramatic pictures of
Irish life that have heretofore occupied the stage, neither you nor I nor your
correspondents nor your readers can say.

My terms for an article in the *Irish World* are $1,000 a column. No
charge for this letter. Yours truly,

Dion Boucicault[19]

The editors objected to Boucicault's claim that his real judges would be the
Irish people at the Theater Royal in Dublin, a theater with the British Royal
insignia. Furthermore, they argued, "New York is the greatest Irish city in
the world. It has a larger Irish element even than Dublin." It is Boucicault's
slighting of the *immigrant* community that stings. Responding to Boucicault's kind offer of the gratis "article," the editors also inform him that
while terms for advertisement were usually $2 a line, they would waive the
fee in hopes that the exchange would be of interest "to the great Irish public,
at least, whom he has done his best—unwittingly, let us hope—to bring into
contempt and ridicule."[20]

Letters in the *Irish World* continued the following week. One is titled
"Is Boucicault Irish?" and another, "Boucicault and Nast." The outrage was
primarily directed at the depiction of Conn the Shaughraun. The backlash
from the community served a constructive purpose: two letters called for an
original Irish theater:

> Such men as Dion Boucicault may by some be ranked as Irish dramatists,
> but the Irish people do not consider them as such. . . . As an auxiliary to
> this undertaking we have a right to emancipate the Irish drama from the
> grasp of a lot of buffoons who have control of it. Indeed, it may seriously
> be doubted whether a *free* country can exist without the aid of the drama.
> Let us see if we cannot, at least in America, make the Irish drama what it
> ought to be.[21]

Indirectly, then, Boucicault constructed coherence in the immigrant community of his audience as well as a dream of cohesion onstage. The anger at

Boucicault's letter even affected the reporting of the testimonial the following week honoring Boucicault from the Irish people in America:

> But of what value is the testimonial of the Irish-American element, if the Irish-American element is not competent to judge? Have you, Mr. Boucicault, honestly changed your opinion? Or do you intend to offer a second insult to our people by using their name as convenience suggests?[22]

Over the next two weeks, discussion broadened to the stage Irishman in general. Actor-manager Barney Williams, who had originally commissioned *The Colleen Bawn,* became involved. When the *World* absolved him from "blame" for portraying stage Irishmen (in other plays), he wrote a letter that included a mini history of Irish writers, with an appreciative nod to Boucicault.

In focusing so intently on Boucicault's attitude to the Irish American community, both papers managed to avoid the touchier issue of the politics of the play. Boucicault, however, did not. On 1 January 1876, Boucicault wrote an open letter to Disraeli calling for the release of the Fenian prisoners in the name of those who had seen *The Shaughraun* and by so doing had expressed their sympathies, placing special emphasis on the Americans: "I have seen, and I know, that toward these twelve or fourteen miserable men are directed the sympathies of 20,000,000 of English hearts in American breasts—English hearts that sincerely respect their mother country, and would love her dearly if she would let them."[23] Boucicault had in fact received a testimonial at the end of the New York run from Irish communities for his contribution to Irish drama.

The *New York Herald* presented a lengthy description of "The Shaughraun Supper" on 8 March 1875, but the *Irish-American,* formerly so friendly, attacked Boucicault for not inviting them to the affair:

> We have, on more than one occasion, expressed our opinion of Mr. Boucicault's merits, both as a writer and as a delineator of the Irish character. . . . But if this presentation was intended to have anything of a representative character about it, whoever had charge of the arrangements took care to divest it of that peculiar feature, by studiously ignoring the existence of the Irish-American press—one of the feats in which small, self-sufficient New York politicians sometimes out-do themselves.[24]

Although these papers were based in New York, all had national circulation, and many of the most impassioned responses to the "Stage Irishman" debate were from St. Louis, Boston, and other cities at a distance from the performance at Wallack's.

Bronson Howard's article "Old and New World Audiences" in the *Celtic Monthly* in December 1874 and the editor's response provide even more context for the meaning of Irish theater to Irish audiences in America. Howard decried the lack of segregation by classes in America, claiming that without such segregation the theater presented a dull, level response. Howard missed the wit and vitality of the pit. The editor expressed surprise at that sentiment from a dramatist and rejoiced at the "respectableness" of American theaters. In America, wrote the editor, men of learning, "intimate with every dramatist from Shakespeare to Boucicault," could be found.[25] Howard had claimed that humble life could seldom be seen on stage, but the *Celtic Monthly* responded that the greatest successes, including *The Shaughraun*, have depicted just that. The theater Howard preferred was the very picture of the Theater Royal in Dublin, the theater that Boucicault reserved for his judges, a place where gallery wits felt free to shout out jokes about the scene onstage.

Clearly the *Celtic Monthly* still admired Boucicault, regardless of the outcry over *The Shaughraun,* and there is no reason to think, as with the slighted *Irish-American,* that the testimonial Boucicault received was not real. Boucicault donated proceeds of some performances of the play to the Fenian prisoners. He was certainly thoroughly rehabilitated into the emigrant community by January 1879, when the *Celtic Monthly* published a precise description of Boucicault's New York apartment. Reprinted from the St. Louis *Republican,* the account glories in the luxuries of this native son:

> The chandelier alone on that floor cost as much as the furnishing of many a handsome house, and the furniture and decorating of the suite—saloon, sleeping room and bath—reached $20,000, exclusive of paintings, some months ago.[26]

In the same issue, the editorial department gushed:

> Mr. Dion Boucicault has many claims upon Irish gratitude and esteem. Unlike some who have risen to fame and fortune, he has never forgotten or ignored the widowed Motherland who prides in calling him her son. . . . We now understand that Mr. Boucicault is to deliver a lecture on the second of next month for the benefit of the relatives of those members of the 69th Regiment who fell during the late war. . . . The mere announcement should

be sufficient to fill the largest hall, whether we consider the eminence of the lecturer of the worthiness of the object it is intended to serve.[27]

Also in January 1879, the *Irish-American* published a paragraph blurb on a revival of *The Shaughraun*, praising its production values and Boucicault's Conn in particular.

On 15 February 1879, the *Irish-American* ran a notice that Boucicault would give a benefit performance of *The Colleen Bawn* for "the widows and orphans of Firemen Reilly and Irving."[28] One month later, in March 1879, Boucicault was elected a member of the New York Friendly Sons of St. Patrick. During this year, Boucicault was an honored guest at the annual dinner of the New York Friendly Sons of St. Patrick, held on St. Patrick's Day. This organization, founded in the late eighteenth century (1771 in Philadelphia, 1784 in New York City) to honor St. Patrick, was devoted to literature and culture and had branches around the country. Originally founded in part to aid immigrant relief, it became a social club as much as a club devoted to good works and charity and did not demand ethnic Irishness as a qualification for membership. At the membership ceremony at Delmonico's in 1879, the speaker proposed he be elected "in return for the music of the quartette which he so kindly contributed" and concluded:

> I have waited a reasonable time gentlemen, and as there is no objection, I will now declare Mr. Dion Boucicault unanimously elected a member of The Friendly Sons of St. Patrick, notwithstanding the fact that his ancestors were born in France.[29]

For the rest of 1879, Boucicault was mentioned regularly in the *Celtic Monthly*, which included stories of his youth and announcements of his success. The *Irish-American*, in a review of a new play by W. B. Cahill called *The Cruitheacawn* in June 1880, still referred to *The Shaughraun* as the watermark for plays on Irish life. As Boucicault's plays had become standards, so his person was increasingly treated as a national treasure. In a "get well" message of November 1879, the *Celtic Monthly* defends Boucicault from charges of dualism:

> While thoughtless Englishmen are laughing at his wit and frolics upon the stage, he tells them—without their being aware of it until his story is done—how their rulers are ruling Ireland with a rod of iron, how the land is being desolated and the people driven to ruin and revolt. He pictures his country in her true, living colors, with the hand of an artist and the heart of a patriot.[30]

The Englishman could laugh because it was the English colonial system Boucicault demonized, not the English themselves. Boucicault maintained his patriotism for the rest of his life, distributing a "Fireside Story" on the history of Ireland for a revival of *The Colleen Bawn* in 1881. Unusually for Boucicault, he cited his sources in it. Boucicault lived on as the grand old man of Irish letters in America: teaching acting class in New York, receiving fellow Irishman Oscar Wilde on his lecture tour in 1882, reviving old plays and premiering new ones—although he never had another really popular success. Boucicault continued to appear in the records of the Friendly Sons throughout the 1880s, attending the centennial dinner of the New York branch in 1884. The obituaries on his death in 1890 were kind and long. The *Freeman's Journal* made special note of Boucicault's attitude toward America:

> Mr. Boucicault was a great believer in Americans and American audiences. He thought they were more intelligent than English ones, and I do not suppose that any one on this side of the water would have disputed with him on that point, though there was nothing in which he took greater delight than in lively controversy. He thought the world a good world and New York the best place in it. It was in New York that he died, and there is no place in which he would have preferred to end his ripe and brilliant life.[31]

Boucicault had finally been forgiven for his slighting of the Americans. In preferring to die in America, he died for Ireland.

After the turn of the century, both the Irish American press and theater declined as Irish Americans integrated more fully into American society. As silent film grew in popularity, however, ethnic stereotypes again found their way into performance. Sidney Olcott, the son of Irish immigrants to Canada, shot seventeen films in Ireland in 1910–11 to counter this trend. Along with a version of Rory O'More and photoplays of poems by Thomas Moore, Olcott filmed several of Boucicault's most popular plays, including *The Colleen Bawn* and *Arrah-na-Pogue*.[32] For the immigrants' descendants, Boucicault's plays were no longer romantic nostalgia but heritage. In their presentation of proud Irishmen able to navigate the tensions of colonialism, Boucicault's plays offered a possibility of reconciliation. To the succeeding generations of Irish Americans they offered a dream of union not so much with the English as with the past and present of their own identity.

6

Kilkenny, Melbourne, New York

George Tallis and the Irish Theatrical Diaspora

PETER KUCH

On the 30th of September 1886, when the seventeen-year-old George Tallis from Callan, Co. Kilkenny, accompanied by his sister Charlotte, stepped off the steamship *Orizba* at Port Melbourne, he would hardly have been aware that he was taking his first steps into theatrical history. Yet, within half a century of arriving in Australia, he would control one of the largest theatrical organizations in the world and be honored with a knighthood that acknowledged him "as head of the theatrical profession" in his adopted country.

First, what was the theatrical culture that George Tallis encountered when he began working in the theater in Australia? By theatrical culture I mean the actors and artistes he would have remarked, watched, or met; the theatrical bill-of-fare he would have experienced—whether light opera, comic opera, opera, Shakespeare, melodrama, pantomime, musical, or serious play; the material culture he would have encountered—the state of the theaters, lighting and sound, costumes, scenery, and special effects—all the so-called furniture of the stage; and finally the management practices that would have engaged his attention—negotiating contracts, advertising, methods of booking and selling tickets, accounting practices, insurance, and staff management. Second, what impact did George Tallis have on the theater in Australia up to and including his first two visits to America—the first in 1902 and the second in 1918? By then, Tallis had been working in the Australian theater for over a quarter of a century. What impact did he make? How did his American visits contribute to that impact? And what conclusions might be drawn about George Tallis's role for the Irish theatrical diaspora?

His background and his reasons for coming to Australia were little different from those that had brought thousands of his fellow Irishmen to the other side of the world—concern for family and the search for work. George Tallis was born on 28 October 1869, the youngest of ten children, to John and Sarah Tallis of 18 Bridge Street, Callan, a small town approximately half-way between Clonmel and Kilkenny. 18 Bridge Street was part grocery store and part off-license and had been purchased by John Tallis eight years before George's birth in 1861 with the proceeds from the sale of a thirty-acre farm he had inherited. The Tallises were Church of Ireland; their family church, St. Mary's, was on the same street as their business. George and his four brothers and five sisters would only enjoy their father's company for a comparatively short time, for John Tallis died at the age of seventy, just as his youngest son was turning seven. Sarah managed to keep the family together for a further seven years, until 1883, at which time she took her youngest daughter, Charlotte, to Dublin, where she set up a couturier's business. George, now fourteen, went to live with three of his sisters in Kilkenny where they set up a similar business. In June of that year two of his brothers, John and Henry, lured by accounts of Australia from Sarah's brother, Richard (Dick) Nicholson, decided to emigrate, partly for reasons of health and partly to seek their fortune. The following year, the fifteen-year-old George secured a job as a cadet reporter on the *Kilkenny Moderator*.

But if things were going well for the Tallis women, they were not going equally well for the Tallis men. Some time in either 1884 or 1885 George Tallis lost the sight of one eye when he was pushed on the stairs of St. Canice's Cathedral in Kilkenny and fell against an ornamental iron barb. Meanwhile, his brothers, Henry and John, who had arrived in Sydney in 1883 and settled in an area known as the Rocks, were finding Australia was far from the land of promise they had crossed the oceans to find. John became seriously ill and died in Sydney Hospital in mid-1884 or 1885. He is buried at Rookwood. Henry, who was a jeweler, found it difficult to obtain work, moving first to Silverton near the great mining city of Broken Hill and then to the long-established Irish settlement of Maldon, about 60 miles north of Melbourne. But when accounts of the parlous state of his health began filtering back to Dublin, Sarah Tallis decided to dispatch her youngest son and her youngest daughter to Melbourne to look after Henry. George and Charlotte left Kingstown on the *Orizba* on 30 September 1886 and arrived in Melbourne fifty-five days later, on 24 November.

Though doubtless both traveled to Maldon to see their brother, it was only Charlotte who remained with Henry until he died in 1888, at which time she returned to Ireland. George, it seems, after the 1886 visit, immediately went down to the city to look for work.

He later told a reporter with a Melbourne newspaper that his intention on arriving in Australia was to find work as a journalist,[1] yet his principal biographers, his grandchildren, Michael and Joan Tallis, claim that the seventeen-year-old George had two letters of recommendation in his pocket when he arrived in Melbourne in 1886—one addressed to Dr. Cunningham, chief-of-staff of the *Argus* newspaper[2] and the other addressed to an American impresario who was then beginning to establish his name and his fortune in Australia—James Cassius Williamson. The possibility of a letter of recommendation addressed to the chief-of-staff of the *Argus* suits Tallis's two-year apprenticeship with the *Kilkenny Moderator,* but the provenance of a letter of recommendation to J. C. Williamson, as he became known, remains a mystery as the only verifiable connection between the two men is that they were a mere generation apart.

But an argument has been made by his biographers for propinquity. J. C. Williamson, who was then in New York, had taken a troupe to Dublin in 1877 as part of a three-year world tour, the Irish papers remarking the immense popularity of :its Irish-American principal players and its Irish dramas,"[3] though no evidence has yet emerged to establish that the then eight-year-old George Tallis, his father having died the previous year, or any of the other Tallises, were so enamored of the theater that they would have taken particular notice of the American actor-manager's visit to a city several hours journey from where they were living. Besides, there is a nine-year gap between Williamson's 1877 Dublin season and the first meeting with George Tallis on the other side of the world in 1886. To date I have not been able to find the purported letter of recommendation to J. C. Williamson among either the Tallis or the Williamson papers.[4]

Not that eminently presentable and obviously enterprising young men needed letters of recommendation to gain employment in Melbourne in 1886. Wealth from some of the largest goldfields in the world was still flowing into the city,[5] with the theaters in particular doing brisk business. A chance encounter outside the Theater Royal in Bourke Street, where it seems J. C. Williamson was working at that time, and the ensuing conversation, would have been sufficient introduction. George Tallis's own explanation, despite its Dickensian ring of coincidence, seems the most plausible. As he told the journalist who was interviewing him late in life: "Fate put me in touch with J. C. Williamson when I arrived here, and, well—here I am."[6] What fate indisputably delivered was a job as a general factotum in the theatrical firm of Williamson, Garner, and Musgrove.

Williamson, Garner, and Musgrove had been founded in May 1882 when Williamson was thirty-six years old, Garner thirty-one, and Musgrove twenty-nine. The company, known locally as "the Triumverate," was as ambitious as its founders were youthful, and as shrewd as they were accomplished. Williamson brought to the company one of its most valuable properties— *Struck Oil*—a play for which he had acquired the rights in 1873, brought with great success to Melbourne in 1874, and then toured internationally from 1875 to 1879.[7] An even more valuable property in his possession was the sole Australian and New Zealand rights to Gilbert and Sullivan's *H.M.S. Pinafore* that he acquired in London during the tour, rights that he protected so vigorously in the Australian and New Zealand courts on his return in 1879 that he not only earned the gratitude and trust of the D'Oyly Carte Opera Company but also ensured that he received preferential treatment in all subsequent negotiations over rights to Gilbert and Sullivan's operas. The other two partners, Arthur Garner and George Musgrove, were as accomplished. Garner was an English actor who had assembled his own light opera company, the London Comedy Company, which delighted Melbourne and Sydney audiences throughout 1879 and 1880,[8] and George Musgrove, at the age of twenty-six, had borrowed money to travel to England to bring out Offenbach's comic opera *La Fille du tambour-major* in 1880–1.[9]

By the time the Triumverate came to hire the young George Tallis in 1886, they had gained control of the Theater Royal and the Princess Theater[10] in Melbourne, the Theater Royal in Sydney, set up an arrangement with the Theater Royal in Adelaide, and taken out short-term leases on several other theaters. And they had also begun touring extensively throughout Australia and New Zealand. A letter written by Williamson in February 1886 gives some indication of the scope and intensity of the firm's operations that year:

> Frank Thornton and our *Private Secretary* company have just returned from New Zealand . . . and are now playing at the Bijou. . . . At our Theater Royal, Melbourne, our opera company are now finishing the ninth week in *The Mikado*, which has been an enormous success. We shall run it through

Easter. . . . At our Bijou Theater in Melbourne, the Majeronis begin a season, on Saturday, with *Queen Elizabeth.* At the Opera House we produce
Falka, at the same date. In Sidney [*sic*] our stock dramatic company, now
in the seventh week to excellent business, produce *The Magistrate* next
Monday. At the Gaiety, *The Great Pink Pearl,* is running well.[11]

Such was the demand for theatrical entertainment in the 1880s that in addition to the Williamson, Garner, and Musgrove Company, Melbourne supported at least two other major companies that were also flourishing—The
Bland Holt Company, and the Brough-Boucicault Company, as well as a
number of independent entrepreneurs. The Bland Holt company specialized in Australian theater, particularly melodramas on local and nationalist
themes. Thereby it not only benefited from the change in Australian taste
that had been taking place since the 1870s when Shakespeare and grand
opera had progressively given way to musicals and melodramas,[12] but it also
benefited from the burgeoning nationalism that would eventually express
itself politically in the Federation of Australia in 1901 and culturally in an
outpouring of Australian poetry, prose, and painting throughout the 1880s
and 1890s that arguably still comprises the dominant discourse for Australian identity.

The third major Melbourne Company, the Brough-Boucicault Company, owed its origins one of the Triumverate's earliest ventures—inviting
Dionysius Lardner Boucicault, the Irish playwright, actor, and theater manager who had reaped enormous wealth from the American theater—*The
Shaughraun* (1874) alone is said to have made him well over half a million
dollars—to tour Australia and New Zealand in 1885. Boucicault, who had
suddenly left his wife Agnes Robertson in New York for Louise Thorndyke,
an actress not much older than the eldest of his five children, seems to have
felt that a discrete season in the Antipodes might prove the best way to
revive his personal and his financial fortunes. Fortunately, this brilliant but
errant Irishman has left a detailed account of his time in Melbourne, a city
he described as "an independent and republican community—clean, bright
and saucy."[13] Of the Theater Royal, where the young George Tallis and J. C.
Williamson[14] would meet in less than 15 months time, he wrote:

We found the Theater Royal to be a large, dusty, primitive building, with
poor accommodation for the audience, and still more wretched arrangements for the actors behind the scenes.

The scenic department, so far as the painting is concerned, was excellent, so was the furniture of the stage; but the disorder, the confusion, the mess. No expense seemed to be spared but such disorder, besides entailing waste, must engender a lack of discipline in other departments. The company was meagre, the principal members having been drafted off to Sydney, where they were rehearsing *The Private Secretary.* The Theater Royal is divided into a pit floor, a dress circle tier, a second circle. The prices are: Dress Circle, 5s., seat 180 persons; orchestral stalls, 3s., seat 568; upper boxes, 2s., seat 300; and pit and gallery, 1s., holding 1300. There are 1600 persons at low price, and 180 at the higher. The result is a popular audience. The 1600 have their own way. I think a smaller theater should be erected in Melbourne, where plays of the higher class, produced with much care and well scened, would maintain a higher standard of taste. Melbourne claims to be a critical public. There is intelligence enough to make one; the soil is rich but uncultivated, and over'run with a rowdy element, than wants no better drama that *The Lights o' London, Struck Oil, The Shaughran* and *The Silver King.* When we were rehearing *The Jilt* the management begged me not to announce it as a five-act comedy, as that would keep the public away; so it was called *A Sporting Play.* It is a pity that the lower taste in dramatic entertainment should be cultivated so assiduously as to threaten with extinction the finer qualities in the public. The two kinds of entertainment may exist and flourish side by side. The more delicate may require to be reared under glass, and need the care of the press.[15]

In the event, Boucicault's Melbourne season, which ran from 11 July to 18 August 1885, and which, in addition to performances of *A Sporting Play,* included performances of *The Colleen Bawn,* produced two successful outcomes. The receipts for the Melbourne season were much higher than expected,[16] and Dion Boucicault, the son, stayed on in Melbourne to found the very type of company that his father believed the theatergoing public of that city deserved. The Brough-Boucicault Company, which leased the Bijou Theatre in Melbourne and subsequently the Criterion in Sydney from 1886 to 1896, soon established a reputation for securing the very best plays staged to the highest standards. In addition to being the first to stage Wilde's plays—*Lady Windermere's Fan, An Ideal Husband,* and *The Importance of Being Earnest*—the Brough-Boucicault Company also staged Pinero, Chambers, Shaw, and Barrie.

Thus, the theatrical world that the young George Tallis entered was rich, various, vigorous, and highly competitive. It was dominated by English, Irish, and European works—whether dramatic, musical, or operatic. In addition, there was a clear preference for local or English actors. As one local theater critic rather bluntly observed, American actors and actresses have not been unqualified successes: "The highfalutin' notices of the United States press by which their advent has usually been heralded have ceased to arouse any feeling but that of amusement, and the result generally has demonstrated that the ability of the *artiste* was in the inverse ratio of the estimate by his or her enraptured admirers."[17]

In his account of his 1885 Australian tour Dion Boucicault senior had likewise cautioned: "It is a great mistake to take out a company to Australia. The audiences there are accustomed to the local actors, and prefer them to strangers. As to actresses, they like new faces, but do not care to criticise much beyond that."[18] In the main the theaters themselves, despite their impressive facades and sumptuous foyers, were akin to the Theatre Royal in that they tended to be "large, dusty, primitive" buildings, "with poor accommodation for the audience, and still more wretched arrangements for the actors behind the scenes."[19] Yet the management practices that the new employee encountered in Williamson, Garner, and Musgrove, were among the best in the world. The key, it seemed, was diversification. This was a lesson George Tallis learned thoroughly and applied assiduously and successfully throughout his impressive career.

Tallis began work in the Theatre Royal in 1886 as a jack-of-all-trades—selling tickets, ushering, cleaning and performing any one of the hundred-and-one other tasks needed to keep patrons satisfied and a huge theater running smoothly. Of the two theaters managed by the Triumverate—the Theatre Royal and the Princess Theater—the Theatre Royal catered for popular taste, though not exclusively. In his first three years, before he received his first promotion, Tallis would have seen a bill-of-fare that ranged from the tenth revival of Williamson's *Struck Oil*, to the Royal Dramatic Company's *The Merchant of Venice*, to Janet Achurch and Dion Boucicault in *Led Astray*, and Janet Achurch and Charles Carrington with the New London Dramatic Company in *The Pointsman*. Appointed treasurer to the Theatre Royal in 1889, Tallis would most likely have conducted all the front-of-house business with Grattan Rigg for his season of Boucicault's *The Shaughraun* (2 weeks), *The Irish Detective* (1 week), *The Octoroon* (1 week), *Shin Fane* (1 week), and *The Colleen Bawn* (1 week) that ran from 9 November to 21 December 1889.

And if he had time to go to the company's other theater, he would have been able to see performances among others of *The Pirates of Penzance, Iolanthe, The Mikado, School for Scandal, Hamlet, Twelfth Night*, and most notably, Janet Achurch and Charles Carrington opening in *A Doll's House* on 14 September 1889, barely a year after the play had premiered in London.[20] Two and a half years later, the same theater would provide the venue for another international celebrity, the "divine" Bernhardt, whose season of twenty-four nights and four matinees involved a program that included *La Tosca, Fedora, La Dame aux camellias, Cleopatra, Adrienne Lecouvreur, Theodora, Frou Frou, Jean D'Arc*, and *Camille*.[21] Though it was the senior management who handled the Bernhardt tour, Tallis seems to have been given some of the management tasks and must have shown himself capable, for a little over six months later, in 1892, he was promoted to treasurer of the more up-market Princess Theatre.

In a sense he could not have been promoted at a more inopportune time, for the opening years of the 1890s witnessed a succession of bank defaults followed by a disastrous drought that plunged the colony of Victoria and the city of Melbourne into a financial crisis. A grossly inflated property market, plummeting commodity prices, opportunism that frequently degenerated into fraud, massive local and overseas borrowing (often unsecured), a vicious competition for deposits that rapidly became corrupt—and what one contemporary commentator quaintly labeled "unbridled mendacity"—soon wreaked havoc with the economy.[22] As George Tallis himself later observed, more damage was done to the fabric of Australian life by the 1890s crash than the 1930s Depression. Understandably, as the economic crisis deepened, theatergoing shifted from modest to luxury costs, and the theatrical bill-of-fare shifted from aesthetic challenge to escapism and fantasy. At first Musgrove left the partnership due to a dispute, then Garner left the following year due to financial difficulties, though shortly after Garner's departure Musgrove rejoined. Yet such management restructures and the worsening economy served only to prove George Tallis's worth. Toward the end of 1892, he was promoted to manager-in-charge-of-touring, business manager, and perhaps most important of all, in terms of what he would learn about the profession, private secretary to J. C. Williamson himself. Tallis frequently credited the J. C. Williamson office for everything he had learned about the theater.

But touring was also a great educator, not only because of the extent to which it tested organizational skills but also because it was highly competitive. By the 1890s the way traveling theatricals moved about the country was so well established that it was being mapped by publications such as *The Dramatic Year Book for the Year Ending December 31st 1891,* edited by Charles S. Cheltnam, a guide that could be purchased from any reputable bookseller that not only set out in great detail the itinerary and the amount of time that should be allocated to each venue, but also provided the basis for calculating projected takings.

> Under ordinary circumstances the theatrical tour can only start from one
> of three places, Melbourne, Sydney or Adelaide; and as Melbourne is the
> central one of the three, and indeed the place usually first opened in, it is
> assumed this is the starting point. . . . Commencing at Melbourne, then,
> after a season of say three months, it will probably be advisable to go to
> Sydney. . . . The following route must be taken and the following towns
> passed through by rail: Seymour, 60 miles, population of district, 2,600;
> one night. Eurora, Benalla, 121 miles; population of town 1,700; of district
> 7,200; one night. Wangaratta, 150 miles; population 1,800; one night.[23]

And so on. By the mid 1890s Tallis found himself managing a circuit that took in all the main cities in Australia and New Zealand and upward of eighty country centers.[24] With his manager-in-charge-of-touring hat he would attend to all the intricacies of co-ordinating train and/or steamship timetables to ensure that the actors, sets, and properties would each arrive at the next scheduled venue at the same time and on time. Then, he would don his business manager hat to ensure that all the receipts were in order for shows such as Bland Holt's *A Million of Money* (1893), The Royal Comic Opera's *The Vicar of Bray* (1894), Mrs. Brown-Potter and Kyrle Bellew's *As You Like It* (1896), Palmer's and Brady's New York Company in *Trilby* (1896), and Wilson Barrett's *The Sign of the Cross,* which, when it opened on 3 July 1897, played for 250 performances.[25]

Though the bill-of-fare at the Williamson-Musgrove Theatres was still predominantly Australian, English, and European and for the most part comprised Shakespeare, light opera, melodrama, and musical comedy, a significant change was about to take place. Early in 1898, when George Musgrove was in America on a three-month tour looking for new material, he saw *The Belle of New York* at the Casino Theatre, and on an impulse signed it for a season at the Shaftesbury Theater in London. *The Belle* opened there in April 1898 and was an immediate success, eventually running for two years. At the end of its first year, Williamson and Musgrove felt sufficiently confident about its success to put aside their prejudices about American shows and sign a second company for an Australian tour. Largely because it was a London hit, *The Belle* played to a packed house when it opened in Melbourne in April 1899, but the audience quickly reverted to type and within a quarter-of-an-hour of the curtain rising there were murmurs of irritation that eventually swelled to cat-calls and jeers. But actors and the company persisted and though audiences were small on the second night, the numbers gradually built throughout the five-week season to the extent that when *The Belle of New York* was given its final night, the five-week Melbourne season was pronounced an encouraging success.

In December 1899, the Williamson-Musgrove partnership was dissolved, though wrangling over the division of assets continued until February 1901. It is a mark of the degree of trust that the aging J. C. Williamson placed in his thirty-year-old business manager and private secretary that he appointed Tallis to resolve the matter in consultation with one of Musgrove's oldest and most trusted friends, the lawyer Theodore Fink.[26] Of the original Triumverate, only J. C. Williamson remained, with Tallis now indisputably established as his right-hand man. More trust was soon shown in him when in mid-1902 it was proposed that he should assume the role once performed by Musgrove and travel to America and England to search for new material.

Fortunately, Tallis's travel diary has survived and is lodged with his papers at the National Library of Australia in Canberra.[27] In his diary Tallis records that he left Melbourne on 13 September 1902 and after calling at Sydney, Auckland, Pango-Pango, and Honolulu, arrived at San Francisco on 6 October. After spending a fortnight in San Francisco and four days in Chicago meeting actors and actresses and impresarios, visiting theaters, and seeing shows, he arrived in New York on Saturday, 25 October, where he put up at the Avenue Hotel. From the entry for Monday, 27 October, to the entry for Tuesday, 16 December, when Tallis sailed for London on the *Campania,* the diary is crowded with details of meetings, impressions of shows, records of cables sent to and received from J. C. Williamson in Sydney, notes regarding negotiations with actors and actresses, and observations about theater setup and theater management that could be employed back in Australia.

Mon 27th Called on Mr Sawyer and Mr Jordan. Recd. Cable from Mr JCW re Sousa & to see Miss Leslie etc. Saw *The Way Down East* and *Tales of Passage.*

Evng. visited the Empire Theatre—Charles Frohman, Manager—and saw Mr John Drew in *The Mummy* and *The Humming Bird*—Delighted— Splendid performance all round especially Drew as Lumley and Barrymore as Guiseppe and Margaret Dale as Lady Lumley. Marie Derickson weak.

Tues 28th Had chat with Mr Sanger? Re Brady contract. . . . Will not recommend Leslie & says fact of *Zaza and Mason* not having been done means losing interest in Australia. Suggested seeing *"Are You Mason"* performance—probably somebody there suitable.

Lunched with Jordan—met Captn Heilbrou afternoon and then evening. Saw Mrs Campbell in *The Joy of Living*—Piece very sombre & talkey & company weak except Mr Chas Bryant as Norbert.

Election Day. Met Welty and Cauby & had dinner with them at 5th Av: Afterwards went to Broadway Theater—met there Sandy Dingwall (Litt's Manager) & Savage's manager—Saw arrangement for calling cabs by electricity

Wed Went to Savoy—Saw Ethel Barrymore in *Carrots*

Evening—went to *Ninety and Nine*—disappointed in play . . . Saw Brady afternoon—waiting advice London—See again Satdy.

Thurs Dined with Wilty—Went to see . . . Olcott and Miss Taylor—bad room—Miss T. re lead? Met Coventry.

Saw Weldon Grossmith in *Night of the Party*—very funny—See him.

MEMO: Front House uniforms—black with braid in front and Epaulettes—name in gold on side & gold buttons Striped Trousers—tall collar.

Monday 15th Saw *Garden of the Gods*—Greatly impressed—splendid production marvellous lighting effects—approached Belasco thro Jordan— waiting reply

Several issues of note emerge from the journal. The first is Tallis's intense interest in what I earlier called the material culture of the theater. The notes to himself about methods for "calling cabs" and the carefully recorded detail of the front-of-house uniforms are part of this. Elsewhere in the travel diary there are equally meticulous accounts of methods for promoting shows; of arranging seating so patrons get the best value for their money; of arrangements for booking and for selling tickets; and of safety precautions—it was while he was in Chicago that he first saw a fire screen in a theater.[28] While it is impossible to detail exactly what Tallis utilized from his American tour when he returned to Australia, it seems safe to assume that someone who made such observations and took the trouble to record them would most likely use some if not all of what they had seen and learned. What he did publicly acknowledge was the indelible impression made by the great American manager Charles Frohman, who he had met on his first full working day in New York. Many years later he would relay the anecdote that Frohman had watched the opening of a $100,000 production "from the furthermost perch in the Gallery"[29] to illustrate what he believed to be the essence of good management—supreme faith in the product yoked with utter self-effacement in its presentation.

Second, it would seem that by the time he went to America, the Firm, as the J. C. Williamson Company was now known, had overcome its prejudice against American actors and actresses and American material. Though it was Musgrove's promotion of *The Belle of New York* in London in 1898 that appears to have begun the process, it was Tallis who decided to continue it with his 1902 visit. And it is not as if he was simply acting on the orders of J. C. Williamson himself. Even as late as 1905, Williamson was publicly of the opinion that any management that imported American shows did so only at a considerable financial risk.[30] But arguably Tallis was sufficiently senior by then to have been actively involved in deciding where the Firm should look for the best material. What emerges from the list of appointments with actresses is that Tallis had been entrusted with the task of assessing the strengths and weaknesses of New York's leading ladies. Personal assessment of performance and face-to-face interviews would remove the risk of relying on industry gossip, reviews, and promotional material. "Thurs. Had appt with Miss Leslie—did not keep it—arranged tomorrow—at 11," reads one entry in the diary. The entry for the next day reads:

Fri Met Miss Leslie—good looking & attractive but appears rather weak physically for heavy work & very expensive. Dined at Players Club with Cauby.

Evening—went to see *Dolly Varden* with Lulu Glasser in title role—rotten show—bad cast and star vulgar.

Finally, what emerges from the diary is the image of Tallis as a business-man engrossed in the theater rather than a theater practitioner with a keen eye for business. Compared with the entries found in Williamson's and Mus-grove's diaries, both of whom had first-hand experience of the stage, Tallis's remarks about actors, actresses, plays, and shows have dollar signs attached to their aesthetic judgments. In fact, as John McCallum has suggested in a forthcoming history of Australian drama that he has very kindly made avail-able, Williamson and Musgrove were the last of the great impresarios who had not only written, acted, and managed, but who also had extensive expe-rience touring. Thus Tallis's 1902 tour marks a significant shift in the history of Australian theater not only in terms of a greater acceptance of American material but also in terms of the way the always precarious balance between art and entertainment shifted even further in favor of entertainment.

By the time Tallis came to make his next visit to America in 1918, signif-icant personal, cultural, and political changes had taken place in both his life and the life of Australia. In 1904 Tallis was invited to become a partner in the company. By then he had married, his first two children had been born, and he and his family were about to move into Santoi, a magnificent mansion built for them in the fashionable Melbourne suburb of Camberwell. Two more children, a daughter and another son, were born in 1907 and 1911. In 1911, the Firm had been incorporated as J. C. Williamson Limited, with a capital of £180,000 comprised of 140,000 fully paid shares of £1 and 40,000 contributing £1 shares paid to 10 shillings. J. C. Williamson held 50 percent of the shares and Tallis and a new partner, Ramaciotti, 25 percent each.[31] In 1911 there was a further restructure, which saw Tallis emerge with 62.5 percent of the shares, Williamson 25 percent, and the Firm's solicitor, Arthur Wigram Allen, with 12.5 percent.[32] In 1913, J. C. Williamson suddenly col-lapsed and died while he was visiting Paris, leaving Tallis indisputably in control of what by now had become one of the most powerful theatrical companies in the world.

The same year, 1913, *Melbourne Punch* published a pen-sketch of the Irishman who in twenty-seven years had gained control of the company that had first employed him as usher, cleaner, ticket-seller and jack-of-all trades.

> He is a man who always works, but who organises his work so that it is made as easy as possible. He is a modest man. The public seldom hears of him. He never advertises himself. He knows that advertisement of a manager is good material wasted. The public are not to be induced to attend the show by any

quality of the manager in it. His creed is that the proper place for a manager is the place he has always occupied—well out of the limelight, with all the glare thrown upon the wares he has to display to the public.

He is the ideal manager—cautious, bland, reticent, retiring—a man who though engaged in show business, displays none of those blatant qualities which so often, unfortunately, go with a showman.[33]

The outbreak of World War I not only saw Tallis throw the weight of J. C. Williamson Limited behind the war effort (for which he received a knighthood), but it also saw him engaged in commercial skirmishing with J & N Tait Limited, another Australian theatrical company that had been growing steadily since the turn of the century. Hostilities reached a peak when Williamson and Tait became engaged in a prolonged bidding war for *Peg o' My Heart* starring Sarah Allgood, with the Tait brothers emerging the victors. One of the reasons for Tallis's 1918 trip to America was to gain a competitive edge in his battle with the Tait brothers for new material. On his return he gave an interview to the *Melbourne Argus* that was published in the issue for 8 November 1918:

> The Americans think Australia is magnificent. The name Anzac stirs them deeply. New York is full of Australians and of people Australians know. It is just like going down Bourke Street.
>
> The secret of success of Australian artists in America is that they have a vigorous style that suits the Americans, they are good workers, and owing to frequent changes of bill in this country they obtain experience that tends to make them versatile. They are not one-type artists, as so many of the British players are nowadays.[34]

In the same interview Tallis announced that he had secured "the greatest film D. W. Griffith had yet produced," *Hearts of the World*. In the event it was film, and particularly American film, that would ensure that American material steadily but remorselessly gained control of the Australian market. By the beginning of the 1920s the film industry had displaced live theater as the preferred form of entertainment. One newspaper of the day estimated that in Australia, with a population of five million, there were seventy million visits to the cinema annually compared with eleven million visits to live theaters, ten million to concerts, and six million to other types of entertainment.[35] Tallis's response was to diversify, not only to source films but also to source shows, musical comedy, light opera, and serious drama. While his

1922 and 1927 visits to New York seem to have been devoted equally to live theater and film, his 1928 trip to New York and London was reported first in the *Adelaide Advertiser* and then in the *Melbourne Age* as seeing him personally yet

> more than 100 plays and select 20. These included two of Frederick Lonsdales, *The High Road* and *On Approval* and *The Silent House* by Harrison Owen, an ex-Melbourne pressman. Others selected were *The Letter*, which would be included among the Vanburgh-Boucicault repertoire: *The Squall*, *The Night Stick* and *The Happy Husband*. In addition to inducing Miss Vanburgh and Mr Boucicault to return to Australia, he had been successful in securing Miss Margaret Bannerman for a season.
>
> Sir George added that he was hoping to conclude negotiations with Robert Lorraine the distinguished Shaw actor to make an Australian tour with his Shaw productions.[36]

It is a commonplace of Australian cultural history, particularly theater history, to decry the J. C. Williamson organization for pandering to rather than shaping public taste. Given his long and significant role in the company, Sir George Tallis stands partly culpable. But to make such a criticism is to overlook a crucial aspect of his approach to management—his skill at diversifying—and to overlook his considerable achievement as an impresario—the creation of considerable wealth that was united to an unwavering commitment to live theater. Were it not for George Tallis's management skills and business acumen theater in Australia may well not have been as rich and as various as it proved to be.

7

The Abbey, Its "Helpers," and the Field of Cultural Production in 1913

LUCY McDIARMID

On Tuesday, 21 January 1913, the Gregory-Yeats play *The Pot of Broth* was performed by the Abbey players at a benefit matinee in Chicago. The purpose of the benefit was to raise funds for the Dublin Municipal Gallery of Modern Art: at that stage in the Gallery's history, the Dublin Corporation was promising to pay for a permanent building if funds could be raised privately to buy a site, and Lady Gregory was doing some of that fund-raising among wealthy, culture-loving Americans. *The Pot of Broth* was the curtain-raiser for Shaw's *Shewing-up of Blanco Posnet* and Gregory's own *Hyacinth Halvey;* it was more appropriate for the benefit than its audience could have guessed.

The Pot of Broth is based on the familiar folk-tale known in some forms as "stone soup." The Gregory-Yeats version (written in 1902) seems already to be an Abbey play, with a "stranger" who visits a house and disturbs the country people who live there. The stranger was originally called a "beggar" in the Abbey version but was redesignated a "tramp," probably in response to the tramp in Synge's *The Shadow of the Glen* (1903). The Gregory-Yeats stranger speaks with the aggressive seductiveness of the character Kathleen ni Houlihan (from 1902) and the rebel ballad-singer in *The Rising of the Moon* (1907). He's a fast-talking rogue who persuades the Coneelys that something wonderful can be made from the magic stone he carries with him:

> It is a mistake you are making, ma'am, it is not asking anything I am. It is giving I am more used to. I was never in a house yet but there would be a welcome for me in it again.

And also:

> No one in the world but myself has one, ma'am, and no other stone in the world has the same power, for it has enchantment on it. All I'll ask of you now, ma'am, is the loan of a pot with a drop of boiling water in it.[1]

He performs a miracle, charming them out of all their food to make a delicious broth that he consumes entirely by himself, before leaving the stone with the Coneelys and departing quickly.

There's a distinct resemblance between this character and Lady Gregory, as least as she functioned in Chicago in January 1913, raising funds for the Lane Gallery: she made people who were giving believe that they were receiving something; she disguised begging as a pleasant social visit; she managed her work with great charm, smiling and flattering and making nice to everyone; and she held out as a glamorous prize something wonderful that ultimately did not come to be as she had promised. And that's why the Lady is a tramp.

The money raised during the winter and spring of 1912–13 at the Abbey's Municipal Gallery benefit matinees in Chicago, New York, Boston, London, and Dublin became part of a notorious dispute.[2] The Dublin Corporation finally voted in September 1913 (as the date of Yeats's poem notes) not to fund the building, so the Abbey directors were left with a fund—called the Guarantee fund or sometimes the guarantors' fund—that no longer had a purpose.[3] In November the Abbey players began demanding the money for themselves. The Abbey directors, Yeats and Gregory, thought the funds (with a few reservations) should be put aside in a special trust account for a permanent site for the gallery, whenever that might be possible. Between the beginning of November 1913 and the end of January 1914, many letters on this subject went back and forth between Yeats and Gregory, Gregory and the Abbey players, Lennox Robinson and Gregory, William Bailey and Gregory, Gregory and John Quinn, and others. The dispute wasn't settled until 2 February 1914, when an opinion of the solicitor-general of Ireland, Jonathan Pim (from an old Irish Quaker family) awarded the entire sum to the players.[4]

From one point of view, the argument over the guarantee funds looks like another in the series of management-labor problems that Adrian Frazier discusses in *Behind the Scenes: Yeats, Horniman, and the Struggle for the Abbey Theatre,* such as the changed relationship between directors and players that resulted after the Irish National Theatre Society became a joint stock company in 1905.[5] Although it makes sense to read this dispute according to the Marxist paradigm Frazier uses, I want to offer another way of understanding it. The benefit matinees took place mostly in the United States and London, and the diaspora's cultural work existed on a different scale from Dublin's. More people and more work were required to advertise, to sell plays, to raise funds. The failure of the permanent gallery building and site to materialize in 1913 and the immediate need to provide a rationale for all the money collected made it necessary to define something that would otherwise never have been discussed, namely, whose labor had earned the guarantee fund. The dispute led to the articulation of a category of cultural workers Lady Gregory termed "the helpers," and it is that new designation I discuss here.

According to Bourdieu's concept of the "field of cultural production," works of art exist as symbolic objects only if they are known and recognized as such; the material production of works of art is accompanied by "the symbolic production of the work, i.e. the production of the value of the work, or . . . of belief in the value of the work."[6] Scholars (according to Bourdieu) need to consider "not only the direct producers of the work in its materiality (artist, writer, etc.) but also the producers of the meaning and value of the work—critics, publishers, gallery directors and the whole set of agents whose combined efforts produce consumers capable of knowing and recognizing the work of art as such."[7] Bourdieu also mentions among those who "help to define and produce the value of works of art," institutions such as "museums, galleries, academies." "In short," he writes, "it is a question of understanding works of art as a *manifestation* of the field as a whole."[8]

The "helpers" introduced by Gregory (and, to a lesser extent, Yeats) into their argument constitute yet another category of people involved in the "symbolic production" of works of art: not the paid professional cultural workers (critics, publishers, gallery owners, and so forth) but the volunteers who donated their skills without pay, the lawyers, bankers, financiers, politicians, civic leaders, society hostesses, "committees," donors and benefactors, the "names" that would be printed on the stationery if they were a "board." These were the people who "worked up" the "special matinees." To support her interests in Ireland—the permanent site for the Lane Gallery, and, more broadly, the establishment of Dublin as a "city of culture"—Lady Gregory created a decentralized, diasporic, cosmopolitan group of cultural workers, the "field" necessary to generate successful benefit performances. In the idiom that would be used today, she "developed" the diaspora.

Of course, Gregory had also used a guarantee fund to establish the Irish Literary Theatre, and the two opening chapters of *Our Irish Theatre* describe in detail her successful fund-raising.[9] But on home territory she only needed to write letters: in America, she had to meet people hitherto unknown to her and ask them for much more. Like the tramp, she had to be able to make friends quickly and persuade them to help her. The helpers were rich, socially prominent Irish and non-Irish, Protestant and Catholic civic leaders in major cities of the Irish Atlantic diaspora; they were diasporic extensions of Gregory herself. In the midst of the dispute, in a letter to Yeats in January, 1914, she wrote emphatically, in a line all by itself, "We represent the helpers outside Theatre."[10] Again and again during the dispute, as if scanning a map or the itinerary of the Abbey players, she listed the people whose vested interest in the funds needed to be taken into account. In a "proposed answer to Players re Gallery" (undated; probably December 1913), she writes that in Chicago there was "a ladies committee who sold seats and brought people in," a "Fine Arts Committee" that "lent the building" for the performance, a local manager of the booking company, a Mr. Donoughy, "who paid for advertisements or part of them as his contribution," Mr. Aldis and Mrs. McCormack who bought seats and distributed tickets.[11] In New York the Wallace Theatre "was lent free at Lady Gregory's request," and "Mr. Roosevelt's sister," Mrs. Douglas Robinson ("a minor poet") and her son "took boxes. . . . to help the Gallery" and so on.[12]

With their important, well-known names, their regular appearances in the society columns of the paper (the women) or the news (the men), these people, in Bourdieu's terms (which Lady Gregory would have agreed with), added "value" to the work of art: they made it stylish to want to go see the Abbey Players in *The Pot of Broth, Blanco Posnet,* and *Hyacinth Halvey.* In the same "proposed answer," she mentions "Mr. Bourke Cockrane," the Sligo-born New York politician and lawyer, friend of John Quinn, whose wife set up the New York benefit and Professor George Pierce Baker of Harvard, "who has helped our general work so much that we must keep our character up to what he expects of us."[13] In London the helpers included Mrs. John Leslie, the mother of the diplomat and writer Shane Leslie and a distant relative of the Churchills, "Mr. Huth Jackson, the financier, a large subscriber (£300) to our theatre fund, and whose wife sent a subscription to the matinee as she could not attend; and Mr. Bernard Shaw."[14]

Lady Gregory had been creating the helpers before the benefit matinees. During the Abbey's previous trip to Chicago, in the winter of 1912,
she was extending the field of cultural production by means of exchanges
of hospitality. On 30 January 1912, John Quinn's friends "Mr. and Mrs.
Hamill" gave a dinner party for Lady Gregory and took her to the theater
afterward. Mr. and Mrs. Arthur Aldis and Mr. and Mrs. Bryan Lathrop
gave a reception for her at which she spoke on "The Abbey Theatre: The
Art of the Drama." Gregory herself gave a tea for some of her new Chicago
friends and was flattered to see a poem written to her published in the *Chicago Tribune*'s column "A line-o'-type or two," which praised her for not
staying at home. To the "great and simple seer of Erin's seers," the author
said, "How we rejoice that thou wouldst not remain/Beside thy hearth,
bemoaning useless years."[15]

Gregory didn't stay beside her hearth the next year, either. A year later,
on 22 January 1913, the *Tribune*'s society column listed all the committee members who helped to raise money for the Municipal Gallery site.[16]
They were wealthy Chicago businessmen and professional people, or their
wives, who were profiting from the boom economy of the end of the gilded
age. Hamill, Quinn's friend, had a "grandly scaled Georgian mansion,"
considered a landmark until its demolition was authorized in 2002.[17] Elsie
McCormick was from the reaper family. Charles Strobel was an engineer
who designed some of the first skyscrapers on the loop; the McKinlocks were
Episcopalians, he was a wealthy businessman who built McKinlock Hall at
Harvard's Leverett House in memory of his son, who (like Lady Gregory's)
died in World War I.[18] The Peabody family founded a coal business that is
still flourishing. Judge Marcus Kavanagh published essays in support of the
death penalty, because he believed it prevented murder; he was married to
the former Herminie McGibney Templeton, the Irish-born author of *Darby
O'Gill and the Good People* (1903).[19]

One of the people attending the benefit performance was Harriet Monroe, a Chicago native who had founded *Poetry* magazine the year before,
which was editorially supported by Ezra Pound. She brought Rabindranath
Tagore with her to the plays; both Pound and Tagore were spending much
time with Yeats in London that year.[20] The list of supporters of *Poetry* magazine included many of the same people on the Abbey benefit committee,
among them Arthur Aldis, Mrs. Charles Hamill, one of the Peabody brothers, and Mr. McKinlock (also Mrs. Potter Palmer, whose real estate baron

husband built the Palmer House Hotel).[21] Lady Gregory had tapped into the Chicago elite for whom patronage of the arts was an important aspect of civic duty, those who built an American public culture from their new wealth. At that time there was no tax advantage for such philanthropy, but without their patronage, there would have been no museums, theaters, orchestras, or literary magazines. European cultural institutions had evolved, for the most part, from state support (or, like the Louvre, been forcibly nationalized). The Comédie Française had been founded by Louis XIV in 1680.[22] Possibly because of that history Bourdieu did not consider patrons of the arts, society ladies, lawyers, and business men as occupants of a corner of the field of cultural production. Moreover, because the Irish, also, in 1913, depended on private benefactors to found theaters and museums, the civic-minded generosity of the wealthy Chicagoans no doubt gave them a ready sympathy for Lady Gregory's and Hugh Lane's cultural projects.

With its listing of names and flattering comments on Lady Gregory's every move, the press, at least the *Chicago Tribune,* was fundamental in helping Gregory with the helpers. The *Tribune* published Lady Gregory's eight-paragraph letter ("Appeal for Art in Dublin") on 5 January 1913, further supporting her efforts with an editorial entitled "Home Rule and the Arts."[23] In January alone there were at least seven separate mentions of the gallery fund-raising, quite apart from reviews of the performances. When the anonymous author of the "Line-o-type" column on 9 January 1913 announced the need to raise funds for the site in Dublin, he wrote:

> A committee of ladies and gentlemen are to meet next Monday forenoon with Mrs. Charles Hamill and discuss ways and means with Lady Gregory; and if we were a wealthy Irish-American gentleman we should spoil the ladies' little game by offering to draw our personal check for the required sum. Is there not such an Irish-American—*or such an American*—in Chicago? What a monument it would be! What an opportunity to link one's name with something that will last through the centuries! And to visit Dublin a few years hence and be pointed out as the man who saved a great art gallery for the city![24]

This decentered, cosmopolitan vision typified the helpers' cast of mind. The passage calls on "an Irish-American" or "an American," as if in matters of cultural patronage nationality does not make a difference that really matters. Ireland is just an extension of America. Or perhaps it is that Dublin is just an extension of Chicago, and a rich Chicago businessman might be just as happy to be a philanthropic celebrity in one city as another.

The Chicago matinee raised $1,000; no letter in the archives details how much was made in any of the others. But back in Dublin in the autumn of 1913, after the corporation voted against funding the building for the gallery, the cosmopolitan vision of American journalists, the generosity of the diaspora (or rich Americans who functioned as an Irish diaspora, such as the Roosevelts), and the value of their important names—all these did not weigh heavily on the players' minds. Twenty-five thousand Dubliners were on strike, many of them locked out from their jobs in the Irish Transport and General Workers' Union. In an atmosphere dominated by fierce and long-lasting debate over the economic value of labor, the Abbey players (who were not members of a union) engaged in collective bargaining. On 7 November, they wrote Lady Gregory:

> As it has now been definitely stated that the subscriptions in connection with the [Art Gallery] are to be returned to the subscribers, we would be glad if you will let us have at your earliest convenience the money raised by us in Chicago, New York, Boston, London, and Dublin. Yours respectfully, Arthur Sinclair, Fred O'Donovan, J. M. Kerrigan, J. A. O'Rourke, U. Wright, Sydney J. Morgan, Eithene Magee, Eileen O'Doherty[25]

Lady Gregory (with Yeats's support and approval) wrote offering them the proceeds from Boston, because they had missed a matinee there when they did the benefit performance.[26] On 18 November they wrote back:

> We are in receipt of your letter which we have considered very carefully and regret that we cannot see our way to accept a portion of the money earned by us as suggested. We are entitled to the whole amount but do not object to your retaining the two hundred dollars subscribed by Miss Osborne and the other lady [these were two women in Boston who had given money directly to the fund and had not bought tickets; it was Lady Gregory who could not remember the name of the second one]. We are also prepared to guarantee (should the Art Gallery question rise up again) £1,000 to be worked off at special performances as before.[27]

And finally, on 4 December, after having read more about Mr. Hamill and Mr. Bourke Cockran and Mrs. Leslie and the rest of them, this letter arrived from the players to Gregory:

We cannot understand your attitude in this matter. No one has any right to this money but ourselves and we are therefore astonished at your reluctance in forwarding to us the amount subscribed. We must now really ask you for our money by return of post as Christmas is fast approaching and we have also the expense of another American tour in front of us.[28]

At this point, in December, Lady Gregory was in London and Yeats in Dublin meeting directly with the players and reporting on the mood of their meetings. When, before Christmas, the directors still refused to turn over the money, the players consulted a solicitor, intending to sue Lady Gregory. In late January (Gregory now back in Gort, Yeats going back and forth between London and Dublin, and London and Sussex, where he was living with Pound that winter), Yeats and the players agreed to put the issue, with statements by both sides, before the Solicitor-General, not as opposed parties, but simply to get his legal opinion as a form of arbitration. Yeats wanted to avoid the direct antagonism of a legal battle. On 21 January he wrote Lady Gregory that if the opinion given awarded the funds to the company, "It will mean peace in the Theatre and general good humour."[29]

Lady Gregory was not in strike-torn Dublin: in the west of Ireland, she was remembering the generosity of the American helpers, and she was furious at Yeats. "Dear Willie," she wrote on 22 January, "I think your proposal the most astounding I ever heard of. . . . You propose that we should accept this award without taking another legal opinion. That means that American and other helpers will be told that money they gave and worked for for one purpose has been diverted without their sanction to another. . . . You propose for the sake of putting them in good humor to accept a decision which will leave us open to the charge of illegally paying our Company money that doesn't belong to them."[30] And so forth. But the plan as agreed to by Yeats and the players went ahead, and on 31 January Jonathan Pim handed down (from 10 Herbert Street) the opinion that "the purchasers of tickets" had gotten the benefit of the performances they saw and so were not owed any money; and that the players "who gave their undertakings, who worked so hard to make the undertaking a success and who incidentally lost money in carrying out their promise, are now entitled to receive the result of the work which they undertook to do."[31] Legal expenses (about £40) and the $200 given directly were deducted from a total not mentioned in any of the correspondence, something over £1,000, and the remainder given to the Abbey players.

Gregory and Yeats were exchanging three or four letters a week in the three months (November through January, 1913–14) taken up by the dispute with the Abbey players over the guarantee fund, which was only one of several items on their agenda. Both of the other episodes show how much of Gregory's and Yeats's time was spent in border areas of the field of cultural production, the symbolic rather than the material production of works of art; in these cases, "producing the meaning and value" of their own work by maintaining the value of their names. In January 1914 George Moore's account of Lady Gregory in *Vale,* in which he described her as an "ardent soul-gatherer," a Protestant proselytizer, in her youth, was published as a chapter in *The English Review* before its appearance as part of a book. Gregory went directly to the offices of Heinemann (Moore's publishers) and saw Sydney Pawling. As she wrote him on 5 January 1914, it would "damage her position" as director of the Abbey Theatre to be known as an "enemy of the Catholic faith." She wrote Quinn that Mr. Pawling was "quite sympathetic" and communicated immediately with Moore. She also wrote Quinn that Wilfrid Blunt had written her, "I have just read George Moore's article about you. It is an outrage and stupid too. A thing of the gutter." And when she told Blunt of her visit to Heinemann, he wrote back, "I am glad you are taking steps against George Moore. It is time he was put a stop to."[32]

Gregory was corresponding regularly with Blunt (another former lover) at this time because she was helping Yeats and Ezra Pound, who were living together most of that winter in Stone Cottage, in Sussex, organize what became known as the "peacock dinner." It was Pound's idea, in late November, to give a testimonial dinner for Blunt, and Yeats had written Gregory about it because she knew Blunt and could advise them about what kind of invitation he might accept.[33] This dinner of male poets, which took place on 18 January 1914 at Blunt's estate in Sussex, grew in importance in Gregory's mind as she came to realize the publicity that it could attract. In a 12 January letter Yeats wrote to Gregory that Pound insisted that they *not* have a photographer, an idea Gregory had apparently suggested. Pound agreed to an account in the *Times* "because that leaves a record for posterity," but not to a photojournalist who would take a picture for the paper.[34] In the event, they had a private photographer, whose photograph of the seven poets has been called "the most famous Georgian literary photograph." But Gregory's suggestion of a photographer appears to have been made only days after her letter to Pawling at Heinemann, and she was clearly thinking of the peacock dinner as an event that could be used to keep Yeats (and, by association, herself and the Abbey Theatre) in a good light in the press, countering Moore's libel and maintaining the symbolic value of their names.

These three episodes—the guarantee fund dispute, the Moore libel, and the peacock dinner—overlapped with one another in chronology, and, viewed together, they show the diasporic spread of the Gregory-Yeats cultural business, with publication in London affecting a theater in Dublin, a dinner in Sussex written up in the *Times* also, perhaps, affecting a theater in Dublin as well as the reputations of six poets living around London, and a strike in Dublin encouraging actors there to demand funds collected in Chicago, Boston, New York, and London on behalf of an art gallery in Dublin. Ezra Pound, who first thought of and helped plan the dinner, was sending poetry to Harriet Monroe, who attended the Chicago benefit matinee and was close friends with Ford Madox Ford, editor of the *English Review,* which had published Moore's offending chapter.

The episodes also reveal how much of Gregory's and Yeats's time was devoted to small easements in the large field of cultural production, interstitial forms of "help," dinners, teas, flattery, hiring of photographers, getting names in print, getting them out of print, threats, visits to lawyers and bankers, and visits designed to get other people to "help" with the dinners and teas and photographers and newspapers—a whole set of behaviors that supported the production of works of art. These skills were not professional labor, at least not in 1913, and no one would have been paid to exercise them, but they were the bread and butter, or the bread and broth, of all the Gregory-Yeats enterprises.

Mac Liammóir's *The Importance of Being Oscar* in America

JOAN FITZPATRICK DEAN

By 1960, Irish theater had reached another of its perennial crises. The Abbey remained, in Eric Bentley's 1952 formulation, a trick on tourists.[1] Two of Dublin's most promising and innovative companies, the Pike Theater Company and the Globe Theater Company, folded in the late 1950s. Phyllis Ryan's companies—Orion, Gemini, and Libra Productions—valiantly carried on with neither subsidy nor a permanent theater base.[2] For nearly nine years, between February 1956 and September 1964, the Edwards-Mac Liammóir Gate Theater Company presented only one play at the Gate Theater and "twice or thrice yearly offerings are made at the Gaiety or Olympia Theater."[3] The late fifties reduced the fortunes of the founders of the Dublin Gate Company, Micheál Mac Liammóir and Hilton Edwards, then also in their late fifties, as they had effectively lost what had, since 1930, been their home base. They and their company had fallen deeply into debt. Even a £3,000 grant from the Arts Council in 1953 only kept what Edwards would call "the more voracious of the wolves from the door."[4]

In 1957 Edwards traveled to London to assess what possibilities remained for them in England. Edwards wanted to leave Ireland, but Mac Liammóir was not so inclined. One of Edwards's wrenching letters to Mac Liammóir concludes by asking

> whether it is worthwhile to give anything more to Ireland considering the prospects she has left us with after thirty years, or whether we should take the tide while it serves and make what hay we can while the suneshines [*sic*]

in this English market. . . . IRELAND WILL NOT THINK ANYTHING OF US UNLESS WE ARE ACCEPTED AND ARE SUCCESSES OUTSIDE IRELAND.[5]

Precisely what Edwards had pointed to, success outside Ireland, would come in the early sixties in what Christopher Fitz-Simon refers to as "an extraordinary turn in their fortunes"[6] and what Micheál Ó hAodha calls "the Reingreencarnation."[7] Edwards and Mac Liammóir were soon involved in two productions that found success outside Ireland, ones that epitomized the major structural changes in theater: Edwards with the international tour of Brian Friel's *Philadelphia, Here I Come!* and Mac Liammóir and Edwards with *The Importance of Being Oscar.*

In 1956, Edwards was casting about for one-act plays that could be assembled into a theatrical evening for a review tentatively entitled "Tales from the Irish Hills," which he described to Samuel Beckett as "ballads, very short plays, and dramatic excerpts from the best that we can find in Irish literature and music."[8] Two features of Edwards's proposed review are worth tracking for their similarities with Mac Liammóir's *The Importance of Being Oscar.* First, it was to be specifically Irish, which brought it in line with the recently established Arts Council, the Dublin Theater Festival, and a number of initiatives designed to present a progressive image of Ireland's involvement in the arts; second, it would create a new dramatic entertainment out of existing work.

First performed on 15 September 1960 at the Curragh Barracks before an audience largely of officers and their wives in a one-night trial run, and then transferred to the Gaiety Theater on 3 October 1960, *The Importance of Being Oscar* was to provide Mac Liammóir the financial security that thirty years with the Gate never could. In *The Importance of Being Oscar* Mac Liammóir would drop his strictures against solo performances and, moreover, abandon his commitment to the avant-garde visual elements in costume, set design, and décor that characterized much of the Gate's work. Such a "one-man" venture, while not unprecedented, was hardly a sure thing. "Would an entire evening devoted to a single controversial figure of so heady a vintage be at once too limited and too cloying?" wondered Hilton Edwards.[9] Just how risky and unprecedented Mac Liammóir's scheme was is evident when Louis Elliman, the Gaiety Theater manager, refused to stage the production until its inclusion in the Dublin Theater Festival indemnified him against potential losses.

In 1960 Wilde's reputation was only in its embryonic rebound from a very low ebb. In 1926 Arnold Bennett pronounced Wilde "outmoded." No Wilde play had been performed on Broadway since a nine-week run of *The Importance of Being Earnest* in 1947. In 1951, the one-time Abbey director and playwright St. John Ervine published a scurrilous biography, *Oscar Wilde: A Present Time Appraisal*. In his unsympathetic portrait, Ervine asserted that Wilde "lacked originality" and disputed the factuality of the incident when Wilde was humiliated by an angry crowd on the Clapham Junction platform.[10] In 1954, Edwards and Mac Liammóir spearheaded a drive to commemorate the centennial of Wilde's birth with a plaque. When, in spite of Bórd Fáilte's refusal to participate, the campaign was successful, some angry Dubliners contacted the *Evening Mail* to challenge the propriety of honoring Wilde.[11] In 1960, however, two British plays were adapted and released as films: one starring Peter Finch (*The Trials of Oscar Wilde*, based on a play of the same name by John Furnell) and the other with Robert Morley (*Oscar Wilde*; based on a 1938 play by the brothers Sewell and Leslie Stokes).

Mac Liammóir, now sixty-one, decided to avoid any impersonation of Wilde (who died at forty-six). Unlike the performances of Emlyn Williams as Charles Dickens (1952), Hal Holbrook in *Mark Twain Tonight!* (1966), or Julie Harris in *The Belle of Amherst* (1976), Mac Liammóir did not take on Wilde's persona, but narrated his life bridging the selections from Wilde's writings, adventures, and quips. He read from the poems and novels, dropped into the characters of Lady Bracknell and Jack Worthing, and recited "The Ballad of Reading Gaol." In addition to the narrative and recitative voices, Mac Liammóir performed a dozen dramatic and historical personages from Wilde's works and life.

The first half, entitled "The Happy Prince and the Green Carnation," drew principally from on Wilde's poetry, his infatuation with Lily Langtry, his visit to Leadville, Colorado, *The Picture of Dorian Gray*, and his plays—although only *An Ideal Husband* and *The Importance of Being Earnest* along with a highly charged reading in French from *Salome* are explored.[12] The episodes of Wilde's life that have attracted the most attention in recent reworkings for print, stage, and screen—the public furor generated by his arrest and trials—were entirely elided by the interval. Part two, entitled "De Profundis," edits Wilde's letter to Alfred Lord Douglas to about fifteen minutes of stage time and incorporates a poignant exchange between Wilde and Tom

Martin, one of his prison guards. Mac Liammóir has Wilde turned away by a "Roman Catholic Retreat" (58) after his release from prison and later encounter with Andre Gide. After a recitation of "The Ballad of Reading Gaol," the play concludes with an account of Wilde covering Constance's "grave with red roses" (68), drifting through Italy, and ending in Paris where "Robert Ross called in a priest, a Passionist father, who baptized and received the Protestant-born Irishman, Oscar Fingal O'Flahertie Wills Wilde into the Catholic Church and gave him Extreme Unction" (70).

The script did not focus on the two features of Wilde's life that have since drawn much attention: his Irishness and his homosexuality. By eliding the legal actions—arrests and trials—against Wilde at the play's intermission, the play was hardly explicit about Wilde's sexuality. *Oscar* presents homosexuality as a choice between heterosexuality and the "Tiger Life," a "hilarious revolt against Victorianism" (26).

Although little is said about Wilde's family, background, and youth, Irishness surfaces ten times: in speculation about a speech from the dock that might have been in the tradition of Robert Emmet, in references to the tradition of Dublin eloquence, and in Wilde's death bed conversion to Catholicism. Intrinsic to Mac Liammóir's reclamation of Wilde was the vision that they were both Irish. If Wilde went to England and became more English than the English, Alfred Willmore came to Ireland and became more Irish than the Irish.

Owen Dudley Edwards quite appropriately describes *The Importance of Being Oscar* as "crowning a lifetime's evangelization of Wilde in the dangerous surroundings of that prophet's own country."[13] Indeed, for more than three decades, Mac Liammóir and the Gate had presented the Irish premiere of *Salome* (then still banned from public performance in England by the Lord Chamberlain) in 1929 and produced *Lady Windermere's Fan* in 1931; *An Ideal Husband* in 1932 and 1945; *The Importance of Being Earnest* in 1933, 1937, 1938, on tour in 1939 and 1943; and Mac Liammóir's adaptation of *The Picture of Dorian Gray* in 1945 and again in 1956.[14]

Mac Liammóir and Edwards were dubious about the project, not least because of what in 1960 was the novelty of its dramaturgy.[15] They hardly envisioned the enthusiasm with which it was greeted. The Dublin reviews were so positive that a London season was quickly organized for two weeks at the end of October. The 800-seat Apollo Theater in the West End was booked. The celebrity stylist Angus McBean photographed Mac Liammóir for the London program. With few prospects in Ireland, Mac Liammóir was eager to tour.

The one-man show proved vastly more portable than many of the previous touring productions from the Gate Theater Company. The set deliberately avoided "any sense of a room" and instead created "an empty, elegant space,"[16] which used a textile floor, originally a stage cloth painted by Molly MacEwen and later a carpet woven in Donegal. The chaise longue, a pedestal with a vase of calla lilies (replaced by autumn leaves for the second act), a table, and chair comprised the set. Mac Liammóir appeared in a dinner jacket. Simplicity was the hallmark of the production design for a show that would tour more extensively than anything the Gate had ever toured.

The London reviews were superlative: "A triumph for Mr. Mac Liammóir" (*Stage*); "an explosion of incomparable richness" *(Daily Mail)*; "superb" *(Daily Mirror)*. Mac Liammóir had almost universally enthusiastic reviews, many of which highlighted his and Wilde's Irishness. In *Punch,* it was Mac Liammóir's "splendid Irish voice." The *London Times* described, "Mr. Mac Liammóir is the last inheritor of the tradition of eloquent Irish conversation."[17]

So successful was the London run that an American season was no less hastily arranged. The first American run in 924-seat Lyceum Theatre on Broadway was for thirty-six performances over a four-week season that began on March 14 and closed on April 8. Although Mac Liammóir reported that seven out of seven reviews in the New York daily papers were positive, they were not comparable to the London reviews; in fact, several of those reviews were mixed and others, outside the seven dailies, were strongly qualified. So although the *New York Post* found it "a theater event of striking and distinguished interest, and a triumph for its one-man cast," the *World-Telegram and Sun* concluded that the "show can have only a specialized appeal. Personally, I found it an extraordinary display of memory and vocal stamina. It was exquisitely entertaining."

Many of the reviews were mixed and their negativity emanated from a distinct discomfort with Mac Liammóir's sympathetic presentation of homosexuality. Walter Kerr in the *New York Herald Tribune* wrote of Mac Liammóir's "index finger, [thrust] at us in such urgent passion," his "always arched hands," often "curled at his forehead" and likened the performance to one by Edwin Forrest, the nineteenth-century actor best remembered for his histrionic acting style. Kerr wrote of "a few excesses in spite of all," especially the dropping of the "gay green carnation" and found the end "anticlimactic as the sentimentality stretches thin." The nationally distributed wire service, the Associated Press, carried an assessment by William Slover that cautioned: " For Wilde fans and the literary congregation, a visit is a must. Let others beware." Likewise, the *New Yorker* judged that "despite Mr. Mac Liammóir's innumerable skills, his performance will of necessity appeal only to a fairly specialized audience."[18] Encoded in the nationally syndicated and even in the New York reviews was a bristling anxiety over any, let alone a sympathetic, treatment of homosexuality.

In America in 1960, as in Ireland, homosexuality was considered not just a disease but also a crime. That Mac Liammóir's script portrayed homosexuality as a choice was shocking, although not unprecedented on the Broadway stage. Because the New York reviews were, as they are today, the gold standard for reviewing in the United States, the American producer, Sol Hurok, recognized that they had what they needed to support a provincial tour: reviews strong enough to be carefully excerpted to fuel the publicity for an extensive tour.

When he returned to Ireland in April after the four-week New York City run, Mac Liammóir held a press conference at Dublin airport. Not all was well. Outside of the universities, he saw little interest in Wilde. American theater was a disappointment. Americans, he reported, responded to his Irishness in one of three clichéd ways: talk of the color green, references to shamrocks, or simply an indulgent smile. "Their [sentimental] image of Ireland," he told the press, "is not only incorrect but belittling." He described New York as "a city where the world is made safe for morons and one is not encouraged to be anything else there." In an article published in *Inniu,* he advised the Irish to rethink "the silly efforts to replace our national identity abroad through the substitution of leprechauns, shamrock and so on for our real national culture."

The Importance of Being Oscar returned to the United States in October after several revivals in Ireland, an appearance in Paris, a week in Amsterdam and Brussels, and nine stops over a month in Central and South America. The American touring schedule originally included twenty-seven, and then expanded to thirty-nine, venues over two months from 9 October to 10 December 1961, but traveled neither south of St. Louis nor west of Cedar Falls, Iowa and concentrated in college towns. There were multinight runs in Washington, Chicago, Buffalo, Boston, and Philadelphia, but not in large or prestigious theaters. The publicity coup of the tour occurred on 18 October 1961 in Washington, D.C., when First Lady Jacqueline Kennedy attended the performance of *Oscar* in the Coolidge auditorium in the Library of Congress. When the show appeared in Cleveland, it was at John Carroll University. In Philadelphia, a Jewish group sponsored the performances at the Young Hebrew Men's Club.

The advance publicity materials for the ten-week tour drew on London and New York reviews, which then as now outweigh local reviewer's opinions. The provincial reviews would largely have been for the record because they only appeared after the tour had moved on in all but a few of the larger cities, such as Washington, Chicago, and Boston, and would have had little, if any, effect on the box office. Most of the reviews were qualified but positive, and there were some overtly negative reviews. Outside New York, several of the reviews carry a subtext that warned readers that the performance touched on Wilde's homosexuality. In Washington, Tom Donnelly in the *Washington News* described Mac Liammóir as "not a particularly subtle artist" who "lacks finesse. His Lady Bracknell is a dowager out of a Hasty Pudding show." He "missed the mark" in readings from *An Ideal Husband* and the "over-long" performance suffered from "an excess of mugging." In Madison, Wisconsin, the performance was described as "over-burdened" and "over-stated." By the time the show reached Toledo in late October, the warnings became more dire: "Unfortunately, it is not precisely what all TCPA [Toledo Civic Playgoers Association] members bargained for." The worst came in Chicago when the reviewer for the *Chicago Tribune* left at intermission but nonetheless wrote of Mac Liammóir's "florid, fruity acting manner" and his "poised Mayfair accent and delivery that conscientiously ignores natural punctuation."

Mac Liammóir's presented Wilde's homosexuality with great delicacy. Éibhear Walshe's contention that "the emblematic figure of Wilde . . . licensed the actor to bring his dissident sexuality more and more to the fore"[19] rightly contextualizes a comparative rather than absolute candor about homosexuality. Today Mac Liammóir's treatment of homosexuality in *Oscar* may seem coy and evasive, but in the day it was audacious. The American reviews of the two 1960 films of Wilde's life frequently mention that Wilde's name was avoided in "polite company" or in the presence of women and children.

The first part of *The Importance of Being Oscar* foregrounds Wilde's heterosexual impulses: his infatuation for Lily Langtry and his contentment as husband and father. Of Wilde's marriage to "a gentle and very beautiful Irish girl called Constance Mary Lloyd," Mac Liammóir says: "They were passionately and mutually in love and supremely happy" (21). Discussed only obliquely, homosexuality emerges midway through the first act in the emblem of the green carnation:

> The Green Carnation by this time in fact had come to mean something much more than a mere buttonhole, and stood for a brief and brilliant season or two as the symbol of the age. And it seems to me that it represented a mood rather than a movement: a mood that was at once indolent, voluptuous, bizarre, witty and deliberately artificial. To many people it seemed a delightful affair, this hilarious revolt against Victorianism, others found in the Green Carnation something faintly sinister. (25–26)

Despite the lyrics from Noel Coward's 1929 operetta *Bitter Sweet:* ("Art is our inspiration/And as we the reason for the 'nineties' being gay /We all wear a green carnation"[20]) in Irish America in the early 1960s, the green carnation carried a very different meaning. It was displayed, as shamrocks once were, as a marker of Irish ancestry. Typically, green carnations were worn by Irish American men on St. Patrick's day and usually only if they dressed in a suit or more formal attire for Mass, a parade, or other explicitly Irish ceremony.

In that day, Mac Liammóir could not have risked more. The 1958 film version of Tennessee Williams's *Cat on a Hot Tin Roof* sanitized almost every vestige of Brick's attraction to Skipper and left Paul Newman a raving if unhappy heterosexual. *Boys Beware,* a ten-minute cautionary tale that has an analogous cult status with *Reefer Madness,* and whose narrator warns, "One never knows when a homosexual is about. He may appear normal and it may be too late when you discover he is mentally ill," was made in 1961, the same year that Mac Liammóir first toured *Oscar* in the United States. By that time, United Artists and Columbia Pictures had acquired options on three properties that dealt with homosexuality: Lillian Hellman's *The Children's Hour,* Gore Vidal's *The Best Man,* and Allen Drury's *Advise and Consent.*[21] All had been successful on Broadway (*Advise and Consent* began as a bestselling novel), one measure that was leveraged in negotiations between the studios and the Motion Picture Association of America to certify these films. All eventually received PCA certification,[22] but *The Children's Hour* received the most restrictive, X, rating in the United Kingdom and was banned outright in Ireland.

In the American reviews of *The Importance of Being Oscar,* homosexuality is typically euphemized, as in the *Christian Science Monitor,* as "the vice which beset" Wilde. Reviewers expressed relief that Mac Liammóir "quite sensibly" or "wisely avoids concentrating on the legal proceedings." Overall the American reviews in fact, implied a preference for the erasure of the subject of homosexuality altogether. Some reviewers were evidently unprepared for even the oblique, equivocal approach Mac Liammóir took and deeply troubled by any presentation to homosexuality.

Reviewers were also insensitive to the Irish dimension of the evening. Despite numerous references to Ireland and the Irish, one reviewer placed Mac Liammóir in "the great tradition of English acting." Although the *New York Times* review by Howard Taubman concludes "[Mac Liammóir] is an Irishman proudly proclaiming a compatriot's expression, in himself and his work, of the spirit of Ireland," Irishness typically did not figure in the reviews. Taubman never suggests what the spirit of Ireland might be. No one attempted to link *The Importance of Being Earnest* with Behan's *The Hostage,* which concluded its Broadway run nine weeks before Mac Liammóir appeared in New York City. Although Mac Liammóir was often identified as Irish, the only other review that commented on Irishness was the *Christian Science Monitor* that saw him as "reveling like a true celt in the flow of words." Of course, Mac Liammóir's Wilde was the very antithesis of the familiar stage Irishman and likely to destabilize most horizons of expectations about what was Irish. With a rich, sophisticated, glamorous Irish American in the White House after January 1961, the very concept of Irishness was extremely fluid.

Mac Liammóir's tour of the American provinces was hardly an unqualified success. He certainly was aware of the negative reviews, carping comments, and quibbles in the provincial press. One of the most offensive reviews came in a theatrically savvy city, Chicago, where Roger Dettmer asked "Is an evening of Wilde, even a second half devoted to his imprisonment for alleged unnatural practices and his sorry final years in Paris, more than the subject or his effete works warrant?" In his scrapbook of reviews and memorabilia in the Gate Theater Archive, Mac Liammóir's handwritten marginalia offered a stinging comparison between Dublin critics and Dettmer's review: "This is the sort of excretia that passes for dramatic criticism in my own 'Windy City'—only by wading thru this whole turgid mess does one realize that this poor tired queen only caught the first half of 'Oscar.'"

An Oscar of No Importance, Mac Liammóir's chronicle of the long life of *Oscar,* does its best to forget the provincial American tour. Whereas Mac Liammóir provides several hundred words on each city he visits in South America, he neglects to mention any of the thirty-nine American cities where he performed *Oscar.* From his "lonely and apprehensive arrival"[23] at LaGuardia airport until his departure, he found little to admire in American culture. He loathed the commotion, jukeboxes, and general racket that enveloped him. Played against autumnal and winter landscapes ("Death in nature is as physically glorious as life" [129]), the chapter on the American tour in *An Oscar of No Importance,* the shortest in the book, is uncharacteristically gloomy and fraught with self-pity. A visit with Denis Johnston and Betty Chancellor reminds him that "none of our dreams have fulfilled themselves" (128). Actors, Mac Liammóir realizes, "almost inevitably must pass from a moment of notoriety into an eternity of oblivion" (129). Returning to Ireland just before Christmas, Mac Liammóir arranged to be photographed reading in bed with a back of his hand resting on his brow to project an image of exhaustion and relief.

Mac Liammóir's *Oscar* toured the world for many years. It was first televised by RTÉ, where Edwards served as the first head of drama, on St. Patrick's Day 1964. Despite his travails in America, Mac Liammóir returned to the United States to play selected venues throughout the 1960s. *Oscar* has also been revived several times in the United States: in 1991 by the Irish Classical Theater (Buffalo) starring Vincent O'Neill, who was directed by his brother Chris O'Neill. In 2001, on the centenary of Oscar Wilde's death, the Irish Repertory Company in New York City produced Mac Liammóir's piece with Niall Buggy. Central Works Theater Company in Berkeley mounted a revival of the play in 2003. The best known revival was by Simon Callow in London's Savoy Theater in 2000–2001.

Mac Liammóir followed the success of *Oscar* with other, less controversial one-man shows: *I Must Be Talking to My Friends,* first produced at the Gaiety Theater on 15 April 1963; *Talking about Yeats,* first performed at the Gate in honor of the centennial of the poet's birth on 20 June 1965; and *Ill Met by Moonlight* in 1969. Although straightjacketed into these one-man shows by financial exigency (Edwards suggested that "the Oscar Wilde work [has] turned into a 'a Frankenstein monster'" [8]), Mac Liammóir's solo performance became a lifeline for the Gate Theater founders. In Micheál Ó hAodha's estimation *Oscar* was "part catharsis, part exorcism for the sixty-year-old-actor."[24] Now venerated for his inestimable contributions to Irish theater, Mac Liammóir chose *Oscar* for his final stage appearance, one attended by Cearbhail O Dalaigh, then president of Ireland, in December 1975.

The Importance of Being Oscar participates in the reclamation of an Irish identity for Wilde that continues in the work of Terry Eagleton, Davis Coakley, Richard Pine, Jerusha McCormack, and others. Mac Liammóir's American tour was important in positioning Wilde as an Irish playwright and in broadening the American perspective on what was Irish. Along with Behan's *The Hostage*, which ran 127 performances in 1960–61 and won Behan a Tony Award as Best Play, and Friel's *Philadelphia, Here I Come!* which reached Broadway in 1966, *Oscar* reshaped what American audiences understood as Irish drama.

Mac Liammóir's account of Wilde offers its own hermeneutic: "The man of genius is not content with merely echoing the age he lives in: he invents it" (22). Many of the central interpretative assertions that underpin Mac Liammóir's presentation of Wilde also inform Richard Ellmann's celebrated biography of Wilde, which ends with the assertion that Wilde "belongs to our world more than to that of Victoria's."[25] That opinion, in its turn, has been corroborated by Peter Ackroyd's *The Last Will and Testament of Oscar Wilde,* Alan Sinfield's *The Wilde Century,* and scores of creative and nonfiction works.[26]

The Importance of Being Oscar challenged audiences with an unfamiliar dramaturgy, an unconventional and disgraced artist, and an expansive sense of what was Irish. In the American reception of *The Importance of Being Oscar* the issue of Wilde's homosexuality, heavily veiled as it was, eclipsed the question of Wilde as Irishman, but Mac Liammóir provided a vital contribution in the eventual reclamation of Wilde.

9

Beckett and America

JOHN P. HARRINGTON

The great Samuel Beckett Centenary of 2006 proved to be truly exhaustive. However, one of the least frequently noticed events of the anniversary year was announcement that the Coconut Grove Playhouse had been declared a historic landmark. Many will remember that this was the site of the out-of-town tryout of the American premiere production of *Waiting for Godot* that drew sensationalist press and hugely self-congratulatory celebration of the magnitude of the artistic disaster. The theater building, in what in Florida is called "Mediterranean Revival," may well be a good example of vernacular architecture of the 1930s in the Miami area. But the only reason given in the press for its preservation for historical purposes is that it was host to the *Godot* "resounding flop," in which, according to the Gainesville newspaper story on the landmark status, "the audience did not understand the play's metaphysical subtleties, and a third of the attendees left at intermission, while others lined up for refunds."[1] None of these three statements is historically accurate. But what is really interesting is the whole legendary quality of the episode: European culture transferred to America in its own fabled 1950s and proudly rejected as such. The Beckett Centenary of his birth is also the Diamond Jubilee of the Coconut Grove production with Bert Lahr and movement of it with him alone to Broadway. Perhaps the fifty-year distance helps us understand our own vanity in gloating over Beckett's remoteness, Florida's superficiality, and Broadway's commercialism. Then, Beckett helps us, Americans, know ourselves.

Some of the most frequently cited occasions on the great Samuel Beckett centenary of 2006 have as emphasis Beckett the European, including the exhibition at Reading, center of European Beckett Studies, called "Samuel

Beckett—the Irish European." One might think that would offend the early "Irish Beckett" enthusiasts. It does not because the "Irish Beckett" is itself a now historical concept formed some time ago, when Ireland was Ireland and Europe was Europe and the differences were evident. The European Beckett, especially as advanced by the *Journal of Beckett Studies,* center of American Beckett Studies, is focused on what it called "genetic criticism," or how his work had genesis in Continental culture. It advances study of that genesis.[2]

Another area of interest has to do with output rather than the input, in what happened when Beckett's characteristic work reached its audience, and this area is extremely interesting when the work meets a distinctly foreign audience, such as American. Instead of genesis, this is advanced through performance history. The record does not argue for a hitherto undiscovered American Beckett; in fact, the interest in Beckett and America lies in the great gap between the producer of the work and the receivers of it, a gap that presumably existed in Paris and in London and in Dublin, but never quite as wide as that significantly greater great yawning gap between Beckett and America, where the differences continue to be evident. Hence the interest: not in identity, but in contrast. I'm delighted to report that, as recorded by his biographer James Knowlson, at the end of Beckett's single visit to America, after a trip to the 1963–1964 World's Fair, and after persisting through the final inning of a New York Mets double header at Shea Stadium, Beckett headed into the departure gate of his return flight from New York with, according to his publisher Barney Rosset, these words: "This is somehow not the right country for me . . . the people are too strange."[3]

To put the matter of contrast on a slightly higher plane than *Waiting for Godot* at the Coconut Grove Playhouse, the idea of contrast as enriching is a wonderful one in Pascale Casanova's book *The World Republic of Letters.* She is very interested in how national literary cultures are evolving into international ones without ever completely obliterating origins, and in her study both Beckett and Ireland are perhaps the preeminent cases. Casanova wants us to forego exclusionary theories of literature and reading and instead engage more complex models in which, in her words, "the literary world needs to be seen . . . as the product of antagonistic forces. . . . [and in which] international space proceeds for the most part through rivalries within national fields between national and international writers."[4] For her, Beckett is a preeminent example for being such a thoroughly "self-translated" writer oscillating between French and English as language of composition or language of translation and equivalently between identity as a national or an international writer. The interest in Beckett and his work in America resides in that contrast, a very effective iconography of which would be an image of the author at the New York World's Fair, confronting its icon, the Unisphere. These certainly are antagonistic forces, and the rivalries are illuminating.

To return to Beckett and America, the lack of fit and the general strangeness of the playwright to the venue and vice versa are both the task and the benefits of the study of cultural exchange. The American Beckett story begins with the 1955 tryout of *Godot* in Miami that was recast and significantly re-represented for opening on Broadway in 1956. The story is most familiarly told in the great director Alan Schneider's account of how the Broadway producer Michael Myerberg acquired the rights, sent Schneider to Paris to consult with the playwright, and in his absence cast the play himself and cancelled the usual preview engagements in Philadelphia and Washington for a guaranteed run at the Coconut Grove in Miami. In Schneider's account:

> The Miami audience was being informed, in large type, that Bert Lahr, "Star of *Harvey* and *Burlesque*," and Tom Ewell, "Star of the *Seven Year Itch*," were to appear in their midst in "the Laugh *Sensation* of Two Continents," *Waiting for Godot*. The name of the author appeared only in very small print.[5]

Contrary to rumor, the show did not close, which would hardly do on a guaranteed booking where deficits did not accrue to the production. After the full run in preview, protecting his rights, Myerberg set about recalculating for New York. For him, the problem in Miami was that "the audiences were in the wrong area of expectation. They expected a farcical comedy, which 'Waiting for Godot,' of course, is not."

Myerberg recast, with Lahr remaining the only known comic type. He redid the advertising, and successfully placed in the *New York Times* a preview feature by Arthur Gelb, from which the quotation above about expectations was taken. Further, the piece announced the producer's intention to take the "precaution of publicly warning theatergoers in search of casual entertainment not to buy tickets to 'Waiting for Godot.'"[6] Largely thanks to the *Times*, he managed to use the contrast of Lahr and the forbidding playwright, here memorably always characterized as James Joyce's secretary, in conjunction with the huckster appeal to readers *not* to buy tickets, to make intellectual provocation a cause. In this he succeeded. There were some sneering reviews, but in general the actual audience enlisted in the cause, fought for it by letters to editors, and brought paperback copies of the play text to the theater for postperformance discussions. Harold Clurman's perspective then is representative: he wrote that, "If this play is generally difficult for Americans to grasp . . . it is because there is not immediate point of reference for it in the conscious life of our people."[7] That is pretty much what Myerberg said, and it is useful reconfirmation of the significant degree of difference, of antagonistic forces and rivalries between Beckett and America, and that, contrary to the myth, the challenge was accepted readily.

Expungement of the low-end production values of the Miami production for the high-end art values of New York did not limit the audience or the success of the play. Contrary to rumors of "disaster," the production record is remarkable for how many productions of *Waiting for Godot* opened how swiftly. The Bert Lahr Broadway show had a respectable run of seven weeks and a significant revenue return as reported in *Variety*. In less than seven months, *Godot* was revived on Broadway with an all-black cast; that failed in a week, but some perceived challenge or some recognition of *Godot* as powerful theater for avid audiences incentivized that risky investment. By 1957, *Waiting for Godot* was playing in places like Iowa City and also in small cities that were not university towns. In a quintessentially American development, the "property" came to interest Hollywood. Barney Rosset was approached by Steve McQueen, who mentioned Brando as co-star; Rosset quotes Beckett as saying that they were "too big" while "my characters are ghosts."[8] Michael Feingold has recalled how in the 1960s, *Godot* became a repertory staple of the civil rights-oriented Free Southern Theater touring in Alabama and how the activist Fannie Lou Hamer told the press: "In every town in the South, you see men with no jobs just standin' around, waiting. Who they waiting for if it ain't Godot?"[9] Memorably, in 1959 Kenneth Rexroth reported that *"Godot* has been put on as a 'floor show' in the Crystal Palace in St. Louis . . . and has run for a whole season to packed houses in San Francisco. . . . there aren't enough *Godot*'s to meet the demand."[10]

It is only a small leap from a floor show to the notable production directed by Mike Nichols at Lincoln Center in 1988. "Beckett's Godot isn't placed in America," Nichols said. "Mine is." So it was cast with Steve Martin and Robin Williams and performed on a desert set with a Vegas skyline on the horizon. Nichols, however, had learned the lessons of Myerberg: the relation of America and Beckett was one of difference. He began by meeting with Beckett and continued to do so through significant Beckett estate protectors, such as Tom Bishop of New York University and the director Walter Asmus, and sought approval from the estate for every change of text (including changing the "Macon" and "cacon" rhyme to "Napa" and "crappa").[11] The distance between Beckett and America and attempts to align, not to integrate, the antagonistic forces is the history of *Waiting for Godot* in America. In the great Samuel Beckett centenary, Atlanta staged Asmus's version first, (criticized for "unbearably long silences") and then followed it with a Theater Gael production (praised as "hilarious" and "the cause of belly laughter").[12] The relation of the authorized Asmus production derived from Beckett's in Berlin to the local American company was one of interaction and not of imitation.

Obviously, issues surrounding production adaptations arose long before the Beckett estate became indefatigably vigilant and purist. One of the well-remembered and bitterly resented cases of the vigilance against production liberties was that of JoAnne Akalaitis's *Endgame* at the American Repertory Theater in 1984. In retrospect the case seems to have run afoul of the estate from poor communication. The origins of vigilance, especially as applied to the great gap in Beckett's mind between his work and the American public, were evident much earlier, in 1953, when he first began to negotiate American rights. "I hope you realize what you are letting yourself in for," he wrote to Barney Rosset concerning North American rights for Grove Press. Beckett insisted first of all on all the obscenities in his recent prose, such as *Molloy*, which, he said, "I am not at all disposed to mitigate." But in addition to translation issues, he referred to a much greater degree of difference as "the heart of the matter." He appears to have believed that problems with fidelity to the text would be especially evident in America. "The problem therefore is no more complicated than this," he wrote to Rosset: "are you prepared to print the result? I am convinced you will agree with me that a clear understanding on this matter before we set to work is equally indispensable for you, the translator, and myself."[13]

By extension, we can imagine a parallel purity on the forthcoming plays: Are you prepared to perform the play? The record, however, is of higher tolerance of freedoms with the texts of the plays in American productions. That tolerance might not extend all the way to *Godot* as a floor show at the

Crystal Palace in St. Louis, but it did extend to remarkable support for the work of Herbert Blau's San Francisco Actors Workshop, which was scarcely bound by the text, and the counterpart it inspired inside the walls, the San Quentin Drama Workshop, which had begun with two prisoner-produced *Godot* productions and one *Endgame* production staged in the gallows room at San Quentin. By comparison, the subway setting and Phillip Glass music of Akalaitis's *Endgame* seems a modest adjustment. In fact, earlier, and more characteristically, Beckett granted great liberties with the text to Joseph Chaikin, David Warrilow, Fred Neumann, Lee Breuer, and others associated with Mabou Mines when Akalaitis was a member of the company. He probably would have extended the same to Akalaitis had he known her association with the same company. On this issue Knowlson concludes that "Becket could appear, and indeed was, inconsistent" on fidelity to play text as written,[14] and one pattern of inconsistency was allowing greater liberties to American productions. Perhaps that pattern derived in part to the transatlantic distance when that still mattered, but in any case the result was some special chemistry of Beckett with his foreign colleagues, the Americans. Frederick Neumann of Mabou Mines has described how the company's well-known stage production of Beckett's text *The Lost Ones* may or not have been approved by the author and how, on being presented with its designs, Beckett very tolerantly replied, "My, you have adapted it, haven't you?" Neumann also reports how allowing liberties never approached open license. On their subsequent stage production of *Mercier and Camier,* he went to Beckett to apologize for "over-production." The reason was that Beckett's advice had always been "the simpler the better, Freddy." Of his reports from others on *Mercier and Camier,* Beckett reported, "Yes, I've received good reports'—and he held his finger up—'with reservations.'" Hence there would be no Phillip Glass music for the subsequent production of *Company*—"I think," Beckett told Neumann, "there are the proper interstices."[15]

There are two particularly resonant examples of Beckett's work with Americans in performing arts, the film *Film* and the radio play *Words and Music,* that can serve as illustrative examples of very positive chemistry between those two very distant agents, Beckett and America. In the case of *Film,* Beckett came to America. In 1963, Rosset, flush with the Grove Press success in defending so-called obscene works and then profiting from the scandal, invited eight of his authors to write a film script. Most declined, Ionesco and Harold Pinter prepared scripts that were never filmed, and

Beckett alone wrote, persisted in logistics, and supervised filming on the set in New York City in 1964. As is well known, his concept was to film a protagonist trying to avoid perception by the camera, failing, and then turning his own eye on it, all this in cinematic illustration of Berkeley's notion that to be is to be perceived. From the beginning, for Rosset, Beckett, and Alan Schneider, hired to direct, the concept was to cast an icon of American silent film. When Chaplin was unwilling, interest shifted to the Irish actor Jack MacGowran, and when he proved overscheduled, interest shifted back to Buster Keaton, who was more than available at a low point in his career. The antagonistic forces could not have been stronger. Schneider described introducing Samuel Beckett to Buster Keaton in New York City:

> When Sam and I came [to the hotel], Keaton was drinking a can of beer and watching a baseball game on television. . . . The greetings were mild, slightly awkward without meaning to be. The two exchanged a few general words, most of them from Sam, then proceeded to sit in silence while Keaton watched the ball game. I don't think he offered us a beer. . . . They had nothing to share. All of Sam's goodwill and my own flailing efforts to get something started failed to bring them together on any level. . . . The meeting was a disaster.[16]

The first meeting may have been a disaster, but the project was not. Keaton wanted to wear a trademark hat; Beckett wanted just that, too. Beckett wanted layers and greatcoats in the summer New York heat; Keaton managed everything. Schneider's choice of Greenwich Village exteriors was changed by Beckett to lower Manhattan, and when exterior shots proved unworkable on budget, the set moved indoors, which allowed Keaton to indulge in routines with animals that were his preference anyway. Both sets were Beckett's choice, and so, the sole recorded images he chose for his work. The most authorized visible Beckett landscape is a wall and a building beside the Brooklyn Bridge. It was scheduled for demolition and survives only in wholly changed form on the outskirts of the South Street Seaport restaurant and retail district. No doubt that redevelopment would have further convinced Beckett that this was not the right country for him.

From Rosset's point of view, where Pinter and Ionesco failed, Beckett succeeded, with the help of New York and Buster Keaton. *Film* had the misfortune to debut at the New York film Festival when the organizers chose to salute the Buster Keaton everyone knew and so positioned *Film,* with a new,

Beckettian Keaton, in between two slapstick shorts. Schneider called the other shorts "the expected Keaton" and *Film* "the unexpected Keaton." Earlier, recounting how the film was made, he wondered whether it would "turn out to be a Keaton film rather than a Beckett film?"[17] Let the record show that "the unexpected Keaton" is no longer unexpected, and *Film* survives as a Beckett film and not a Keaton film. The outcome of the cultural transaction was not imperious, philistine American vulgarization of European art, but American work fundamentally altered by the external influence and alien presence of Samuel Beckett brought to America. That is equally true about the match of Bert Lahr and the Coconut Grove versus Samuel Beckett and *Waiting for Godot.*

The second example, *Words and Music,* is not about what Samuel Beckett brought to America, but about what America brought to Samuel Beckett. In 1976, Beckett was working on productions of his work at the Schiller-Theater Werkstatt in Berlin. It was while working in Berlin at this time that Beckett, increasingly protective over productions, met frequently with members Mabou Mines and officially established it as an exception to his international prohibition on adaptations, especially of his prose works for the stage.[18] At the same time, Beckett met Morton Feldman, the American composer and quintessential New Yorker. Feldman's adulation of Beckett was of such proportion that he nearly passed out on meeting him. Then they discovered some common ground. In Feldman's account:

> He said to me, after a while, "Mr. Feldman, I don't like opera." I said to him, "I don't blame you." Then he said to me, "I don't like my words being set to music," and I said, "I'm in complete agreement. In fact it's very seldom that I've used words. I've written a lot of pieces with voice, and they're wordless." Then he looked at me again and said, "But what do you want?" And I said, "I have no idea!"[19]

What he got was a scribbled text, later revised into four unpunctuated lines and relayed by postcard with the title "Neither," which became of title of Feldman's composition on it, which was first performed by the Rome Opera in 1977. Feldman did not frequently set texts; I believe there are nine such musical compositions, two are for Beckett texts, and the other, Feldman's last large composition before his death in 1986, was a chamber piece called *For Samuel Beckett.* The encounter was quite formative for Feldman: in a later interview, counting up "the important people in my life," he counted

Beckett last and most: "I spent one afternoon with Beckett; it will be with me forever. Not his work; not his commitment; not his marvelous face, but his attitude."[20]

On the basis of *Neither* and subsequent knowledge of Feldman's work, Beckett, in the 1980s, suggested Feldman as composer for a new score for his radio play *Words and Music,* which became Feldman's penultimate composition. There had been previous music compositions for this work, written in 1961, but none had been entirely successful and so the text of the play had been published without score. The match of Feldman and Beckett happened thanks to Everett Frost, who was producing new recordings of all of Beckett's radio plays, and in *Words and Music* produced a highly successful recording with stalwart Beckett interpreters of the American stage, David Warrilow and Alvin Epstein, along with the resonantly named Bowery Ensemble. The requirements of the piece are thirty-three musical intervals in which the character Music speaks on themes when prompted by a master, Croak, and in competition with a rival, Words. Feldman's description of the task, in conversation with Frost, was: "I never liked any one else's approach to Beckett. I felt it was a little too easy . . . they're treating him as if he's an Existentialist hero, rather than a Tragic hero. And he's a word man, a fantastic word man. And I always felt that I was a note man. And I think that's what brought me to him."[21] Beckett's opinions of the result are not known, but Feldman, late in life, certainly knew that he had benefited from the foreign and somewhat forbidding influence.

Words and Music, Samuel Beckett and America. The synergy is difficult and it is improbable, and it is a product of difference, not identity, and of resistance. This was understood by Harold Clurman in 1956: "This play [*Godot*] is generally difficult for Americans to grasp." This was also the end of the Morton Feldman interview with Everett Frost: "It's very difficult; Beckett is very difficult."[22] Pascale Casanova's work in *The World Republic of Letters* is mostly concerned with print literature, but her sense of the complex evolution of new forms out of rivalries and antagonistic forces, none of which are ever completely effaced, is a terrific rhetoric for discussing competing identities in performing arts.

It was a great leap for America be introduced to Samuel Beckett's work in the 1950s, and we are the beneficiaries of it. Beckett may not have benefited particularly from the relationship: as he said at JFK airport, "This is somehow not the right country for me . . . the people are too strange."

But his work may have. In the British version of the great Samuel Beckett Centenary of 2006, age and youth, Peter Hall and Conor McPherson, both deplored what the first calls "too much respect" and the second "apostolic awe" embedded in Beckett productions in Britain.[23] But in America there is Beckett via popular culture in Bert Lahr and Buster Keaton as well as revisionist modernism via Mabou Mines and Morton Feldman. The relation of none of them to Beckett is characterized by excessive respect or awe, and that is a good for the future of Beckett's work.

The strangeness of it all may even have pleased Beckett. In 1984, in Paris, Beckett kindly met Kenneth Brecher, the director who at the time was doing Beckett in Los Angeles. When they met at the usual place, the hotel on Boulevard St. Jacques, Becher warily confessed that he was doing that grimmest of plays, *Catastrophe* with, in the female role, Leigh Taylor-Young, a television actress familiar from the popular American television series *Dallas* and *Perry Mason Presents*. Becher described her as "a very attractive woman whose legs were shown to advantage" in the play. To which Beckett responded, "No harm in that."[24]

10

Another Look at Those "Three Bollocks in a Cell"

Someone Who'll Watch Over Me and the Shackles of History

CLAIRE GLEITMAN

When Frank McGuinness's *Someone Who'll Watch Over Me* premiered on Broadway in 1991, it seemed perfectly pitched to bring its author the international recognition that had so far eluded him.[1] Though McGuinness's work was largely unknown in the United States at that time, *Someone Who'll Watch Over Me* secured both a Broadway run and an illustrious cast that included Stephen Rea, who was then enjoying wide acclaim as a result of his leading role in *The Crying Game,* which had just arrived in U.S. cinemas. Moreover, the play itself appeared likely to have broad appeal, given its timeliness. Its subject is three men—one Irish, one British, and one American—who are taken hostage in Lebanon and are imprisoned together in a single cell. Throughout most of its nine scenes, the men are chained to the wall and must maintain strength, sanity, and sense of humor as best they can while their offstage captors determine what to do with them. These circumstances clearly call to mind the experiences of Brian Keenan, John McCarthy, and Terry Anderson who were held hostage in Lebanon in the late 1980s and early 1990s and were confined together for a portion of that period. Yet McGuinness's play also evokes other, more literary associations. Summarized differently, *Someone Who'll Watch Over Me* stages the efforts of immobilized men to pass the time while they await release, death, or some other unfathomable fate whose shape depends on the whims of an inscrutable, insistently absent force. By implicitly quoting *Waiting for Godot,* McGuinness places his

124

play in two landscapes simultaneously: one historical and political; the other literary and archetypal. These two landscapes have much to tell us about the play itself, about its relationship to the historical moment in which it was written, and about the different ways in which we might view it in the wake of 9/11 and the Iraq War—events that were unimaginable when McGuinness wrote his play but that cast long shadows upon it when we return to read or see it today.

Despite the fact that *Someone* appeared to have all the necessary ingredients for success, the crushing review it received from Frank Rich—then the notoriously influential chief theater critic for the *New York Times*—might well have brought about a hasty closing. In Rich's judgment, the play was both "facile" and "dull." Its characters, he wrote, were "schematically and . . . stereotypically drawn" and the play itself was "sporadically amusing without being riveting, moving or . . . credible":

> Not even Beckett always succeeded in keeping plays about boredom from being boring. And Mr. McGuinness, if a charming writer in spurts, is no Beckett.

The review heaped particular scorn upon McGuinness's depiction of the character Adam, whom Rich described as "an Irish writer's laughably clichéd notion of a contemporary black American: a saintly, muscle-bound doctor who, amazingly enough, bursts into an angelic rendition of 'Amazing Grace' while the white folks look on in dumbstruck awe."[2]

As it turned out, Rich's review was not lethal; *Someone Who'll Watch Over Me* ran on Broadway for a respectable 216 performances and garnered Tony award nominations for both its author and for Stephen Rea. Yet other American critics also complained that the play's characters are "neat types" and that, with his representation of the African American, "McGuinness flirts, no doubt unwittingly, with insult"—particularly when Adam goes so far as to brag about his penis size.[3] It happens that, although a black actor was cast in the original British and U.S. productions of the play, the role of the American was not originally conceived for a black man and has often been played by white actors. Regardless of whether Adam is read as African American, a careful look at McGuinness's drama will reveal that most of his insults are not unwitting at all, nor is his manipulation of character types.

As has been noted often, McGuinness purposefully manipulates stereotypes in order to break them down and show their danger. Yet, as Helen

Lojek has claimed, he breaks down stereotypes to varying extents and, in the case of the offstage Arabs, barely breaks them down at all.[4] Instead, to some degree McGuinness reifies the stereotype of the essentially impenetrable, irrational Arab because doing so helps facilitate a thawing of relations between his increasingly humane British and Irish characters, who are better able to recognize their common humanity with the foil of the inhumane, bodiless, fundamentally unknowable Arabs to set them off. As for Adam, whatever his color, his function as a character (at least in the second half of the play, when he is dead) corresponds more closely to the Arabs than it does to his Irish and British counterparts; he becomes in the other men's imagination what they need him to be to solidify their burgeoning relationships.

Nevertheless, McGuinness's larger project in *Someone* is surely to dismantle hardened notions of national, sexual, and personal identity through an insistence on fluidity that is manifested in his treatment of (some) characters and in his treatment of texts, which interweave and penetrate one another in such a way as to undermine their apparent autonomy. When the Irishman Edward declares: "Save us from all who believe they're right," he locates what the drama classifies as the gravest threat to humanity, which is certainty, or single-minded interpretations of nations, history, texts, or people.[5] McGuinness counters certainty with an insistence on indeterminacy, fluidity, and play. The play enacts its indeterminacy by creating an ambiguous "no-man's-land" between the two landscapes it evokes: the literary (suggested most overtly by the invisible, inscrutable "Godots") and the historical (conjured by that visible, very material prison wall as well as the prisoners' chains). Persistently, the play tempts us to see it as timeless, while just as persistently insisting upon its fixedness in time. This ambiguity has contributed to telling shifts in the play's reception during the decade and a half since its New York premiere, an issue to which I shall return.

Someone Who'll Watch Over Me opens with Edward and Adam alone together in the prison cell. The first scene swiftly introduces to their dissimilarities, as each man exhibits the stereotypes associated with his nation so flamboyantly that he might as well be wearing a placard on his chest reading: *The American* or *The Irishman*. Adam says little at first, because he is exercising. (That's what we Americans do.) Edward, by contrast, is gabbing incessantly and, of course, quite giftedly, about what he would choose to bring to a desert island, which turns out to be—you guessed it: a beer-making kit and a guide to brewing it. As the scene progresses, the characters' embodiment of national stereotypes becomes an explicit topic of conversation, as Edward complains about Adam's relentless exercising: "Do yous Americans ever stand still?" (4). Later, speaking of the scientific research that brought Adam to Beirut, Edward notes that Adam came here merely to do "a job. Very professional. . . . Very profitable. Very American" (5). Yet after sharply dichotomizing his characters along national borders, McGuinness brings them together as they acknowledge their common separation from homes that may be different but that merge by virtue of the men's shared longing for them: "I miss my home," says Adam, to which Edward replies: "I want to go home." Moments later he adds: "I want to go home. Arabs, Arabs," which prompts the final lines in the scene, in which the men give voice to a deeply felt mutuality as they agree that they are not at home but somewhere quite alien and strange: "I'm in Lebanon," says Adam, and Edward agrees: "So am I" (6). Thus, this opening scene sets in motion a movement that continues throughout the play: the national stereotypes that divide the men are shown to be artificial and dissolve as they recognize all that they share, and that recognition is aided and abetted by the realization that—different though they are—they could not be as different from one another as the Arabs are from both of them.

In scene 2 the stereotypes come to the fore again, as does the habit of stereotyping that the play critiques. As the scene opens Adam is reading the Bible, which prompts Edward to wonder why his Irish compatriots are often so religious. Adam replies that it is because "they are always thanking God"; Edward asks, "What for?" and Adam replies: "That they're not Belgian" (8). While this joke betrays some uncertainty on McGuinness's part as to which nationalities Americans ridicule (the answer is the Polish and, thanks to *South Park,* more recently, the Canadians, never the Belgians), it paves the way for some broader musings about the peculiarities the two men associate with a wide variety of countries and locations: "The Germans and the Dutch, they're buying up the whole of the West of Ireland"; the Arabs "don't masturbate"; and girls from California are kinky (8–9). When Adam proceeds to brag about his "dick" that can "choke a donkey" (9) and their new comrade in chains, Michael, awakes from unconsciousness to reveal himself as a prissy "Brit Boy" tailor-made for Edward the Irishman to mock, we may begin to perceive (as Frank Rich apparently did not) that McGuinness is up to something.

After some initial slagging of the new arrival by Edward, the men introduce themselves in such a way as to underline the importance of nationality to their sense of self:

> My name's Adam Canning. I'm an American.
> Edward Sheridan. Irish.
> I'm an Englishman. (10)

Given that their national origins are fundamental to their understanding of who they are, it irks the men keenly that the Arabs make no distinction whatsoever between them. When Adam predicts that surely Edward will be released, as he hails from a neutral country, Edward replies: "Didn't I think that? Wasn't it me waving the green passport in their faces, roaring, 'Ireland, Ireland'? They still stuck the gun up my arse and dragged me in here" (4). Later, his mental state deteriorating, Adam cries out with exasperation: "I'm an American. How dare you do this? I'm an American" (21). Yet the Arabs refuse to embrace the meanings with which Westerners imbue these categories. Still, the hostages cling to familiar markers of national identity in the hopes of stabilizing their sense of self in a context that threatens to erase it.

In scene 3, they devise another means of passing the time, which is to collaborate on making a "movie" whose shape is determined by their present, doleful circumstances and by the cultural reference points familiar to each man. Edward provides the film's beginning, which features a guitar-carrying nun who comes to Beirut "to do her Christian duty to the orphans of that troubled city"; she wins converts by singing to goats and small Arab children. When this apparent burlesque of *The Sound of Music* dissolves into carnage, Adam steps in and transforms Edward's film into a "shoot-'em-up" by the American maestro of gratuitous cinematic violence, Sam Peckinpah: "A band of machismo Arabs arrive on white steeds" and shoot off the heads of the vultures feeding on the body of the now dead nun. Michael, as new to this ritual as he is to the cell, attempts to annul the violent fantasy with a Richard Attenborough antidote: a "man preaching peace" and wearing a loincloth arrives on the scene (16). Michael's subsequent commentary stresses the ways in which Attenborough depicts Gandhi as a beacon of British middle-class liberal values; the film, he says, is "a testimony to [Attenborough's] decent, well-crafted and honourable political views" (18).

At this point, Edward intervenes with yet another narrative. Among the peasants on the scene, he declares, "there is one disabled, who has a

dream—to be an artist. With the help of his mother, and his own determination, he . . . wins an Oscar, which he collects with his ear" (16). Edward's
rendition of *My Left Foot* conjures the familiar romance of the Irish peasant
artist who overcomes seemingly insurmountable obstacles due in part to the
dogged energies of his indomitable mother. In short, each character conjures
an essentialized version of his nation through the vehicle of film. The figura-
tion of Arabs is also noteworthy: they are children, vultures, and murderers;
they are "machismo" and "cruel." Thus this digression into self-reflexive play
gives access to what might be called the postcolonial political unconscious.
Even in fictive flights of fancy, the characters cannot escape the troubling
complex of attitudes and historical determinants that helped forge the horror
in which they are (they think, randomly and nonsensically) enmeshed.

The men's montage of competing directorial styles gives way to a fleet-
ing concord between Edward and Michael, who agree that "fucking Americans" are "all quite mad" (18). Adam is brought back into the fold when the
trio collectively ponders the enigma that is their captors; yet his momentary
isolation, as he briefly becomes an object of scrutiny for the remaining pair,
foreshadows the emblematic status he will take on later and that he begins to
assume as early as scene 4. Here, we learn that his parents were rarely avail-
able to him because of their preoccupation with the "too many foster kids"
that the family took in. Adam, whose very name connotes the new man in
the new world, was raised in a home that was itself a little melting pot that
gathered into itself "all our unfortunate little brothers and sisters." Though
he felt neglected, Adam admits that his parents were troubled over him:
"If we let him, he'd take on all our worries" (20). For now, Adam shows
little interest in embracing the Christ-like status that this line assigns to him
and rails against the supposedly beneficent American market economy that
reduces all human beings to commodities sold at whatever price the market
will bear, a price over which they have no control. "Whoever has no control
is fucked," Adam concludes. "I am an American, I am Arab. I am fucked. We
have that much in common" (22).

Adam's recognition carries great weight, as it is one of the few moments
in the play when the divide between Westerner and Arab dissolves: here,
they have in common the shared condition of being "fucked," or equally
powerless within a system indifferent to both. From this moment forward,
Adam's role is largely to act as peacemaker and dissolver of boundaries, and
his Christ-like status is often made explicit; scene 4 ends with his recounting

a dream in which he is resurrected by his father's touch (26). Even in advance of his death, Adam's distinctness as a character diminishes as he focuses his attention on mediating between Michael and Edward, who quarrel about (among other subjects) Irish history, the Irish language, Irish historical memory, and the Bloomsfield/Chomsky controversy in linguistics. Adam takes no position on these matters, though he tries repeatedly to put a stop to the squabbling: "Guys, please, guys" (31). When the subject of the American Civil War is raised and Michael and Edward engage in a dispute about whether Irish Americans fought in it "to retain slavery," Adam steps in only to delicately change the subject (33). His failure to express an opinion on the issue, even after Michael's provocative reference to *Gone with the Wind*, is particularly surprising if we read him as African American. But Adam, I am arguing, has become more iconic than "real," in contrast to the gradual stripping away of posture and stereotype that occurs with the other two men. Throughout scene 5, he mostly listens to the others' battles, worries about what will become of Michael after his own death (which he forecasts), and is the deciding voice when Edward—who has initiated a game in which the trio imagines having drinks—asks whether their captors might be invited to join. When Adam nods his assent, Edward welcomes them in, saying: "Bit of a song. A story. The same the world over" (35).

This scene of communion, in which a "same the world over" oneness is achieved, is only imagined, of course. Yet a longing for it is felt throughout the play and in its most idealized form it tends to occur through performance, story or song. Later in the same scene, Edward asks Michael to tell a story; Michael begins by proposing the "terribly sad" story that is "The Wanderer," but Edward demands a happy story instead and so Michael obliges with "Sir Orfeo." This fourteenth-century variation on Ovid's version of the Orpheus myth puts a cheerful spin on Ovid's heartbreaking original: in the medieval version, Sir Orfeo retrieves his beloved wife from the Underworld rather than watching her vanish forever. Michael's chosen version is meant to offer comfort to his listeners, who have themselves been "stolen by death," and also to Michael himself, whose wife was killed in a car crash. When Edward asks about her death in a later scene, Michael notes that she was "Full of love and goodness. Gone" (51). While telling the medieval tale, Michael describes Orfeo's wife identically, as "full of love and goodness" (37); yet he erases the irrevocable horror of "Gone" with a story of hopelessness overcome. It is significant that the anonymous author of "Sir Orfeo" is believed to have been a Londoner who adapted a Celtic story-form, the Breton-lai, in order to write his own adaptation of the classical myth. Woven through Michael's retelling of this classical story rewritten by a medieval Britain with a Celtic twist is a reference to the Book of Ruth: "for he knew," he says of Sir Orfeo, "whither thou goest, I will go with thee, and whither I go, thou shalt go with me" (37). Thus, the moment displays the marvelous elasticity of texts and the productive cross-pollination that can occur between different eras and cultures. Finally, it shows an emotional depth in Michael that we could not have glimpsed in the self-described "sanctimonious prig" whom we met in Scene One (18).

Scene 5 ends with Adam singing "Amazing Grace," a moment that Rich picked out for special ridicule. One can defend the moment by noting that in this scene each man sings a song or tells a story associated with his home culture; in selecting a song strongly linked with the antislavery movement in America, Adam merely does what the others have done. Yet, I am arguing, Adam's character *does* develop differently from his fellow captives, though I would not attribute this (as Rich does) to an author's bumbling but rather to careful design: as layers of cliché are stripped from them, Adam becomes increasingly fixed in goodness. Between scene 5 and 6 he presumably is killed, though Edward resists believing it; to dislodge him from denial, Michael offers as evidence the fact that one of their captors "actually wept" (39). The word "actually" is telling: in Michael's view, this glimpse of the Arab's humanity is astonishing, but it is equally telling that it is Adam's death that elicited it. As Edward moves toward acceptance, he delivers a eulogy for his dead friend: "He could be cruel, . . . [but] he was not often cruel. He was brave, he could protect himself, and me, and you. He was beautiful to look at. . . . He was innocent. Kind, gentle. Friend, I believe it goes without saying, love, so I never said" (41). Even as Edward admits to an inability to express deep feeling that his "gift of the gab" conceals, he completes the process of deifying and objectifying Adam, whose physical beauty pierced Edward's macho shell as his bravery and sweetness pierced his heart.

Of course, what we know about Adam's terrible fate undermines portions of Edward's hagiography: clearly, Adam could *not* protect himself; it is not obvious that he could protect his fellow captives either (though perhaps as sacrificial "lamb" he will save them); and Edward does not explain in what respect Adam was any more "innocent" than the other men with whom he was imprisoned. Surely Edward's deification of Adam results in part from his own need for solace; Adam is partially "rewritten" by Edward as the author of "Sir Orfeo" rewrites Ovid. Yet McGuinness positions Adam in such a way as to make Edward's representation of him seem not unearned. When Michael recites the George Herbert poem, "Love (III)," at the end of scene 6, in which Love is a figure for Christ, he merely makes blatant what has been implicit in Adam's character for some time now.

With Adam gone, the historical combatants, British and Irish, are left to face one another alone, and this face-off is the real heart of the play. While Rich maintains that McGuinness is "more Beckett than Costa-Gavras," *Someone Who'll Watch Over Me* is hardly apolitical; on the contrary, it stages its own version of what the first George Bush dubbed proudly, at the end of the Gulf War, a "new world order." In McGuinness's depiction of it, the Old World antagonists, Irish and English, are beset by complex postcolonial relationships and locked in endless games. Their New World accomplice strives to cajole them into getting along as, meanwhile, all three are held captive by a shadowy Third World that they barely attempt to understand. McGuinness, it must be conceded, partly colludes with them in this, as he too is a prisoner of his time: he does not ever really attempt to examine what is on the other side of the wall. Rather, the Arab context functions mainly as a screen against which (for the play) the more pressing colonial and postcolonial conflicts of England and Ireland can be dramatized. Fluidity is the play's proffered antidote to the absolutist thinking that is diagnosed as the source of such antagonisms, and the most exuberant manifestation of this is the men's reenactment of the 1977 Wimbledon Ladies' Final, in which Great Britain's Virginia Wade defeated "poor wee Betty Stove" of Holland. This reenactment opposes the seeming implacability of history with destabilizing play. "To hell with history," Edward proclaims, taking on the role of the doomed Betty (43). Alas, history triumphs and Betty Stove is defeated, but an undaunted Edward shifts into the role of the Queen, who lasciviously admires Virginia Wade's sweat. Later, Michael sings "Run, Rabbit, run," the captive men take turns playing hunter and hunted, and Michael impersonates Edward impersonating a rabbit (45).

Through this series of plays within the play, the men perform a potent deconstruction of the categories through which their cultures maintain the status quo. Having stripped away nationality as a meaningful signifier of personal identity, they now jettison gender, the great organizing principle of social order. When they take turns impersonating a hunted rabbit they strip away the human, reducing themselves to the wretched, naked animals that lie beneath the costumes they have worn throughout their lives. Michael and Edward conclude the rabbit game by pronouncing it "ridiculous," which prompts them to observe that much of the history in which they have been implicated is ridiculous:

MICHAEL: It is really our fault for your troubles at home?
EDWARD: Ridiculous.
MICHAEL: Is it our fault we're here in the first place?
EDWARD: Ridiculous.
MICHAEL: Do those children holding us captive have a reason to hate us?
    (46)

Thus, the culminating recognition implies a dissolution of boundaries that is not unlike Adam's earlier pronouncement of American and Arab as equally "fucked." Here, Irish, English, and Arab historical conflicts are said to have in common the shared condition of being ridiculous. Yet the scene does not end with this recognition. Instead, the men proclaim that there *is* a logic to history, however absurd:

EDWARD: There always has to be a loser. In every game, a loser.
MICHAEL: Yes, that's history. (47)

In short, the plays within the play lead the surviving prisoners to a fundamental realization about the fluidity of gender and, indeed, of human nature—to a declaration, in short, of a kind of essential humanity—but this recognition fails to rescue them, or us, from history, or the divisions, categories and consequences it imposes upon us.

The concluding scenes carry the men further along the *via negativa* they have been following in their enforced exile, as each confronts a crucial memory involving his father. In the process, the last vestiges of Edward's cynicism are stripped away and the bond between the two prisoners is cemented. This bond is made manifest in their last moment together onstage, when Edward has been released and Michael is to be left in appalling solitude—a fate that Vladimir and Estragon feared but from which Beckett spared them. Before Edward departs, the two men imitate the Spartan ritual that Michael learned from his father, combing one another's hair in a powerful gesture connoting love, a determination to soldier on, and a redefinition of the meaning of strength that recalls the lines from the Koran that Adam read in scene 4:

"Peace it is, the Night of Power" (23). While "peace" and "power" are ant-onyms in some contexts, the Koran draws them together as synonymous as does the Spartan ritual, which is at once a battle cry and a celebration of the tenderness that would make battling obsolete.

The play draws to a close with Michael alone and quoting from "The Wanderer," an Old English poem to which he referred in two previous scenes. The poem, significantly, is about a man who has lost everything—friends, family, and country—and whose desolation prompts him to pon-der the inexorable stripping away of all we hold dear. When Michael first quoted from "The Wanderer" in scene 8, he remarked that he heard his father's voice "in that ancient poem, speaking with the voice of England, talking to itself, for the first time. Our beginning, our end, England's" (51). In its originary moment, Michael asserts, England is talking to itself about its end. Thus England, the great colonial power, begins in Michael's imagination in a state of solitude and despair, and that is also where it ends. This is made doubly poignant by Michael's declaration that the study of the literature recounting these early English moments is itself dying: "They're not teaching much Old and Middle English these days. A dying concern" (12–13). The entire English enterprise, it seems, is hedged about with loss and despair.

When Michael returns to "The Wanderer" in the play's final scene, the staging literalizes the assertions he made previously. England, in the person of Michael, is now alone and chained to the wall that its history played a role in constructing. Moments later, Michael recites again from an even older foundational text from which he also quoted before: "Whither thou goest, I will go with thee, and whither I go, thou shalt go with me" (58). This famous line is Ruth's response to her mother-in-law, Naomi, who instructs Ruth to return to her homeland after she is widowed. But Ruth chooses instead to renounce her ties to her homeland in favor of a new one based on a deep relationship to Naomi and the spiritual values she represents. The lines, in other words, are a declaration of independence from country and religion and a pledge of allegiance to personal relationships. Michael's quotations thus reenact the process of stripping away that we have witnessed through-out the play. But his voice does not fall silent with Ruth. Instead, he utters what amounts to a benediction, intersected by the aural and visual image of the historical particulars entrapping all of us: "Good luck. [*He rattles the chains that bind him.*] Good luck" (57). This final line seems a benediction on Edward, on Michael himself, and on us: all still chained to our histories, however "ridiculous."

Our response to this drama today is inevitably complicated by the historical situation of the play itself, the time of its writing versus the time in which we now read or view it. Beirut is no longer the world's code for the vagaries of history. 9/11 and Baghdad have transformed the terms within which *Someone Who'll Watch Over Me* took shape. In those faraway days of the early 1990s, it was possible to *not see* the Middle East even while the action of your play was set directly within it. Even the most negative critical commentary from those prelapsarian years is intently focused on the English, the Irish, and the American, accepting the play's conceit that the Arab world is a screen, albeit one constituted in the play's discourse by colonialism. Not only is it not possible, now, to imagine the silence of the Arab context, the relative positions of England, Ireland, and the United States have transformed in ways that make the play's arrangement of them seem almost a period piece. As we have seen, Edward and Michael unfix themselves from hardened, oppositional positions in part because the fixed figure of the dehumanized Arab helps to facilitate that unfixing, as does, in its different way, the fixed figure of the judicious, moderating American.[6] Both 9/11 and the Iraq War have made it difficult to imagine either the Arab world or America being portrayed in this fashion today.

Still, it is my contention that McGuinness succeeds in interrogating the terms by which the impasse of the Middle East persists in bedeviling our history. As I have noted, when Edward and Michael recognize "ridiculousness" as the root condition of their lives and their world, they appear to disavow the divisions that separate them from each other and their captors. Yet Michael's crucial line—"Do those children holding us captive have a reason to hate us"—has the effect of installing Michael and the other hostages in the role of fathers of rebellious sons. To think of all relational conflicts through the paradigm of the family drama limits the available positions for all players, resulting, *Godot*-like, in a repetition of the same drama perpetually. While Michael and Edward are able to resolve their differences, their inability to jettison the synecdochal identification of family drama and national dynamics merely takes them out of one cell to land them in another. By chaining his emblematic characters to an emblematic wall, McGuinness suggests, to some degree prophetically, the current state of the West. In the years since the play first premiered, England and Ireland have made their way toward a fragile concord. Yet the Arab wall remains and before it the worlds that Adam, Michael, and Edward represent are still chained—in stubborn, frightened, and bellicose incomprehension.

Indeed, shifts in the play's reception in recent years reveal both how much and also how little has changed since 1991, when Frank Rich took the play to task for what he regarded as its formulaic nature. As we have seen, Rich was not alone among early 90s critics in complaining about the stereotypical nature of McGuinness's characters without recognizing the degree to which this is a purposeful device that shows how firmly shackled the men are in their historically constructed identities. Commentary on more recent U.S. productions largely ignores the stereotypes as well as the play's troubling interrogation of historical particulars, while embracing McGuinness's characters as timeless portraits of an essential humanity. Thus, *Someone Who'll Watch Over Me* becomes consolation in the wake of the 9/11 tragedy. For instance, in October 2001, the Circle Theater in Fort Worth, Texas, chose to revise its season of plays because of the terrible events that had transpired in the preceding month. The theater issued a press release explaining the change as follows:

> We admire playwright Bruce Graham and had hoped to present his play, *Desperate Affection,* here this fall [said the theater's artistic director, Rose Pearson]. However, since *Desperate Affection*'s plot revolves around an attempted presidential assassination . . . in New York, we felt this was not an appropriate time to produce this particular piece. . . . So, we elected to present *Someone Who'll Watch Over Me,* a play about 3 hostages [taken captive] . . . in the Middle East. While the subject is serious, the message is clearly inspirational.[7]

It is more than a bit puzzling that a play about the attempted assassination of a president in New York City should be regarded as less appropriate to the immediate aftermath of 9/11 than a play about the violent relationship between the Arab world and the West. While acknowledging the play's "serious" subject matter and its relevance to "what's happening in today's world," Pearson described *Someone Who'll Watch Over Me* not as a play about the vexed politics of postcoloniality, but as a celebration of "man's ability to bond together as brothers" and "to have pride in their country." In the appalling haze of the disaster of 9/11, Pearson felt that McGuinness's play could bring "hope to audiences' hearts" along with "tears to their eyes." Ovid becomes "Sir Orfeo."

In 2005, just after the bombings in the London transport system, the Interplayers Ensemble in Spokane, Washington, chose to revive the play with a keen sense of its historical relevance: "I settled on [*Someone Who'll Watch Over Me*] right after the London bombings," the play's director, Nike Imoru, told a writer for the *Spokesman Review,* who went on to note: "Funny how things don't change. This play was timely back in 1991, too, when it was first a smash hit in London and on Broadway." In the same article, Imoru is quoted as saying that *Someone* seemed to him to be an apt choice because it fit "perfectly with the overall themes of Interplayers' 25th anniversary season: 'triumph and celebration of the human spirit.'"[8]

Thus, we learn, it was the immediate context of an eruption of terrorism within the cosmopolitan centers of the West that impelled the Interplayers Ensemble to revive McGuinness's play. And yet, as was the case with the Circle Theater production, the play is also said to be chosen because of its timeliness, a timeliness that is yoked to the timeless verities of "triumph and celebration of the human spirit." My intention here is not to deny that *Someone Who'll Watch Over Me* resonates beyond its own historical moment, but to argue that it is also circumscribed and defined by that moment in fashions that declarations about its "timelessness" obscure. McGuinness's characters remain figuratively confined in separate prisons because they cannot release themselves from historically determined modes of thinking that persist, to some degree, right to the end of the play. Hence, the wall remains, as do the chains. As I have attempted to demonstrate, the play counterpoints its gestures toward timelessness with recurring indications of its characters'—and its own—imprisonment in time. Ultimately, *Someone*'s fundamental indeterminacy destabilizes any attempt to enlist it in a celebration of an essentialized human spirit that somehow transcends the particular contexts within which that spirit struggles. The play's canny deployment of its intertextual geography within the specifics of its political, cultural, and historical contexts, all against the looming yet all but invisible absolute alterity of the Arab world, demonstrates the paradoxical situation within which we all struggle. We stumble about with the hobbling attitudes and postures our cultures have bequeathed to us. Occasionally, and painfully, we are able, for brief moments, to see our way beyond those hobbles, only to find that we are still shackled to a history that we did not start but that we perpetuate. As Michael says: "That's history."

11

Faith Healer in New York and Dublin

NICHOLAS GRENE

Faith Healer was revived by the Gate Theater in Dublin in 2006. After a sell-out run of six weeks in Dublin, it transferred to Broadway where, in spite of somewhat mixed reviews, it won a Tony nomination for Ralph Fiennes as leading actor and a Tony award for Ian McDiarmid as best featured actor. The box office was sufficiently strong to warrant an extension to the fifteen-week run originally planned. This Broadway success in 2006 makes it the more interesting to look at the play's original production, because *Faith Healer* is unusual among Brian Friel's plays in having opened on Broadway and unique in opening with a non-Irish director and an international cast. It flopped in New York in 1979, in spite of having James Mason in the lead, but when revived at the Abbey in 1980 it became one of the landmark productions of its time, helping to confirm Donal McCann's reputation as one of Ireland's great actors. Why did it fail on Broadway, why did it succeed in Dublin? Were there significant differences between its reception in one venue and the other? These questions, however, are underpinned by other issues having to do with the origins of the play and how it came to be produced on Broadway in the first place, issues that relate also to the 2006 revival. To study *Faith Healer* in New York and Dublin is to be brought up against the marketplace facts of theatrical production as well as the broader matter of how we construct theatrical history.

The play *Faith Healer* as we know it had a quite extended pre-history. In October 1975, Brian Friel sent to his London agent Warren Brown the text of a one-act monologue called *Faith Healer*.[1] It was a project he had been working on since back in April of the year, deeply uncertain about what form it would take, experimenting with all sorts of different modes of action and narration, including the intercutting of film or still images. The only things that had remained constant were the story of the faith healer, his involvement with his wife/mistress Grace, his manager Teddy, and the ending in his violent death in Ballybeg. It was not until a very late stage that Friel decided to confine it to a single monologue by Frank, a monologue substantially like the final text except that he tells out the story to its very end.

Warren Brown wrote back expressing doubt about finding a commercial venue for a one-act play, and probably for that reason we find Friel in March of 1976 negotiating for a production at the Queen's University Festival.[2] What was being planned was a fully professional production—they were talking of leading actors and directors—but on the reduced scale and modest budget of a university arts festival. Then, unexpectedly in September, very close to the date of the projected production—the QUB Festival was to take place in November—Friel sent along a second monologue, called "Faith Healer's Wife," to be played as a companion piece. He even suggested Billie Whitelaw for the part of Grace.[3] Once again, this monologue was quite close to Grace's speech in the final play, though Kinlochbervie was not yet the crucial location it was to become. Michael Barnes, the festival director, was naturally delighted. But he must have been surprised to receive, weeks later, yet a third script, this one called "The Game," to be played with the other two. "The Game," which has never been published, is a two-hander about an unsuccessful alcoholic commercial artist and his wife who work out the peculiar dynamics of their marriage by a game in which they lock eyes and the loser is the first to look away.[4] Friel proposed the three one-acts should be billed as "Bannermen": the *Faith Healer*'s banner advertising the Fantastic Frank Hardy was to be echoed in the vulgar posters that the Omagh artist Noel has to paint for a living at the start of "The Game." Obviously, "The Game" was to provide parts and interaction for the two performers of the Frank and Grace monologues.

"Bannermen" did not get produced at the 1976 Queen's Festival, perhaps not surprisingly given how late it came together as a script. But in January 1977 on a suggestion from the actor Niall Toíbin, who had read "Bannermen," Friel set to writing a third monologue by Teddy to bind the two by Frank and Grace together. A second intervention by a theater professional then helped to re-shape the play once again, this time in the direction of its final form. The British producer Oscar Lewenstein, with whom Friel had worked before, suggested to him that the three-monologue format ending with Teddy would present difficulties in terms of attracting actors, especially for the part of Frank. It was in discussion between Friel and Lewenstein that a reconstruction was proposed: "First, a monologue by the faith healer, which would not contain the description of the final episode in his life, then the monologue by the faith healer's wife, then the interval, then a shorter version of Teddy's monologue [it was very much longer in the first draft], followed by a monologue by the faith healer."[5] In other words, what was planned here was the play *Faith Healer* as we know it.

Two things are striking in this prolonged genesis of the play. The first is how tentative and uncertain Friel was throughout on the form it was to take. He had played around with different ideas in the early stages of composition. The decision to go for the monologue format was a hesitant one. It took him a long time, one substantial wrong turn, and two crucial practical prompts from theatrical colleagues to yield the four-part play. The other remarkable thing is how rapidly *Faith Healer* was taken up as a strong commercial prospect once its final form did begin to emerge. The possibility of a Queen's Festival production in 1977 was rapidly ditched. Lewenstein urged Friel not to give the play to the Abbey but let him take it on as commercial production. Friel's London agent, by this time Sheila Lennon, would not even countenance an opening in Dublin, where Lewenstein wanted to co-produce it with Noel Pearson at the Gate Theatre. Instead, she maintained that "the best start for the play . . . is . . . either the West End or Broadway."[6]

There is an oddity here. *Faith Healer* is one of Friel's most intellectually and artistically demanding plays. Its monologue format is terrifically challenging for audiences. Of all his plays, this would seem to be the one that most obviously belongs in the subsidized theater. Why then were agents and producers so determined to try it in the West End or Broadway? One answer is obvious in the correspondence between Friel, his agents, and Lewenstein over the period from March 1977 to October 1978. They all saw the play as a vehicle for a major star in the male lead. The first choice was Peter O'Toole, the second Richard Burton, and after them Anthony Hopkins, Paul Scofield, Nicol Williamson, and Milo O'Shea were all canvassed, in some cases approached. Directors were less important in their deliberations; the currently successful British director Michael Blakemore was mentioned; at one point Alan Schneider appeared seriously interested. The prospect of a production hung fire for so long in part because it was always difficult to get figures such as Peter O'Toole and Richard Burton simply to read the script, much less make a decision on it. There was a problem too with location. Lewenstein, based in Brighton, had his sights first set on London, and once he shifted his ideas to a Broadway opening there were difficulties in finding an active New York co-producer. Finally, in October 1977, after Lewenstein's option had run out, a letter came from Friel saying that he has decided to accept an offer of Morton Gottlieb, with whom Friel had also worked before, to produce the play in New York with James Mason in the lead.

Friel was, of course, not an unknown on Broadway at this point in time. There had been the huge breakthrough success with *Philadelphia, Here I Come!* (1966) and a follow-up with the two one-act plays *Lovers* in 1968, which Gottlieb had produced. On the other hand, there had been failures with *The Loves of Cass Maguire* (1966), with *The Mundy Scheme* (1969), which closed after just two performances, and with *The Freedom of the City* (1974). Friel's was a recognizable name in New York theater but by no means one that was associated with surefire hits. The talking-point about *Faith Healer* in the pre-publicity was the return to the stage of James Mason, who had last appeared on Broadway thirty years before, but who had a considerable current reputation as a movie star. There was also a feature story having to do with the casting of his wife, the Australian Clarissa Kaye, opposite himself. Mason had been on a longlist for the part, but fairly well down that list, as he was considered at sixty-nine to be too old for Frank, whom Friel envisaged as a man at most in his early forties. It is pretty clear that Mason took on the role as a vehicle that allowed him and his wife to act together in the theater.

The prestigious Panamanian-born director José Quintero, who had made his name with productions of Tennessee Williams and Eugene O'Neill, was hired; Ed Flanders, Tony-award winner for *A Moon for the Misbegotten*, directed by Quintero, was cast as Teddy. Rehearsals began in January 1979, with tryouts first in Boston and then in Baltimore before an opening in the Longacre Theater on Broadway in April. There was mixed reaction from Boston and Baltimore, in which the play divided critics down the middle. The nay-sayers had the more striking headlines: "The *Faith Healer* Sends First Nighters Scurrying for Exit" read one; "*Faith Healer* Could Use a Miracle" was another. But there was real appreciation as well.[7] The play arrived in New York with a change from the original Boston cast, with Donal Donnelly having replaced Ed Flanders as Teddy in Baltimore. At one extreme among the overnight reviews was William Raidy in the *Star-Ledger:* "*Faith*

Healer is an exciting, provocative and highly inventive drama wonderfully acted . . . and wonderfully written. It is Brian Friel's best play and the season's best opportunity to see a play of substance."[8] On the other hand, there was Clive Barnes, writing in the *New York Post*. His review, headed "Friel's *Faith* Beyond Healing," ended with the knock-out punch: "No acting could save this play. Pretentiousness carves its own tombstone."

The later reactions were on the whole much more thoughtful and more positive. There was a very enthusiastic review from Brendan Gill in the *New Yorker* and a fine, extended appreciation by Walter Kerr in the *New York Times*. But by the time Kerr's piece on the play appeared on 25 April, *Faith Healer* was already on its way out: it closed after twenty performances. The reviews taken collectively suggest that this was a fine production of a play that was in the end just too challenging for all but its more discerning critics, who loved it. The star name of James Mason, excellent acting, and sensitive direction could not convince enough New Yorkers to go to see this experimental work, and it went down as a result.

There is, however, another inside story of the production, as Friel tells it himself.[9] According to him, it was a very unhappy show from the start. James Mason was excellent in the part of Frank: icy, a killer, yet capable of immense charm. Clarissa Kaye, though, was a complete disaster. Her background was apparently as a contortionist rather than as a straight actor. She wept her way through all the rehearsals, evidently aware that she could not manage it. Publicly, Mason made no attempt to help or defend her, only once speaking up to say that Clarissa had difficulty understanding Mr. Quintero, a snide remark because Quintero, though he had worked in the United States for many years, spoke a heavily accented English. Privately, Mason insisted on her talent as an actress—"She is splendid, Brian, isn't she?" he would say to Friel over a drink—though everyone else could tell she was terrible. There were crisis meetings on Broadway planning how to get rid of her. Substitute names were prepared of actresses who could take over, and the only issue was the financial implications of her being sacked or withdrawing voluntarily.

Ed Flanders, the man originally cast to play Teddy, was terrifically gifted and very fine in the part, though he was a very heavy drinker and Friel had had to spend a good deal of his time during rehearsals in Boston accompanying him to bars to keep him in some sort of shape. Flanders took against Clarissa Kaye from the start and declared that he would rehearse the show and open it in Boston, but would not go into New York with it. He was as good as his word. Donal Donnelly, who replaced Flanders and who had been so successful in *Philadelphia, Here I Come!* was seriously under-rehearsed and not really right for the role. What is more, Jose Quintero, able director that he was, also has his problems. On the day before rehearsals started, when in the company of Tennessee Williams, he had been beaten up by a homophobic gang on the streets. Moreover, he was sufficiently addicted to whatever drug he was using at the time to require frequent visits to the bathroom to keep himself going.

Much of this is the sort of greenroom gossip that no one would expect to surface in newspaper reaction to the play. But it is staggering to read the reviews against Friel's own account of the production. There are a few negative comments about Kaye's acting at the Boston opening; otherwise it is a complete chorus of praise.[10] Whether the critics loved or hated the play, they were almost uniform in their enthusiasm for the playing of Grace: "An impressive New York debut"; "Miss Kaye . . . is an extraordinary performer;" "Clarissa Kaye . . . reveals herself as an awesome technician"; "Miss Kaye gives a strong dynamic performance," this last from a review headed "'Healer' Can Cure Insomnia." Oddly enough, though most of the reviewers admired Mason's performance—Clive Barnes was wonderfully eloquent about it—there was more criticism of him than of Kaye, criticism of his attempt at an Irish accent, of his voice as too cut-glass for the part. In Baltimore, one reviewer suggested that Flanders did not yet know his lines, but in the New York reception there is no suggestion that he was under-rehearsed. On the contrary, some reviewers thought he stole the show.

Which should we trust, the playwright's own version, as the inside but possibly biased account, or the multiple, presumably objective reviews of the actual production? In terms of the normal principles of evaluating evidence, the latter would seem more likely to be trustworthy. And yet there are some other small clues that might make us doubtful about the credibility of the 1979 reviewers' representations. For example, reviews of a 1983 off-Broadway revival in the intimate Vineyard Theater suggested that *Faith Healer* was lost in the larger Longacre Theater. The original production, said one critic tartly, "closed quickly—in part because the leading man was largely inaudible, even in the 7th row where I sat/slept through it."[11] That makes sense of a complaint by Brendan Gill that the actors were miked in the Longacre, a "theater" as Gill notes, "where actors have gone unmiked for half a century."[12] It seems likely that Mason, for so long a movie actor, simply did not have the technique to project for the stage and the producers were forced to resort to amplification in later performances: Gill would not necessarily have seen the show on opening night. For the original Broadway failure, another reviewer of the Vineyard revival comments, "The main blame then was placed on the performers rather than on Mr Friel's technique or theme." At least as far as the 1979 reviews went, that simply is not true: with a very few exceptions, they all suggested that the play failed in spite of the actors not because of them. But could it be that this was some sort of truth about the production leaking out belatedly, or was it merely a retrospective reconstruction of the reception?

The same questions arise in relation to the Abbey production of the play. It was staged at the Abbey with a nervous awareness of its Broadway failure. Joe Dowling, the director, tried to suggest that "there was nothing wrong with the show on Broadway, that the venue rather than the play was the problem."[13] A pre-production interview with Friel was headlined, "Broadway, Who Cares?" In fact, the reactions to the Abbey version followed much the same pattern as those in New York. There was a rave review from David Nolan in the *Irish Times,* who had also seen and admired the play on Broadway. Desmond Rushe was just as hyperbolic—"as richly stimulating evening of theater as could be imagined." But Con Houlihan in the *Evening Press* complained that "Its main fault is a familiar one: the characters are far too articulate." According to Tim Harding in the Sunday Press, the play "fails to satisfy the excitement it stimulates. . . . Brian Friel . . . commits commercial hara-kiri in quest of an elusive ideal." Colm Cronin in *Hibernia* maintained that "the greatest difficulty about *Faith Healer* is to accept its structure." There was by no means universal acclaim for Donal McCann's performance either: Gus Smith in the *Sunday Independent* praised John Kavanagh as Teddy at the expense of McCann.

What is striking is that by the time the play was revived at the Abbey in 1990, with McCann returning to the part of Frank, both the play and McCann's performance in it had been canonized. Only Richard Pine in an RTÉ radio review, expressed reservations that echoed my own personal reaction to seeing the revival.[14] Like Pine, I thought McCann's performance had coarsened and that Dowling's direction was much less confident: he put in a back-projected video that realized Frank's final exit into the yard, as though he had lost faith in the monologue as a self-sufficient form of theatricality. But apart from Pine, no critic said that in 1990. Instead, this was universally treated as the classic, heroic treatment of one of the great contemporary Irish plays.

Ulf Dantanus, in his pioneering 1985 study of Friel, represents the early stage history of *Faith Healer* as it has commonly been perceived since:

> The play's failure in the commercialized theater of Broadway was completely predictable. . . . The triumphant success of the Abbey Theater production in August 1980 . . . can have been no surprise. *Faith Healer* demands, to an unusual extent, the idea of a shared experience between stage and audience, of collaboration between the two. Perhaps that collaboration, in this play, comes more easily from an Irish audience.[15]

In the light of the background explored in this essay, there are a number of things wrong with this. First of all, the play was not the predictable failure in New York that Dantanus suggests. There were appreciative reviews; there were positive reactions. The trouble was that, for a Broadway show with an investment of $325,000 in it, audiences had to come in numbers quickly or it had to close. For those basic economic reasons, the damning overnight reviews were killers. These are the well-known facts of life on Broadway. The critical reaction in Dublin was not initially much more affirmative. But in the subsidized theater it was possible for the Abbey to keep the play on for a six-week run, by which time enough people had come to see it and been mesmerized by McCann's performance to turn it into a success. There is no question here of some innate superiority of Irish over American audiences, or of some greater sympathy with story-telling due to our age-old tradition of the *shanachie*. We are talking about differences in theatrical structures and theatrical economics.

Two things seem to emerge from this effort to reconstruct the story of *Faith Healer* in New York and Dublin. One is the notion of the play as a star vehicle, particularly a movie star vehicle. There is correspondence in the NLI archive concerning a projected Gate Theater revival of the play in 1999 as part of a season of Friel's work to celebrate his seventieth birthday. This once again turns on casting Frank Hardy.[16] The names mentioned this time are Richard Harris (doubtfully), Anthony Hopkins (again)—Friel in fact calls Hopkins "the model [underlined twice] Frank Hardy"[17]—John Malkovitch, and Alan Rickman. There are letters from Hopkins, Malkovitch, and Rickman all more or less reluctantly turning it down. There is a still longer list in a fax from Noel Pearson to Friel later in 1999, after the Gate production failed to materialize, and it is to this list Friel has added a whole set of supplementary names, including that of Ralph Fiennes.[18] We all know that movie-star names sell theater tickets. The point about *Faith Healer* is that an audience is allowed to see the movie star on his own; he is able to strut his stuff there in front of you, with no special effects, no beautiful backdrops, no supporting cast. For an actor, equally, this is an opportunity to show just how good he is. That may be why this apparently most uncommercial of Friel plays should have attracted producers against the odds to try to bring it to Broadway, and why major actors such as Mason or Fiennes should have been prepared to give it a go.

The other thing has to do with the business of theater history itself, of how we tell the story of a given play in production. It is not possible to establish definitively, in view of the conflicting evidence, what that initial staging of *Faith Healer* was like or how good or bad Clarissa Kaye was as Grace. A filmography for Kaye shows that she did a good deal of television and film work from 1979 through her death from cancer in 1994, but there is no indication that she ever played in the theater again. *Faith Healer* is her only Broadway credit.[19] In spite of what the reviewers said, you cannot always believe what you read in the newspapers. What does seem to emerge from both the New York and Dublin productions of the play is how different accounts come to be constructed retrospectively, out of folk memory perhaps, out of changed perspectives, out of piety toward the past or a skewed privileging of the present. It is a hard, complicated business trying to find out the truth about theater.

12

"Dancing on a One-Way Street"

Irish Reactions to *Dancing at Lughnasa* in New York

PATRICK LONERGAN

Brian Friel's *Dancing at Lughnasa* is an important example of the inter-relationship of American and Irish theater, particularly since 1990. Its script draws heavily on American culture, bringing us songs by Cole Porter and an approach to the narration of remembered events that is highly reminiscent of the work of Tennessee Williams. And its production was one of the first of many Irish successes on the New York stage from the 1990s onward, being followed by productions of plays by Martin McDonagh, Conor McPherson, and indeed by Brian Friel himself, whose *Faith Healer* was a critical and commercial success on Broadway in 2006.

Dancing at Lughnasa premiered on 24 April 1990 at the Abbey Theater, where it was directed by Patrick Mason. It toured nationally and internationally until 1993, giving rise to a 1998 film starring Meryl Streep. In 1999, the play was revived as part of a "Friel Festival" held to celebrate the author's seventieth birthday, where it was presented as a "vessel of celebratory nostalgia," according to Karen Fricker. This, as Fricker notes, is "deeply ironic": Friel's achievement with *Lughnasa,* and throughout his work, is "to question the instinct for nostalgia, to expose the gap between experience and understanding, words and meaning, what is institutionally categorized as history and what really happened."[1] Throughout its production history in Ireland, audiences seemed unaware of the challenging aspects of Friel's script, instead focusing on the play's sentimental and nostalgic qualities. Rather than reading the play as a critique of Irish society in the early 1990s, audiences were instead encouraged to see its international success—particularly on

Broadway—as evidence of Ireland's newfound self-assurance on the global stage. The production of *Dancing at Lughnasa* thus appears to have been received in ways that are not only unsupported by the script, but which also seems to undermine the themes considered by the play. How can play and production give rise to such divergent responses?

To answer this question, I want to suggest that, as Nicholas Grene argues elsewhere in this publication, different accounts of a play's reception can be constructed retrospectively, perhaps as a result of a misplaced or inappropriate piety toward the past. Just as there is a mythology of sorts about *Faith Healer,* something similar has happened with the original Abbey Theater production of *Dancing at Lughnasa,* whereby the canonical status of the play within Ireland was earned not through its reception before Irish audiences, but instead through those audiences' knowledge and appreciation of its success in America. This "mythology" reveals the way in which culture moves from Ireland to the United States and back again, allowing us to deepen our consideration of the performance of Irishness on the international stage.

The nostalgic attitude to the 1999 Dublin production of *Lughnasa* is relatively easy to account for: the Ireland of 1999 was considerably different from the Ireland of 1990. An explicit example of this can be seen in comparing different audience responses to scenes in the play. For example, at the opening of the second act of *Lughnasa,* in which Maggie and Michael talk together in the Mundys' kitchen, Michael says that he is writing a letter to Santa Claus, to which Maggie replies, "In September? Nothing like getting in before the rush."[2] In the 1990 production, this scene was played for comedic effect, and the audience responded with laughter to the idea of a child thinking of Christmas in early September. In the 1999 revival of the play, this line was again delivered to produce laughter but, on that occasion, none was forthcoming. During the intervening nine years, Christmas had become so commercialized a part of Irish life that the idea of a child thinking of Santa Claus in September was greeted not with amusement but weary recognition.[3]

Ireland in 1990 was of course on the verge of transformation, but the atmosphere that had characterized the 1980s—of economic gloom and political turbulence—remained when *Dancing at Lughnasa* premiered in

April 1990. Kate's fear of losing her job should have resonated with an Irish audience in 1990. Unemployment was at that time running at 13.3 percent, after a decade of serious job loss and redundancy. Similarly, the decision of Agnes and Rose to flee Ireland, and their ultimate fate of poverty, alcoholism and homelessness, was a dramatization of the tragedy of Irish emigration, which in 1990 remained a major part of Irish life: in 1990, 56,300 people—or 1.6 percent of the entire population—left the Republic of Ireland. However, by 1999, Ireland had become a country of net immigration, with 47,500 immigrants arriving to the country. This net immigration has led to a major demographic shift in Ireland whereby one in ten people resident in the Republic of Ireland in 2002 was born outside the country. A large proportion of those new arrivals come from Africa: in 1996, only 4,867 people living in Ireland had been born in Africa, but by 2002, that number had grown to 26,515.[4] In relative terms, this is a small number, representing less than 1 percent of the entire population, but it is also an increase of over 600 percent in only six years, during which time the revival of *Lughnasa* was taking the Abbey stage. This transformation created a new way of thinking about the treatment in *Lughnasa* of the relationship between Irish and African cultures, which moved from being a debate about postcolonial affinities between Ireland and Africa to becoming an actual social relationship being enacted on the streets of Dublin and other Irish cities or towns.

The representation of Father Jack was also potentially shocking in 1990. During the 1990s, a series of absurd or flawed priests would appear on the Irish stage. Father Welsh in McDonagh's *Leenane Trilogy* (1997) and Father Billy in Tom Murphy's *The Wake* (1998) are two prominent examples of an altered Irish attitude to religious authority, as is the appearance during the decade of the television series *Father Ted*. Keegan in Shaw's *John Bull's Other Island* (1904) appears to be a prototype of Father Jack; Friel himself had portrayed a rather ridiculous priest in *Living Quarters* (1975); and Synge had caricatured the Catholic priesthood in *The Tinkers Wedding* (published in 1907, although his play was not produced in Ireland until 1971). There were, however, few previous instances in Irish culture of a priest like Father Jack, who had rejected Catholicism not for theological reasons, but from a sense of its irrelevance, who recommends having "love children," and who appears to have had an intimate relationships with his "house boy," Okinawa. By 1999, however, the status of Catholic clergy in Ireland had altered radically. *Lughnasa* appeared two years before it was revealed that Bishop Eamon

Casey had a son—an initially shocking revelation that would seem minor in relation to later revelations about institutional abuse of children and women by Irish clergy. So if in 1990 there was a risk of the characterization of Father Jack provoking controversy for appearing to denigrate the Catholic Church, by the end of the decade the reputation of the church had so declined that any performer playing Jack had to work hard to gain sympathy from the audience for his character.

Another taboo of the early 1990s challenged by the play was its morally and ethically neutral presentation of single parenthood. Single-parent families in Ireland in 1990 accounted for 14.5 percent of all births in Ireland. Yet within Irish discourse, the "normal"—as well as the legal—family unit remained the traditional heterosexual two-parent married family. Roddy Doyle's *The Snapper* (1991) was one of the first mainstream attempts to normalize the phenomenon of single parenthood within Irish culture. Friel's presentation of Chris and Michael disrupts contemporaneous notions of normality in a similar way to Doyle's novel: Chris's unmarried state is rarely mentioned and in no way problematized in the play. By 1999, however, single parenthood was considerably less controversial: when figures were counted in 2003 it was revealed that 31.4 percent of all births in the Republic of Ireland were to single and/or unmarried parents.

Furthermore, audiences in 1999 appear to have seen the play through their memories of *Riverdance*, a show to which *Lughnasa* is sometimes compared, and with which it is occasionally confused. The choreographer for the 1990 and 1999 productions of *Lughnasa* was Terry John Bates, who explains that for the latter production he was forced to add more steps to the dance in the first act. "There were far more steps the second time because people *were expecting* the energy then. You had to satisfy the audience." He admits frankly that "I had to redo it again after *River Dance* [*sic*] again you know. The audience were conscious of *River Dance*—totally."[5]

Finally, and perhaps most significantly, the play focused on a group Irish women at a time when the status of women within Ireland was changing considerably. The play premiered six months before Mary Robinson became Ireland's first woman president and before Garry Hynes was appointed to the Artistic Directorship of the Abbey Theater in 1991. The decade saw the emergence of many Irish women playwrights, the most important of whom is Marina Carr; and there was a general perception that the status of Irish women within both theater and society had improved. This improvement was imperfect, however. Garry Hynes's tenure at the Abbey lasted only until 1993, and although women dominate many areas of Irish theater, the majority of mainstream productions on the country's largest stages are by male playwrights. The 1990 production of *Dancing at Lughnasa* may have represented a celebration of female physicality, but the mobility of the play internationally contrasted starkly with state attempts to control female movement in Ireland during the decade. Such events as the February 1992 "X-Case," in which a fourteen-year-old girl who had been raped was prevented from traveling to England for an abortion, exemplify a confusion in Ireland about state control over the bodies of Irish women. If the 1990 dance scene in *Lughnasa* was presented as celebratory, its 1999 revival ought to have been a reminder that much work remained to be done to protect the status of Irish women.

Yet the gender politics of Friel's play have received little attention. Friel's respected status in Irish letters appears to have made critics excessively inclined to read Michael as an onstage representative of the author himself, to see the play as being directly autobiographical in an uncomplicated sense. Friel's decision to put five strong women characters at the center of his play is not unusual in world drama—one thinks of *The House of Bernarda Alba* or *Three Sisters*—but there had been few comparable examples of plays for, by, or about women in the Irish mainstream dramatic tradition before 1990. The possibility that the representation of the five Mundy sisters might have been equal to, or more important than, the narrative of the lone male did not seem to occur to many Irish commentators. This arose from the absence of an appropriate vocabulary in Irish criticism for describing work by and about women, which had been pointed out by Victoria White in an influential article published shortly before *Lughnasa* opened. Writing about Charabanc Theater Company, which was established in Belfast in 1984 as a way of counteracting the absence of challenging and substantial roles for women, White suggests that the Irish media marginalized Charabanc "by concentrating on their being women." Because Charabanc produced work by and for women, it was, White states, represented as "catering for a minority audience" despite the fact that, as one of the company's founders Eleanor Methven points out, women represent "a minority of 52% of the world!" Charabanc was often referred to as "the best all-women theater company in Ireland," which as Methven pointed out, "wasn't much of a compliment," since Charabanc was also the only all-woman theater company in Ireland. "Why can't they just say we're one of the best theater companies in Ireland?" she asked.[6] In the year before *Lughnasa* premiered, many plays by Irish women appeared, such as Mary Elizabeth Burke-Kennedy's *Women at Arms*; and the play's premiere coincided with a celebrated Gate Theater *Three Sisters,* adapted by Frank McGuinness and starring the three Cusack Sisters. Friel cannot be credited with changing the place of women on the Irish stage, but *Lughnasa* may be seen as one of the first examples of mainstream Irish theater being affected by a process that had stretched back into the 1970s, when women such as Deirdre O'Connell, Garry Hynes, Lynne Parker, Marie Jones, Carol Moore, Eleanor Methven, and many others began to have a greater impact on drama in Ireland.

All of these changes can explain the sense of nostalgia toward Mason's production of *Lughnasa*: it seemed by 1999 to have emerged from an Ireland that was gone forever. Furthermore, many critics suggest that Irish audiences in the late 1990s needed to distance themselves from a perceived version of the country's past as a way of asserting their growing sense of modernity—as has been argued in relation to the plays of Marina Carr and Martin McDonagh by Joe Cleary and Victor Merriman.

That sense of nostalgia is important, however, because it obscures the extent to which the script of *Lughnasa* could have been used to challenge many Irish taboos and problems, both in 1990 and 1999—about priests, single-parent families, homelessness, unemployment, gender, emigration, and so on. It seems worth considering why these challenging aspects of the play went unremarked and unremembered. To consider that issue, I want to discuss the production that played at the Abbey in 1990 and that transferred to New York the following year.

Catherine Byrne, who played Chris in the play's 1990 premiere and Agnes in its 1999 "Friel Festival" revival, states that Patrick Mason's *Lughnasa* was intended to be seen as a "golden production." "There's a bleak side to Brian's plays but he doesn't always like that highlighted," she explains. Mason's *Lughnasa* was "all golden corn and poppies, beautiful lighting; the women were colour-coordinated." "But," Byrne adds, "there's another production of *Dancing at Lughnasa* we haven't seen yet. We haven't seen how dark it is."[7]

Byrne's comments suggest that the direction and design of this "golden production" were intended to produce sentimental rather than genuinely emotional responses. The set design by Joe Vanek has now become iconic, presenting a field of grain that dominated the right of the stage, creating the impression of the Mundys' lives being played out against a landscape of abundance. This image could be said to work against Friel's script: while visually striking, Vanek's design may have worked against the play's frequent use of images of barrenness, impoverishment, and infertility. Such images pervade the action: *Lughnasa* is set at harvest time, but represents a failure of regeneration. The Mundys are a family of six, which produces only one child. Two of the six will have left the family home within a year of the conclusion of the action; a third will have died. Furthermore, all of the sisters are vulnerable to the risk of poverty: theirs after all is a household in which three eggs must be made to feed seven people.[8]

The lighting design by Trevor Dawson further obscures such themes. He used soft yellows and golds in his design, so the overall atmosphere created was of warmth and perpetual sunshine. The playing area was almost entirely open: the walls of the Mundys' house are not presented on stage, and no other structures dominate the space. This openness would have diminished the audience's sense that the sisters' lives were claustrophobic. Furthermore, a set in which none of the structures casts a shadow is unlikely to alert the audience to the possibility that there is an undertone of sadness and loss in the play.

Similarly, the sound design of *Lughnasa* has influenced its reception. Patrick Mason added a number of sound effects not included in the script, the purpose of which was to draw attention to the similarities between Ireland and Africa. A piece of African chant called "Celebration Dance" was played at the end of the first act and the beginning of the second to establish a relationship between Irish traditional music and African song, for example. Mason's most influential decision relates to his treatment of the dance in the first act. As Abbey sound director David Nowlan explains, a "major bone of contention for the show" was (as he revealingly terms it) the "big dance number." The "Mason's Reel," Nowlan states, is "quite a short tune and would have been very, very repetitive. So one of the musicians suggested a reel which is in the same key, called 'Miss Macleod's Reel,' just to get into the whole excitement of 'The Mason's Apron.' . . . We did it by doing a lot of bodhran over dubs, making it very, very heavy and percussive." Furthermore, says Nowlan, "another part of the brief was that Patrick wanted to give it a kind of African ethnic vibe. Brian quite liked that idea."[9]

This direction by Mason of the dance scene contrasts strongly with Friel's own stage directions. The movements of the sisters should seem caricatured, Friel writes; the sound should be too loud, the beat too fast, and "the almost recognisable dance" should appear "grotesque." He states that there should be "a sense of order consciously being subverted, of the women consciously and crudely caricaturing themselves, indeed of near-hysteria being produced."[10] However, as Patrick Burke points out, the intensification of the rhythmic aspects of the dance, when performed, worked against Friel's instructions:

> In its premiere production at the Abbey Theater, Dublin, and subsequently in New York and London, that dance was generally lauded in terms of the energetically celebratory, an evaluation supported by the *joie de vivre* of the Chieftains' music which, anachronistically and counter to Friel's stage directions, accompanied it. Such an emphasis on celebration tended to ignore the text's emphasis on the ugly aspects of the dance.[11]

Some of the casting and directing choices further skewed interpretations of the play. Kate was intended to be presented as a forty-year-old woman: her tragedy is that she has been classified as redundant by her society while still relatively young. The part was, however, originally performed by Frances Tomelty, who, contrary to the script, presented Kate as an elder woman and delivered her lines in a histrionic manner, encouraging audiences to laugh at her character. Kate's romantic interest in Austin Morgan was, for example, presented as undignified and inherently absurd, instead of arising from a legitimate desire to form a relationship with someone whom she appears to respect. This part was subsequently taken over by Rosaleen Linehan, a respected actor who, nevertheless, is known mainly for comic roles. Irish audiences were probably predisposed to find Linehan funny before she appeared on stage, a problem to which the actor herself seems alert. Referring to "the nature of my temperament," Linehan admitted in 1999 that "there's a large streak of sarcastic wit" in her personality, which was also revealed in her performance of Kate. While *Lughnasa* was on tour in the United States, Friel approached Linehan to discuss this matter with her: "'Just one thing, Rosaleen,' he said. 'I don't write irony.' That wiped out the performance for that week!" said Linehan, implying that her portrayal of Kate was "ironic" for every other week during the production's run.[12] As a result, it may have been difficult for the original audiences of *Lughnasa* to attribute to Kate any qualities other than the superficial.

It might be easy to criticize Patrick Mason's decisions in relation to casting and design, but many of his choices were praised. His use of a beat on "The Mason's Apron" is regarded by many as a brilliant directorial choice, even if it overshadowed or undermined Friel's attempt to communicate a rejection of authority to his audience. Similarly, his casting of Tomelty and Linehan makes sense from a commercial perspective. Both were well known, respected actors in 1990–91, and it is customary for Irish producers to manage the risks associated with premieres by emphasizing a play's humorous elements while curtailing any potentially offensive content.

It appears, however, that the darkness implicit in the play was not only ignored but that it may even have been suppressed in favor of a less provocative presentation of the play; it seems also that it emphasized euphoric release where Friel wanted grotesque near-hysteria, and that it made characters such as Kate appear ridiculous rather than sympathetic.

I would suggest that one reason for such decisions may be that the play was seen from an early stage as a strong candidate for commercial success and that, rather than producing the play in a way that would have been of exclusive interest to an Irish audience, the Abbey instead emphasized the qualities of the play likely to make it appealing internationally. The Broadway run of *Lughnasa* was produced by Noel Pearson, who brought to it an entrepreneurial spirit that drove the play to international fame: as Anthony Roche points out, Pearson later portrayed the move from "Ballybeg to Broadway" as an inevitability.[13] Pearson had been appointed to the Board of the Abbey in 1987 and acted as artistic director between 1989 and 1990. He explains that:

> In 1987 I took over the Abbey and [Friel] wrote me a very warm letter and I asked him to give me a play. He gave me *Lughnasa* in 1988, two years before it moved to London. Nobody wanted it there. Nobody wanted it on Broadway, either, at first. An Irish play had not been successful there since [Hugh Leonard's] *Da*.[14]

The "golden" quality of the 1990 production may not have been a deliberate attempt to make the play commercially attractive, but those features of the production certainly appealed to audiences in London and New York.

What is interesting here is that the premiere of *Lughnasa* was not especially well received in Dublin, perhaps because the issues that would have been relevant to an Irish audience at that time (homelessness, poverty, emigration, etc.) were not given much emphasis. Its reception was further conditioned by a number of significant events that coincided with its opening. *Lughnasa* was, for example, the first play to be performed at the newly renovated Abbey Theater. In the original Michael Scott design for the building, the theater comprised a large concrete façade with small doors at the front. This aesthetic was intended to suggest that the theater space was a kind of magic box; that, by peeking through the small opening of the doors, one might get a glimpse of amazing goings-on inside. In practice, most visitors to the theater found the austerity of the façade alienating; rather than being encouraged to peek inside, they instead felt shut out. The theater's 1989–90 renovations were an attempt to address some of the resultant criticism. The Abbey's management wanted to present the theater as more relevant to its community and country, and the new façade was a physical manifestation of this desire for openness: a new bar area with windows overlooking Abbey Street exposed the theater to public view. The new façade attracted a great deal of public attention and discussion; indeed, much of the pre-publicity for *Lughnasa* focused more on the building than the play.[15] For these reasons, audiences for *Lughnasa* would have been predisposed to read the play in the context of the celebratory atmosphere associated with the reopening of the building.

Another important factor in the reception of the play was Friel's decision not to offer it to the Field Day company, which had produced four of his previous five works. Friel explained his movement away from Field Day as an attempt to prevent his work from being "associated with institutions or directors. I don't want a tandem to develop. Institutions are inclined to enforce characteristics, impose an attitude or a voice or a response. I think you're better to keep away from all that. It's for that reason that I didn't give *Dancing at Lughnasa* to Field Day."[16] This decision was characterized as a departure from Field Day (although Friel's resignation from the company did not formally occur until 1994) and hence as a move away from the overtly political work in which he had been engaged since 1980. This may have had the effect of discouraging audiences and critics from attempting political readings of the play or of considering the play in the context of Friel's earlier work.

Material in the Friel archive shows that the play was certainly liked—there is some interesting fan mail from Bono and Christy Moore, among others—but it was by no means treated as a contemporary masterpiece. Ticket sales were respectable, but the production rarely appears to have reached full attendance. The critical response was similarly mixed. The *Evening Press* paid most attention to the play's running time, noting with mild disapproval that it did not end until 10.25 (a mere half hour before pub closing time). The *Independent* declared that it was a "many layered sandwich—but it lacks real meat," and the Irish edition of the *Guardian,* damning with faint praise, stated that "it will be a play loved in Ireland."[17] Fintan O'Toole, writing in the *Irish Times,* was generally positive about the play, but criticized Friel's characterization of Father Jack, whom he saw as a "metaphorical version of a Field Day pamphlet."[18]

It was not until *Lughnasa* transferred in November 1990 to the Royal National Theater in London that Irish reactions toward the play became more positive. "The Abbey Stuns the South Bank," declared the *Sunday Independent* while the *Irish Times* approvingly noted that London "Raves for Friel Play." However, it was the transfer of the play to Broadway in 1991 that cemented its reputation. There was huge excitement in Ireland about the New York run even before *Lughnasa* opened there. The Abbey's Martin Fahy enthusiastically told the media that "if *Dancing at Lughnasa* gets a good reception from the New York critics, Brian Friel will never again have to buy another Lotto ticket"—a nice reminder of an Ireland where the only way to make a million was by winning the Lotto or going to Broadway. Dublin's Lord Mayor hosted a civic reception at the Mansion House to celebrate the transfer of *Lughnasa* to Broadway a full nine months before it opened there. The Taoiseach Charles Haughey sent a personalized fax to the cast on the Broadway opening night. RTE's Arts Show dedicated a special edition to the New York production. *Irish Times* readers were invited to enter a competition to win tickets for two to see *Lughnasa* in New York for Christmas 1991.[19] And in November of that year, one month after the play opened in New York—but eighteen months after it had premiered in Dublin—a distinctly uncomfortable looking Friel appeared on the front page of Ireland's newspapers, seated beside Charles Haughey as one of the winners of the "People of the Year" awards.[20] This enthusiasm continued for most of the play's Broadway run, with regular media updates telling the Irish public which magazines had interviewed or profiled Friel, which celebrities had attended the Broadway production, and how much better the Irish actors were than the American cast who took over from them in 1992. In short, Friel generated far more excitement by bringing *Lughnasa* to Broadway than he had done by producing it in Ireland.

The only person who seemed uncomfortable with this was Friel himself. Accepting his Tony Award for best play in 1992, he expressed ambivalence about the reception of his play by alluding to Graham Grene's comment that "success is only the postponement of failure."[21] With his next play, *Wonderful Tennessee* (1994), Friel presented a set of characters who were almost completely static to an audience expecting more dance. *Molly Sweeney* (1994) portrays the negative consequences when a visually impaired woman has her sight restored, and thus may be seen as a dramatization of the proposition that success is the postponement of a failure. Crucially, in this play, Friel gives us another dance scene, this time ensuring, through his use of monologue, that no one will misinterpret his intentions:

> As soon as Tom played the last note of "The Lament for Limerick," I found myself on my feet in the middle of the sitting-room and calling, "A hornpipe, Tom! A mad, fast hornpipe!" And the moment he began to play, I shouted—screamed, "Now watch me! Just you watch me!" And in a rage of anger and defiance I danced wild and furious dance round and round that room; then out to the hall; then back to the kitchen; then back to the room again and round it a third time. Mad and wild and frenzied. . . . It must have been terrifying to watch, because when I stopped, the room was hushed.[22]

Give Me Your Answer, Do! (1997) might also be seen as a reaction against—or as contrasting with—the perception that *Lughnasa* was a joyful play. *Give Me Your Answer* is shockingly frank in its treatment of authorial fear about reception, presenting a writer whose child cannot speak for herself, and whose (commodified) work is being evaluated for inclusion in an American archive, with the success of the deal hinging on the author's revelation that he has secretly written two pornographic novels. It cannot be assumed that Friel was commenting directly in these works on the misinterpretation of *Lughnasa,* but it is notable that his subsequent plays diverge from any expectation that might have been generated by the production of *Lughnasa.* Subsequent Irish productions of *Lughnasa* have attempted to tackle the script's darker elements: there was a Belfast production directed by Friel's nephew Conall Morisson in 1995, a Joe Dowling production at the Gate in 2005, a very successful version from An Grianan in Donegal in 2002, and an Irish language version called *Damhsa ag Lughnasa* which toured Ireland in 2001. So we are beginning to see productions that are closer to Friel's script. Yet audiences' ideas about *Lughnasa* persist.

I would suggest that the cause of this continued misinterpretation of Friel's play arises because the international success of *Lughnasa* occurred at one of those periods when the performance of Irishness on the international stage is extremely important within the country itself. Ireland's delight with the international success of *Lughnasa* did not happen in isolation, but was part of a growing awareness of the country's status in relation to the rest of the world. Shortly after the premiere of *Dancing at Lughnasa*, the Irish football team took part in the 1990 Football World Cup, the first for which a team from the Republic of Ireland had qualified. That team included second- and third-generation expatriates and crossed religious and ethnic divides; its fans believed that they had distinguished themselves for their good behavior and good humor, which contrasted (they were told) with the hooliganism of their English neighbors. The performance on the world stage of an inclusive and admirable Irish identity created a sense of national confidence, which is encapsulated well by Dermot Bolger's *In High Germany* (1990) and Roddy Doyle's *The Van* (1992). In 1991, Dublin became Europe's "City of Culture," and the resulting influx of tourists and exuberant media commentary again focused Irish attention on the status of the country abroad. This association of national self-importance with the perception of people abroad dominated the 1990s, and appears to have affected Irish audiences' attitudes to *Lughnasa*. The generally mixed reviews for the play's 1990 premiere were forgotten after it achieved success overseas; its return to the Abbey in 1992, and its subsequent Irish tour were wildly popular. *Lughnasa* toured the world, and Ireland, until 1993. The celebration of the place of Irish culture internationally gained momentum even as *Lughnasa* stepped away from the Abbey stage. Roddy Doyle won the Booker Prize for *Paddy Clarke, Ha, Ha, Ha* in 1994, and Seamus Heaney won the Nobel Prize for Literature in 1995.

It thus appears to be the case that *Lughnasa* required international endorsement before it was unreservedly admitted into the Irish dramatic canon. In this respect, it might be seen as similar to previous Irish plays, such as *The Playboy of the Western World* (1907), *A Whistle in the Dark* (1961), and *Philadelphia, Here I Come!* (1964). What distinguishes *Lughnasa* is that its international success occurred at a time when Irish culture in its entirety was redefining its relationship with the rest of the world, so that the play's success was not seen as an isolated phenomenon, but as part of a number of Irish successes during the 1990s. This celebratory approach to Irish writing was unlikely to lead commentators to suggest that *Lughnasa* had been misinterpreted in some respects. This may explain the fact that the revival of *Dancing at Lughnasa* in 1999 was seen as a celebration, not just of Friel's seventieth birthday, but also of the international triumph of the play.

The production history of *Dancing at Lughnasa* is an example of the growing impact of the ideology associated with private business on Irish theater: the key concept for an understanding of the reception of the play in Ireland is *mobility*. The play was considered more valuable when it traveled, and was given canonical status within Ireland only when it was endorsed abroad. Irish commentators could not declare the play to be a success until it had been a success internationally, indicating an insecurity about the relative value of Irish critical judgments. Yet the play became mobile only by removing or moderating those aspects of it that might have engaged directly with Irish life. In its 1990 premiere, its humorous and sentimental qualities were emphasized at the expense of the way in which its script engages with contemporary Irish life. In both 1990 and 1999, its dance scene was presented as emancipatory and celebratory, rather than as a refusal of order or an expression of claustrophobia. In order for the play to become mobile, the production first had to divest itself of those elements that might have made it a more substantial and rewarding experience for specifically Irish audiences.

This means that we have tended to forget or neglect many important elements of the play's original production—including two interesting aspects of it that pertain to the relationship between Irish theater and America. The first is that, while *Dancing at Lughnasa* was being performed on the Abbey's mainstage, *The Glass Menagerie* was being produced downstairs in the Peacock, directed by Friel's daughter Judy.[23] There are many obvious similarities between the two works. Both involve women living in restrictive, claustrophobic environments. Both are set in 1936 to the backdrop of the Spanish Civil War, locating a claustrophobic and hemmed-in social setting within a global context. Both involve a male character who represents the "long-delayed but always expected something that we live for." Both are narrated by someone who does not witness many of the scenes he describes. Furthermore, *The Glass Menagerie* defines a memory play for Friel's purposes: "In memory," writes Williams, "everything seems to happen to music," a line that Friel reproduces almost directly in his own play.[24] The relationship between the productions of *Lughnasa* and *The Glass Menagerie* is dialogic: Friel draws from Williams, but *Lughnasa* allows a deeper understanding of *The Glass Menagerie*. Moreover, the Abbey's decision to present these two plays in partnership illustrates its sense of the importance of international work for Irish theater, both in production and in dramaturgy.

Another significant feature of the production was that its American rights were licensed to Ferndale Theater Productions, a private company owned by Noel Pearson and others. Although the production was billed as "the Abbey Theatre on tour," it was in fact a product from a private enterprise that had effectively leased the Abbey brand for marketing purposes. This exposed Pearson to the accusation that he had abused his position as acting director of the Abbey for financial gain, at a time when the theater was undergoing a period of financial crisis. Pearson was called before the Public Accounts Committee to explain his involvement in the American tour, and there was also an internal investigation by the Abbey's auditors and solicitor—in which it was found that nothing improper had occurred. Even so, it should be noted that the international success of *Lughnasa* was of little financial benefit to the Abbey, due to decisions made by the Artistic Director who would later produce the international tour. The long-term significance of this is that it set an important precedent, establishing that, as a theater in receipt of public funds, the Abbey should not expose itself to the financial risks associated with a Broadway production; it also blurred the lines between private interests and the national remit of the Abbey. This issue has persisted since that time, most recently in the controversial staging of *The Shaughraun* at the Abbey by *Riverdance* director and Abbey board member John McColgan, which transferred to London's West End in 2005.

These issues also highlight the different ways in which it becomes possible to think of the performance of Irishness abroad. The success of *Dancing at Lughnasa* in the United States may be related to the way in which it appeals to international audience expectations about Irish drama (an issue discussed in more detail by Christina Hunt Mahony in chapter 13). Yet we might also see the presence of *Lughnasa* on the American stage as another form of performance: as a sign to Irish audiences that the national culture has value, as a sign that Ireland itself might take an equal place on the world stage. The meaning of *Lughnasa* to the Irish public does not therefore arise from Friel's script, nor directly from Mason's production. Instead, the status of the play arises from Irish audiences' understanding of the success of its American production.

Dancing at Lughnasa may be understood as a play in which several attempts at communication are made, but none of them adequately. The radio always breaks down, presenting a disembodied musical performance to which the sisters respond physically. Jack's sentences will always fizzle out, Gerry will continue to be "unbelievable," and Michael will never answer when his aunts call for him. Michael the narrator will try to hold his characters in tableau at the play's conclusion, but those characters will move as he talks; Kate will cry throughout his final speech. It is ironic that this play about a failure to communicate would itself be so widely misunderstood. The production history of *Lughnasa* shows that the play's value was determined not by its reception in Ireland but by its mobility. Just as Martin McDonagh would joke in *The Cripple of Inishmaan* that Ireland can't be such a bad place if sharks want to go there, there's a sense in which *Lughnasa* on Broadway was used to suggest to the Irish public that Ireland can't be such a bad place if Americans—especially famous ones—want to see our plays. That is of course significant, but it provides a very limited sense of what the relationship between these two countries' theaters was, and might be.

13

"The Irish Play"

Beyond the Generic?

CHRISTINA HUNT MAHONY

The title of this essay is not intended to indicate an Irish take on MacBeth; rather, its intention is conveyed by the subtitle. My approach is not scholarly, but speculative, an informal intervention into an ongoing debate about what "the Irish Play" is, and what it means to audiences outside of Ireland. It is a subject admirably and convincingly addressed by Nicholas Grene in the final chapter of his book *The Politics of Irish Drama*, to take one fine example, and also by Anthony Roche in the recently published two-volume *Cambridge History of Irish Literature*.[1]

The immediate impetus to explore this subject, however, came in the form of two essays written by Fintan O'Toole, both of which appeared in the *Irish Times*—one after The Dublin Theater Festival of 2005, and the other in the annual year-end arts roundup at Christmas of that year.[2] O'Toole, long a proponent of the literary play and an advocate for the essential role of the playwright in the collaborative art of theater, is, at the same time, a critic interested in and open to a full range of theatrical undertakings and experiments of many kinds.

In his October essay O'Toole wrote:

Is the era of the playwright as the dominant figure in the theatre coming to a close? . . . This is a big issue for Irish theatre, especially in terms of its international standing. What we can claim (as opposed to great companies or actors or directors in large numbers) is an extraordinary contribution to the play as a literary form. . . . [We have] the abiding self-image of our theatrical culture as one in which the writer matters. . . . But does the writer—in the old sense of the solitary genius who labours in isolation on a text that is then interpreted by actors, directors and designers—[does that writer] really matter any more?[3]

O'Toole's questioning of the continuing primacy of the playwright, and the validity of that primacy in the twenty-first century, was precipitated by his rather stunned realization that the Theater Festival had not included even one new Irish play written by a single author. He went on to list the differing types of creative undertakings, collaborations, imports, and partnerships that predominated instead. The productions included plays written collectively, plays co-authored by directors and companies, verbatim theater, and other formats.

O'Toole may be right, but I must also suggest that audiences for Irish plays outside Ireland seem always to have been not devoted fans of "the Playwright" but much more devoted to the concept of "the Irish Play" or what they have come to think of as "the Irish Play." It could be argued that this generic Irish Play is, in a sense, the single-authored play of which O'Toole writes, but more specifically it is a language and/or a story-telling play. Furthermore, the average overseas playgoer's concept of "the Irish Play" includes some stereotypical or démodé elements that Irish writers, actors, and directors now try to avoid or minimize, or in which they are no longer particularly interested.

Reception of Irish plays abroad varies greatly from country to country, and this assessment is based solely on an American response, accumulated during more than two decades. The sampling is not scientific, nor is it probably extensive enough, and is based on informal canvassing of both student audiences and general audiences. Reference to the student audience is excluded because it is atypical and does not inform the wider and relevant assessment of reception, marketing, advertising, or other commercial theatrical realities. American theater audiences for Irish plays, in my context here, can be broken down into four types: the Theater Goer; the Irish American; the Big Nite Out-er; and the Socialite. Sometimes these categories can overlap, but not to a degree significant enough to dispense with the categories.

The Theater Goer is just that, and in a New York audience he or she is immediately recognizable, but the type is not found throughout the country at large by any means. There is also a provincial "Theater Goer" found in a limited number of smaller urban centers, and I will discuss this group later as it relates. The Theater Goer in New York, and only a couple of other major cities, is someone who has no connection necessarily to Ireland, but often has a subscription or subscriptions to area theaters or attends regularly. This Theater Goer attends Irish plays as they occur in subscription or as they attract critical interest. In the most informed circumstances, this person reads dramatic criticism regularly and understands trends, recognizes theatrical names—writers, directors, actors—and knows the history of these artists. It is a small category outside the parameters of the immediate theatrical, journalistic, and academic worlds (that is, people who earn a living in full or in part by being engaged in theatrical productions or writing or commenting upon them).

The Irish American, the second group, goes to Irish events, including theater, often as consistently as the theatergoer attends new theatrical offerings. The Irish American's frame of reference is, in the first instance, not theatrical but Irish and often not more specific than that. He or she might be just as involved in attending sporting fixtures or going to musical performances simply because they are identifiably Irish—and those are his or her co-ordinates.

The Big Nite Out-er only intersects with "the Irish Play" when it becomes a mega-success and its reputation has trickled down in the media to the level of popular magazine coverage or large-canvassing television, radio, and newspaper advertisements. On annual or infrequent expeditions to major cities, this theater patron tends to favor musicals or spectaculars and seeks a bang for his theater buck. Good examples of Irish Plays intersecting with these playgoers in recent memory would include such blockbusters as *Dancing at Lughnasa* for stage drama and *Riverdance* or Michael Flatley's alternatives to same, which are staged events in the same blockbuster category. If, for instance, Alastair McGuckian's recent musical *Ha'penny Bridge* were to travel abroad, it would have the potential to attract such an audience. With its plot à la O'Casey, productions numbers aspiring to the level of *Oklahoma!* and modish lighting and sets evocative of the mega-hits *Cats* and *Les Miserables, Ha'penny Bridge* has broad popular appeal. The Big Nite Out-ers who head for huge commercially successful theater experiences do not have access to major theatrical fare on a regular basis, largely because of geography. They are in search of a good night's entertainment as part of a larger urban cultural tourism package on occasion.

The Socialite, my final category, attends an Irish Play only if it becomes the place to be seen, part of a large fund-raising effort, or is included in a decidedly up-market subscription series. This audience type has in the past been nearly unique to the United States, but is a growing market now in Western Europe where previously high levels of government subsidy of the arts is being supplemented by private sponsorship. Often such subscriptions are corporate; and the Socialite, though informed or cultured, doesn't necessarily care about theater per se, nor about things Irish. In this respect the Socialite is rather like the Big Nite Out-er in a sense, but is simply on the higher end of the economic scale and might live in the city.

If one chats with people from these four types of audiences, especially when identified as an Irish Studies professional, one of the first things to emerge is that with few exceptions it is only the first group—the bona fide Theater Goers—who can identify the authors of Irish plays that they have seen. The varied audiences may indeed, and do, have perceptive insights, have enjoyed the play thoroughly, are able to recite the plot in detail or make informed comments on theatrical theme and values, but they will not be able as a general rule to name the author.

There are exceptions—Brian Friel broke the barrier—once *Lughnasa* was out there his name became a known, a marketable commodity, and for a while thereafter people would book again at the theater simply because a play was one of his. His *Faith Healer* was recently on Broadway and drew predictably large crowds. (It is, however, a cautionary tale that Brian Friel was also nearly a household name decades earlier with the success of *Philadelphia, Here I Come!* in the 1950s, but it wasn't exactly déjà vu all over again when he cropped up with a big success with *Lughnasa* in 1990. Instead, two generations later, 1990s audiences in the States for the most part didn't remember him by name, and some of the fanfare that heralded *Luhgnasa*'s success gave the impression that Friel was a new discovery. I would be very interested to be able to accumulate more specific information about whether the *Faith Healer* phenomenon of 2006 was a matter of the presence of leading man Ralph Fiennes, or whether the majority of American theatergoers who obtained tickets for *Faith Healer* were aware it is a Friel play or indeed an Irish Play at all.)

When academic critics and journalists assess the kind of Irish plays on offer abroad which were well received in the United States—possibly going back as far as Boucicault—what we realize is that if it isn't spectacle in the first instance, then language and story telling prevail. Confining our attention here to contemporary plays, though, we know that what has gone down well in New York and elsewhere in recent decades not only includes Friel's *Lughnasa* but Sebastian Barry's *Steward of Christendom*, Frank McGuinness's *Someone Who'll Watch Over Me*, and Conor McPherson's *The Weir*, to take a few obvious examples. Not only are these all language and/or storytelling plays, more significantly they are linguistically beautiful and, in the end, what they share is that they are edifying.

Martin McDonagh is a writer whose work has not gone down consistently well until very recently with large audiences in major venues in the States. His earlier ventures seemed to be either loved or hated, and in the latter case, were considered too postmodern and irreverent by many. Although McDonagh's work is certainly linguistically memorable and also highly poetic at times, it is not so in the rather pretty way that has come to be associated with the Irish Play. Here one can begin to refine the key ingredients for major Irish theatrical success in the United States—it is not just poetic language that is required, but a particular kind of poetic language. McDonagh's luck changed dramatically in 2006 with the arrival of *The Lieutenant of Inishmore* on Broadway. Inarguably more violent and anarchic than *The Beauty Queen of Leenane* or *The Cripple of Inishmaan*, McDonagh's latest major stage venture, one of the first plays he wrote, seems to have channeled American anxiety and antiterrorist sentiment into a play that has audiences howling with laughter while aghast at onstage torture, dismemberment, animal abuse, a psychotic female guerrilla, random assassination, hostage-taking, and tons of blood. The catharsis provided for a post-9/11 audience is an obvious factor in the turnabout of McDonagh's American reception.

Lack of prettiness, refinement, flowery poeticism, and also obvious forms of edification can instantly explain Tom Murphy's relative and continuing lack of popularity in the United States. Murphy's language is only at times beautiful in this sense, such as in his *Morning after Optimism*, and in some soaring passages in *Bailegangaire* and *The Gigli Concert*. The latter two plays have had only limited American success in repertory, and Murphy's work does not appear on Broadway. The work of Marina Carr, linguistically stunning in the main, joins McDonagh's and Murphy's—too outré, too violent, and/or too gritty, and not immediately grasped as being edifying, although edification is there to be found in the works of all of these authors for the seasoned playgoer. In such plays poeticism of language is, importantly, directed toward less than palatable versions of Irishness and Irish people. The problems of reception are compounded when, as in Marina Carr's work and that of fellow Midlands' playwright Eugene O'Brien, plays are written in dialect which is not easily accessed by overseas audiences.

So, it is not just language which that up "the Irish Play," it is language plus what I am reluctant to call "values," in just the sense that we have learned recently to be dubious about that word. An Irish author can write a play with poetic language, but if it deals directly with major criminal acts (murder, mayhem, incest, or rape), or dares to deal honestly with sensitive subjects (dysfunctional families, loss of faith, venality, or alcoholism), it becomes less than the Irish Play of most mainstream American theatergoers' definition. Most American theatergoers do not want their Irish play à la Tarantino. Often what will be tolerated, or indeed sought out (after some years of hesitation) in Irish films like *The General*, *The Crying Game*, and *The Butcher Boy*, does not appeal to theater audiences who are older and have different expectations from that of the younger demographic of film audiences raised on a diet of postmodern art.

It should be emphasized that the amnesia factor regarding Irish playwrights' names and reputations, and the lack of awareness of their body of work, is not a new phenomenon. It is not simply that there are many more Irish playwrights being touted abroad these days, making it hard to keep them straight. Rather, I have learned in fairly detailed conversations with mature people who have seen *The Playboy of the Western World* and *Riders to the Sea* more than once that they do not know Synge's name at all. Often these same people cannot remember O'Casey's name unless prompted. What is even more astonishing is that I have never heard anyone in the profession comment upon this phenomenon, although it is apparent and consistent.

In a related discovery, I have learned that people in the United States who have seen a Shaw play or two, though they may know his name and remember it, are sometimes astounded to learn that Shaw is Irish because his plays do not intersect with their expectations of the Irish Play and most of them do not take place in Ireland, of course. Diasporic and other audience members may thoroughly have enjoyed *The Importance of Being Earnest* or perhaps another of Wilde's plays (and Wilde's is a name they know), but Wilde seems in the popular perception at times to suffer the same fate as Shaw. Too often people are convinced that Wilde is not only English, but that his plays are the epitome of English plays. Often Wilde's linguistic brilliance, conveyed in foppish terms, renders his plays in people's memory as being quintessentially English. Furthermore, Wilde's plays were always taught in American schools as English plays. They are, after all, period-costumed, and peopled with aristocrats, and in the overseas view of such things, conditioned by years of viewing English period dramas on film and on television (Merchant-Ivoryitis?), these plays do not connect in American audiences minds with Irishness. Wilde in particular offers an oblique and complex view of conventional morality that is definitely not associated with the Irish Play. In the consciousness of American audiences, the Irish Play is meant to be informed by Down Home Virtues, including the sort of public virtue that is Wilde's target. The complexity and nuance of Wilde's unique and specifically Irish perspective on English upper class society—all that postcolonial response—seems lost on the average American punter.

Where does this put us with the Irish Play and overseas audiences, especially today? Audiences in America (and I do not think that they are unique in this regard) go to an Irish play in the first instance to hear the talk—to relish the language. They are not just lulled by the lilt; they also listen to the poetry of it all. If that poetry is served up with humor, so much the better, although humor is not an essential for the success of the Irish Play. These audiences seek a rather old-fashioned form of what I am calling edification, in which sorrows are heartfelt, mourning is articulated, the boy gets the girl in the end through virtue or stamina, or the girl loses the boy because she failed to see his worth. We might think that that is corny, but for a reason that I have not quite been able to figure out, it is what is expected from the Irish Play. The decision does not reside in the audience's consciousness of the work of a single author, but it may well reside in the use of language toward an edifying purpose that only a single creative artist can provide.

People in the United States and in other countries go to theater for a variety of reasons. The more adventuresome among them do certainly look for innovation, shock value, political dialectic, brilliant physicality, suspense, or other elements. They might be more adventuresome about theater that is imported from other places, but if they are in the mood for poetry, articulate expression of yearning, or of life's shortcomings or disillusionments—in short a feel-good factor or perhaps even a feel-bad factor close to the edge of sentimentality, conveyed in the right sort of poetic language—they go to the Irish Play expecting to experience just that. They do not necessarily expect this combination whenever they go to theater, but they do expect it when they are off to an Irish Play.

If we look at some Irish Broadway successes of recent decades we can see readily what appeals. Let's take *Lughnasa* as the obvious example. On the face of it, it is hardly a cheery story. Five unmarried women on a subsistence farm in a remote area have kept going since their parents' death on the strength of one outside income of any worth, now threatened, and all this is set on the eve of a worldwide Depression. One sister has an illegitimate child whose father visits from time to time, making her, and by extension her family, something of outcasts locally. Another sister is "simple" (to use the locution that would have prevailed at the time and in that place) and not entirely able to make her way in the world independently. There is a spinster schoolteacher, another sister who does piece work in a defunct cottage industry, and a hard chaw who is plucky but not always appealing. The play is narrated by the bastard child grown-up. Why did this play seem cheery enough or acceptable in a feel-good sense for an overseas audience?

Well, first there is the perspective of the narrator. All is told in flashback through gauze, to evoke a kinder time before the realities of those sisters' predicament impinged fully—a golden summer for the then-child. The story is told in highly poetic language and espouses family solidarity, abounding joint maternal love for the sole child produced by these sisters, and a sympathetic, if somewhat daffy, portrayal of the only son of the family—a priest who "sacrificed all," including his sanity, in the name of proselytizing in the foreign missions. The total effect is helped greatly by the now-famous atavistic dance sequence that erupts in the play. One might call it a major "*craic* event" if using the language of theater advertisements. One might even label the dance scene hedonistic, except that, despite its primitive appeal, it is danced by five unattached women most of whom will die virgin. *Lughnasa* was a success with diasporic audiences in part because it demonstrates the way that life sends us curve balls. It memorializes those familiar characters we all relish from our own childhoods and crazy families, and it benignly excuses mistakes made in the past.

But what if a playwright takes some of these mistakes and shows their logical outcome—as Tom Murphy did *A Whistle in the Dark,* a play that predates *Lughnasa* but ventures far beyond the overseas definition of the Irish Play. In Murphy's play people do not go to England to clean toilets humbly and die tragically, as we were told was the fate which befell two of the sisters in the dramatic afterlife of *Lughnasa*. Instead, in Murphy's play, the story of five brothers, not five sisters, the emigrant sons become thugs and pimps and petty criminals, and the father who bullied and deceived them in Ireland is not conveniently nor tragically dead, but turns up in England to goad them to do it all over again.

Another Irish play that was a large scale success here, and significantly does not take place in Ireland, is Frank McGuinness's *Someone Who'll Watch Over Me*. Not only is the play superbly funny, with crackling dialogue, but in it we have the classic Irishman, Englishman, and American joke writ large on the stage. Everyone performs at first to type, not disappointing diasporic audiences in the slightest. The Irishman is a wise-cracking, highly ironic Belfast journalist; the Englishman, almost a lampoon figure at first, is a bland middle-aged medievalist widower who lives with his Mum; and the American is an athletic, positive-thinking, gung-ho type, who may or may not be a spy. As grim as the situation of these captives in the Beirut cell becomes, their basic honorable values, their solidarity in adversity, prevails. They may squabble, as do the sisters in *Lughnasa*, but basically the men in McGuinness's cell and the sisters in Donegal are in it together—as families and pals should be. The only death in *Someone Who'll Watch Over Me* is that of the American, and yet, again, as in *Lughnasa*, it takes place conveniently offstage. Meanwhile, the Irishman drops his cynicism at a crucial moment to perform a dutiful and moving aria to his dead father, the Englishman turns out to be a mensch in the end, and all this is delivered in the most splendidly inspiring language imaginable.

Despite the menacing atmosphere, no one in *Someone Who'll Watch Over Me* gets hacked into pieces for his political views or otherwise—for that we have to go to Martin McDonagh, who also took the *Lughnasa* model as a baseline in his breakthrough play in the United States, *The Beauty Queen of Leenane*. McDonagh, long before he reaped success on Broadway with *The Lieutenant of Inishmore*, tried to push far beyond the strict definition of the Irish Play. He rang a logical change on Friel's basic premise to explore what it might have been like if the mother in that Donegal farmhouse had been around to torment all those unmarried daughters, or worse still, to torment the one daughter who got stuck at home looking after her. Obviously there's no gauze in McDonagh, no fond memories of the past. The real strictures of life on a desolate patch, in a cottage up an unforgiving hill are chillingly conveyed in *Beauty Queen*, along with the tyranny and desperation of an aging parent who guards viciously against just such indiscretions as the mother of the illegitimate child had engaged in in Lughnasa. As has been noted often, McDonagh's play also echoes Synge's *Riders to the Sea*, but the elderly widows in each play suffer very different fates and the exasperation levels of the daughters does not compare. Audiences mesmerized by the stark and primitive tragedy of the aged mother in Synge did not find much that was appealing in McDonagh's matricide, complete with poker in brain on display.

A decade ago, when Sebastian Barry's *The Steward of Christendom* arrived in Brooklyn, the definitive qualities of the Irish play were already getting a bit challenged. American audiences might not have quite known what to make initially of Irishman Thomas Dunne. They would not have been immediately in synch with his views on Victoria and the empire, and certainly the Irish American playgoer did not come to hear these sentiments in the Irish Play. Dunne's paean to Victoria could only have sounded like treachery at first to the Irish American ear, although the Theater Goer might have been more open to the experience—to return to two of my categories. However, Barry brought them all around, all the disparate diasporic audiences. After all, what is Thomas Dunne, but a simple Irish country man, raised on a farm? Furthermore he is a widower with three girls and a boy to raise on his own. He loved his wife, who died in childbirth, and remains crushed by his loss of her. Thomas Dunne represents traditional values and his loss is palpable from the start, especially given his predicament as the curtain opens, reduced to wearing dirty longjohns and biding his time in the local asylum. In *The Steward of Christendom* we don't know what we learn in Barry's later novel *Annie Dunne*, in which Barry creates a fictional sidebar to the narrative of the play. With a postmodern sleight-of-hand, Barry later tells us that Thomas Dunne, in his dementia, had attacked his devoted daughter Annie with a sword. It had been the last straw in a series of alienating and antisocial behaviors which landed him in the asylum where we find him in the earlier play. In *The Steward of Christendom,* the sword episode is mentioned, but the dementia is presented much more sympathetically, as a sad tale of loss—lost wife, lost position, a lost son killed in World War I. Furthermore, in his fallen state Dunne recites some of the most glorious poetry for the stage written in the last century. The play also includes a heart-winning combination of little-boy-ghost and the young-son-in-uniform ghost, rather like Friel's narrator as child and grown-up. In *The Steward of Christendom* we also do not know what is revealed in Barry's most recent novel *A Long*

Long Way, that Dunne father-son relations were not at all cozy before the son left for the war, and that Thomas and his son Willie were estranged at the time of Willie's death.

What is apparent from *The Steward of Christendom*'s success, however, is that it is unalloyed language and an unmitigated version of family feeling which carry the play. Barry appends the poignant story of Thomas Dunne's own childhood, complete with a dog that his father heroically refused to put down for his child's sake. This multigenerational story, filled with heartbreak and filial devotion, is a masterpiece in which the playwright manages to pull off the three-card trick of poetic language, unswerving loyalty, and the winning story of a boy and his dog, a combination that is very hard to beat. Thus the play fits tidily into the generic Irish play template, especially if one chooses to overlook or ignore the crucial and rather pesky Victoria factor, and some in the American audiences did just that, as Irish and English audiences did not, or could not.

With these ingredients—family memory, solidarity in adversity and poetic language—Conor McPherson's *The Weir* was enthusiastically received in the United States. McPherson brilliantly took a totally hackneyed venue— the country pub and its denizens, all male and all in various stages of hopelessness, ineffectuality, and stagnation. He then injected into it a slightly less than classic stranger—a pretty young divorced university lecturer from the city. When we learn that the stranger is also a grieving mother who has lost her only child, her less than classic marital and social status fades, she is accepted, and nearly everyone else on stage gets the chance to tell a key story from his past too—thus uniting all in the cast in dramatic bonds of loyalty, discretion, and forgiveness. The ghostliness of the tales each tells, with the implication of access to the supernatural or the spiritual, just serves to intensify the "Irish" factor in a different guise. Access to the spiritual is another manifestation of virtue or edification—something the modern world has lost sight of or lost the ability to access, a relic of the old purity, one might say. McPherson's characters are not religious, but they seem to accept that they are living their lives parallel to another world, to which the playwright provides glimpses, with a nice little frisson of spookiness added to fix the audience's attention.

So, the Irish Play is a melange of poetic language, some storytelling, an acceptable level of honorable behavior, and maybe a bit of spirituality. This is not a formula used as a paradigm for successful recent American or British drama. So why are the Irish commissioned with writing these plays? Is it a bad case of malingering Thatched Cottage Syndrome or a form of Residual John Hinde Disease? I do not think so. Only theater audiences who are very, very far out of the loop would still be suffering from these maladies. American theater goers know about the Celtic Tiger, and though they might not fully understand the social and economic impact of Polish immigration on contemporary Ireland, the people in these theater audiences have most likely figured out that the spinning wheel in the corner of the Irish home, replaced by the television and its foreign soap opera fare in *Beauty Queen,* has been updated to an iMac. It is false and lazy for Irish journalists and cultural commentators to discuss the difference in theatrical audiences at home and abroad and their differing expectations in terms that imply otherwise.

I would suggest this—that the Irish Play as conceived or understood abroad is not a relic, but it may be a totem. In an era of rapidly changing technologies, bombardment of information, international unrest, shifting populations, and deterioration of public conduct and private mores, people are often exposed against their will to rather more than they want to be and often to artistic output or entertainment that is not particularly to their tastes. Perhaps the Irish Play is a bulwark, a defense, an identity or boundary marker, totemic of an ethos that is remembered in western culture and which, in the English language world, is perceived to have been last manifest in Ireland. This is a perception that is only partially defensible, but there could be a very valuable knock-on effect deriving from the appeal of Irish plays which feature traditional values and are written in a traditional format.

After looking at the factors that made the Irish Play successful in mainstream theaters in the United States, one can respond to Fintan O'Toole's question. Yes, if the single author of Irish plays, the literary model for Irish theater that has been such a success, is threatened with extinction, there is perhaps something to worry about in the Irish theater. However, contemporary Irish theater is far more than this answer suggests.

One must discuss the other strands in the diasporic reception of Irish plays—strands that even now provide the artistic scope and appropriate venues for the work of many Irish playwrights who do not fit the larger export mode of the classic Irish Play. Marina Carr, Donal O'Kelly, Tom Kilroy, and Tom Murphy's plays are performed often enough in United States provincial repertory companies of good standing, and these companies are largely kept going by ardent subscribers. They thrive in such smaller metropolitan areas as

San Jose, Minneapolis and Princeton. Newer Irish plays also appear in small fringe and alternative venues. In large part the appeal for fringe and alternative companies is that of the gritty urban themes and postmodern treatments of violence, drug addiction, and the slacker life which inform the work of young Irish playwrights such as Mark O'Rowe and Edna Walsh. Theirs is not fundamentally an Irish appeal, in fact sometimes Irish elements in the script are stripped out or downplayed in American productions. Lesser plays by better-known playwrights often are attractive for the same reasons—plays such as *This Lime Tree Bower* or *St. Nicholas,* both by Conor McPherson, neither of which needs to be played very "Irish."

Apart from fringe and alternative venues, there are also Irish special interest theater groups in Boston, New York, Washington, and Pittsburgh, to name a few—and there are only a few. These companies have been created largely to showcase new Irish playwriting talent in the United States, and many of them operate on shoestrings and disappear too often. In Washington we have Solas Nua, who have very recently made it their mission to introduce newer Irish works to Washington audiences in small warehouse spaces in the city, something which the city has experienced in years past but audiences always welcome. Scena Theatre also has a fairly established reputation for Beckett productions and mounts lesser-known plays by McPherson, Kilroy, and other contemporary Irish playwrights; Woolly Mammoth had a recent remounting of the Gigli Concert, a revival of its own earlier production. It is helpful for these smaller and under-funded companies that the newest of Irish plays share a quality common to new plays everywhere. They are usually plays for only two to four people, and require minimal sets and costuming.

The connection with these smaller, nontraditional Irish artistic offerings staged for the benefit of United States audiences and the overarching traditional concept of the Irish Play is quite simple. If major Irish lyric playwrights of the traditional mode had not originally attracted large-scale popular interest in the Irish theater among American audiences in recent decades, there would have been no entrée for the newer, less traditional playwrights and their themes. Irish plays enjoying well-deserved outings in American fringe and regional theaters in recent times are the beneficiaries of trickle down effect from the major hits with their traditional themes and aspirations. So while some of the theatrical community can get rather uppity at times about something like the *Dancing at Lughnasa* phenomenon, the wisest among them will be grateful. For every *Lughnasa* production American playgoers are exposed to, another Irish writer, another Irish play, gets a toehold on an American small stage.

It would be a pity indeed to see the single-authored literary Irish play, complete with its hallmark lyricism and its promulgation of traditional mores, its spiritual tinges and acceptable comedic frame, go the way of the music hall or the melodrama, but I do not seeing this happening any time soon. There is much to recommend the genre on its own—but I would also hope that overseas reception of Irish plays will grow and change, bringing mainstream America audiences beyond the generic.

Notes

Bibliography

Index

Notes

Abbreviations

AG   (Lady) Augusta Gregory
BF   Brian Friel
JQ   John Quinn
NLI MS National Library of Ireland manuscript
NYPL   New York Public Library
WBY   William Butler Yeats

Introduction

1. Transcript, Belinda McKeon and Joseph Hurley, "Press Perspectives," *Irish Theater in America: Third Annual Conference of Irish Theatrical Diaspora*, New York Univ., 28 Apr. 2006.

2. Seamus Deane, introduction to *Selected Plays of Brian Friel* (Washington, D.C.: Catholic Univ. of America Press, 1984), 16.

3. Nicholas Grene and Chris Morash, eds., "Introduction: Theatre and Diaspora," in *Irish Theatre on Tour* (Dublin: Carysfort Press, 2005), xiv, citing S. E. Wilmer, ed., introduction to *Writing and Rewriting National Theatre Histories* (Iowa City: Univ. of Iowa Press, 2004), 18.

4. Robert Welch, *The Abbey Theatre, 1899–1999* (Oxford: Oxford Univ. Press, 1999), 61.

5. Grene and Morash, xiv.

6. See http://www.irishtheatricaldiaspora.org/fellowships.html.

7. Fintan O'Toole, *The Ex-Isle of Ireland* (Dublin: New Island Books, 1997), 20–21.

8. John P. Harrington, "The Abbey in America: The Real Thing," in *Irish Theatre on Tour*, ed. Nicholas Grene and Chris Morash (Dublin: Carysfort Press, 2005), 47.

9. Mick Moloney, *McNally's Row of Flats: Irish American Songs of Old New York by Harrigan and Braham* (Nashville: Compass Records, 2006).

2. From Scapegrace to Grásta: Popular Attitudes and Stereotypes in Irish American Drama

1. Nicholas Grene, *The Politics of Irish Drama: Plays in Context from Boucicault to Friel* (Cambridge: Cambridge Univ. Press, 1999), 264. The phenomenon of Irish drama as a

commodity of international currency has a counterpart in prefamine fiction, which like Irish drama was valued for its "otherness." The heroes of Maria Edgeworth's *The Absentee* and *Ormonde* and Gerald Griffin's *The Collegians* visit their estates or return home after a period away and meet an old family retainer or local character who interprets the native culture to the protagonist at the same time as he interprets it to the reader.

2. Describing his experience becoming an American citizen, Roger Cohen wrote, "The United States is about the endless possibility of self-reinvention through hard work. It is inseparable from change. When I became an American citizen last year, I was given a short English test in the form of a dictation. The first sentence was, 'I want to be a good American.' The second was 'I plan to work hard every day.'"

3. Asenath Nicholson, *Ireland's Welcome to the Stranger, or Excursions Through Ireland in 1844,* ed. Maureen Murphy (Dublin: Lilliput Press, 2004), 257.

4. Part of the discussion of history of Irish American drama is material previously published in Maureen Murphy, "Irish-American Theater," *Ethnic Theater in the United States,* ed. Maxine Schwartz Seller (Westport: Greenwood Press, 1983) 221–37. William Philip's *St. Stephen's Green: or, the Generous Lover* (1699 or 1700) was the first Smock Alley production set in Dublin, but it was Charles Shadwell's Squire Dandle's speech about his maid in *The Hasty Wedding* that first urged the Irish to take pride in their heritage: "It is not above two years ago, sure she was taken out of an Irish Cabin, with her Brogues on, and yet begins to despise her own Country, and is fond of everything that's English." William Smith Clark, *The Early Irish Stage: The Beginnings to 1720* (Oxford: Clarendon Press, 1955), 159.

5. Caoimhín Ó Danachair lists several studies of Irish mummers' plays in *A Bibliography of Irish Ethnology and Folk Tradition* (Dublin: Mercier Press, 1977), 42. The best source is Alan Gailey's *Irish Folk Drama* (Cork: Mercier Press, 1969). A survival of mummers' plays was collected by the American folklorist Marie Campbell in Kentucky in the 1930s. Marie Campbell, "Survival of Old Folk Drama in the Kentucky Mountains, in *Buying the Wind,* ed. R. M. Dorson (Chicago: Univ. of Chicago Press, 1964), 215–33.

6. Seán O'Súilleabháin, *Irish Wake Amusements* (Cork: Mercier Press, 1967), 89–90.

7. Maurice Bourgeois, *John Millington Synge and the Irish Theater* (London: Constable, 1913), 109–10. See also J. O. Bartley, *Teague, Shenkin and Sawney* (Cork: Cork Univ. Press, 1954) and George C. Duggan, *The Stage Irishman: A History of the Irish Play and Stage Characters from the Earliest Times* (London: Longmans, 1937).

8. Margaret G. Maryoga, *A Short History of the American Drama* (New York: Dodd, Mead and Co., 1943), 247.

9. William Carson, *The Theater on the Frontier* (New York: Benjamin Blom, 1932), 202, 289, 297, 303, 313; Joseph Gaer. ed. *The Theater of the Gold Rush Decade in San Francisco* (New York: Burt Franklin, 1970), 30–31. In addition to the stage Irish plays, plays about Irish history such as H. P. Grattan's *The White Boys: A Romantic Drama* (1836) was first performed earlier in the year as *Rebel Chief.* Another play of the 1830s was William Bayle Bernard's two-act farce, *The Nervous Man or Man of Nerve.* An anonymous commentator described the hero McShane as "an Emeralder of the first water; his confusion of meum and tuem is carried to the utmost limit of Hibernian imagination, he takes a man's place in the mail, seizes possession of his friend's estate, reduces tenant's rents, invites the country

to a series of entertainments and gives away a friend's daughter with the most consummate impudence."

10. Joseph Jefferson, *Autobiography of Joseph Jefferson,* ed. Alan S. Downer (1890; reprint, Cambridge, Mass.: Harvard Univ. Press, 1964), 315. John P. Harrington noted the *New York Herald*'s praise Brougham for "his efforts to elevate the Irish character and help to dispel the prejudice which exists upon our fellow citizens of Irish birth." "Irish Theater," in *An Encyclopedia of the Irish in America,* ed. Michael Glazier. (South Bend: Univ. of Notre Dame Press, 1999), 900.

11. Written in pen on cover of National Library of Ireland copy of *Po-co-hon-tas* is the note "Afterpiece performed as 'La Belle Sauvage' after *She Stoops to Conquer* at the opening of the Gaiety Theater, Dublin in 1872." The lines quoted are from the acting edition of the play published by in New York by Samuel French (n.d.)

12. John Brougham, "Po-co-hon-tas, or the Gentle Savage," in *Drama from the American Theater (1762–1909),* ed. Richard Moody (Cleveland: World, 1966), 3, 8, 12.

13. Earl F. Niehaus, *The Irish in New Orleans, 1800–1860* (Baton Rouge: Louisiana State Univ. Press, 1965), 124–25.

14. Richard Dorson discovered Mose and numbered him among America's authentic folk heroes. See "Mose the Far-Famed and World Renown," *American Literature* 15 (Mar. 1943-Jan. 1944), 288–300.

15. Walt Whitman, "Song of Myself," *Leaves of Grass: Inclusive Edition* (New York: Doubleday, Doran, 1928), 70–71.

16. Joann Krieg, *Whitman and the Irish* (Iowa City: Univ. of Iowa Press, 2000), 60.

17. Dunne's Mr. Dooley describes the Bridgeport fireman Mike Clancy's last fight when Clancy dies trapped under a falling wall. Finley Peter Dunne, "The Popularity of Firemen," in *Mr. Dooley and the Chicago Irish: An Anthology,* ed. Charles Fanning (New York: Arno Press, 1976), 161–65. In recent years, Mose had another incarnation in Dennis Smith's *Report from Engine Company 82* (1972), and in his fire-fighter novels *The Final Fire* (1975), *Glitter and Ash* (1980) and *Steely Blue* (1984). The New York Irish fire fighter is one of the iconic figures of the rescue attempt of people trapped in the Twin Towers on 9/11.

18. Richard Fawkes, *Dion Boucicault: A Biography* (London: Quartet Books, 1979), 109.

19. Jefferson, 108.

20. The first Fenian attempt to invade Canada occurred on 1 June 1866, and the Clerkenwell and Manchester episodes followed in English in 1867. Thomas D'Arcy McGee, who opposed Fenianism, was assassinated in Canada in 1868; he was Canada's first political martyr. There was a second unsuccessful Fenian attempt to invade Canada in 1870.

21. Dion Boucicault,"Arragh-na-Pogue," *The Dolmen Boucicault,* ed. David Krause (Dublin: Dolmen Press, 1964), 115.

22. Boucicault borrowed Dan the Fireman in *The Poor of New York* from the figure of Mose.

23. There are parallels to these characters in prefamine fiction, notably Myles na gCopaleen in Gerald Griffin's *The Collegians* (1829).

24. Anne Nichol's popular *Abie's Irish Rose* (1937), based on the author's 1927 novel, offers a comic example of the tensions among families of inter-faith couples who marry.

Abraham Levy and Rose-Mary Murphy meet in the common ground of World War I France and marry after the war. The comedy turns on the humor of two ethnic groups when the Yiddish dialect meets English, their misunderstandings, and their resolution through the convention of twin grandchildren. It was made into a popular film in 1946.

25. Harrigan's plays were widely admired in their time. William Dean Howells, the American novelist, saw in the New York plays the beginning of American comedy. William Dean Howells, "Editor's Study," *Harper's,* July 1886, 315–16.

26. Irish American politics featured in fiction as well as drama. There are a number of Irish American political novels, the best of which is Edwin O'Connor's *The Last Hurrah* (1956).

27. There was not a corresponding Irish political drama until recently: Marina Carr's *Ariel* (2002) with its debt to *Iphigenigia in Aulis* where the protagonist Fermoy Fitzgerald sacrifices his daughter to satisfy his political ambition, and Sebastian Barry's *Hinterland* (2002) based on the personal and political downfall of Charles Haughey.

28. Donnelly wrote about contemporary American politics: *'84, a Political Revelation. A Political Prophesy: Proceeds of the Republican and Democratic Conventions of 1884 That Nominated Blaine and Butler* and *The Coming Empire, a Political Satire by Americus Free* (1900), a satire on American imperialism.

29. In fact, there was no election in Brooklyn in 1890, the year the Brooklyn Dodgers played their first baseball game (19 Apr. 1890). Alfred Clark Chapin (1848–1936) served as Mayor from 1888 to 1891. Alfred said that Staunton was based on a member of his family who did, in fact, throw his Kathleen down the stairs. Alfred's great aunt found him with the dead woman in his arms. She led him over the rooftops to his saloon, returned herself across the roof, walked down to the saloon, and announced that Kathleen had fallen down stairs. While he beat the rap, he was full of remorse and became self-destructive and eventually mad. *Hogan's Goat* opened American Place Theater on 11 Nov. 1965. A musical version of the play with the title *Cry for Us All,* the curtain line of *Hogan's Goat,* ran for only one week in Apr. 1970.

30. William Alfred, *Hogan's Goat* (New York: Farrar, Straus and Giroux, 1966), 136.

31. Ibid., 138, 142.

32. The play opened at the Savoy on 4 Dec. 1906. The play was later adapted and revised by Harry F. Vickery as *Man of the Hour.*

33. The Metropolitan St. Railroad fraud led reformist Seth Low, the reformist mayor of Brooklyn (1882–86), to seek and win election as mayor of New York in 1901. He defeated the Tammany candidate.

34. Other plays about loyalty and politics include Edward Sheldon's *The Boss* (1911) and Emmet Lavery's *The First Legion* (1934), a play about church politics and the question of a young priest's loyalty to his superior about a whether a miracle has happened.

35. Lady Augusta Gregory, *Our Irish Theatre* (1913; reprint, New York: Oxford Univ. Press, 1972), 222.

36. Maryoga credits Yeats's visit to America in 1903–4 with inspiring a group of New Yorkers under the direction of Joseph I. C. Clarke "to promote a movement for the endowment of an arts theater." Montrose J. Moses attributes the establishment of Mrs. Lynn W. Gale's little theater in Boston directly to the Abbey tour. Beginning in 1915, the works of Irish playwrights

Lord Dunsany (Edward John Morton Plunkett), George Bernard Shaw, W. B. Yeats, and James Joyce were produced under the direction of Helen Arthur, Agnes Morgan, and Alice and Irene Lewisohn at the Neighborhood Playhouse on Grand Street in New York City. Alice Lewisohn Crowley, *The Neighborhood Playhouse* (New York: Theater Arts Books, 1959), 61.

37. John Henry Raleigh,"O'Neill's *Long Day's Journey into Night* and New England Irish Catholicism," *O'Neill: A Collection of Critical Essays,* ed. John Gassner (Englewood Cliffs: Prentice Hall, 1964), 125.

38. Some 188,346 families were served with eviction notices or actually evicted between 1846 and 1854.

39. Eugene O'Neill, *Long Day's Journey into Night* (New Haven: Yale Univ. Press, 1956), 148.

40. Frank Gilroy, *The Subject Was Roses* (New York: Random House, 1965), 192.

41. Alfred, 13.

42. Their Irish counterparts use music and dance as well, nowhere with more success than Brian Friel in *Dancing at Lughnasa* (1990).

43. Delanty's poems allude to Máirtín Ó Direáin's poems from his first collection *Rogha Dánta* (1949): "Coinnle ar Lasta" and "Cuireadh do Mhuire."

44. Greg Delanty, "To President Mary Robinson," *American Wake* (Belfast: Blackstaff Press, 1995), 12.

45. Antoine O'Flatharta, *Grásta I Meiriceá* (Indreabhán: Cló Iar-Chonnachta, 1990), 60.

46. Ibid., 23.

47. Ibid., 41.

48. Ibid., 56.

49. Shanley's successful other plays are *Danny and the Deep Blue Sea, Women of Manhattan, The Dreamer Examines His Pillow, Italian American Reconciliation, Four Dogs and a Bone, and Sailor's Song.* Shanley won an Academy Award for the screenplay for *Moonstruck* (1987). He directed the film *Joe Versus the Volcano,* a blend of satire, comedy, melodrama, romance connected with existentialists.

50. Michael Portaniere and Matthew Murray, "Second to Nun: *Doubt* Wins Pulitzer Prize," *Theatre News* 4 Apr. 2005. http://www.theatermania.com/content/news.cfm/story/5867.

3. Ireland Rearranged: Contemporary Irish Drama and the Irish American Stage

1. Anthony Roche, "Against Nostalgia: The Year in Irish Theater, 1989," *Éire-Ireland* 24, no. 4 (1989): 114.

2. Fintan O'Toole, "Irish Theater: The State of the Art," in *Theater Stuff: Critical Essays on Contemporary Irish Theater,* ed. Eamonn Jordan (Dublin: Carysfort Press, 2000), 47–58.

3. Declan Hughes, "Who the Hell Do We Think We Still Are? Reflections on Irish Theater and Identity," in *Theater Stuff: Critical Essays on Contemporary Irish Theater,* ed. Eamonn Jordan (Dublin: Carysfort Press, 2000): 8, 13.

4. Irish Repertory Theatre, http://www.irishrep.org.

5. Ciarán O'Reilly, e-mail message to author, 18 Apr. 2006.

6. Ibid.

7. The quotes in this and the next paragraph are from Súgán's Web site, http://home. earthlink.net/~poreill47/about_us.htm.

8. Solas Nua, http://www.solasnua.org/about.html.

9. Linda Murray, e-mail message to author, 19 Apr. 2006.

10. Ibid.

11. Ibid.

12. Ibid.

13. O'Toole, "Irish Theater," 51.

4. Between Two Worlds: Boucicault's *The Shaughraun* and Its New York Audience

1. George C. D. Odell, *Annals of the New York Stage,* vol. 9 (1870–1875) (New York: Columbia Univ. Press, 1937), 522.

2. Elizabeth Butler Cullingford, *Ireland's Others: Ethnicity and Gender in Irish Literature and Popular Culture* (Cork: Cork Univ. Press, 2001), 27.

3. *Irish World,* 20 Feb. 1875, 6.

4. *Era,* 28 Mar. 1875, 10.

5. *New York Times,* 15 Nov. 1874, 7.

6. *New York Daily Tribune, Evening Post, [New York] World, New York Times, New York Herald, Irish World.*

7. See James Paul Rodechko, *A Case Study of Irish-American Journalism, 1870–1913* (New York: Arno Press, 1976).

8. *Irish World,* 19 Dec. 1874, 3.

9. Kerby A. Miller, *Emigrants and Exiles: Ireland and the Irish Exodus to North America* (New York: Oxford Univ. Press, 1985), 534.

10. *Irish World,* 9 Jan. 1875, 6.

11. Ibid., 19 Dec. 1874, 3.

12. Gary A. Richardson, "The Greening of America: The Cultural Business of Dion Boucicault's *The Shaughraun,*" *American Drama* (Spring 1994): 1.

13. *Irish World,* 16 Jan. 1875, 6.

14. Ibid., 6 Feb. 1875, 6.

15. See the parallel discussion of the Boucicauct letter in Gwen Orel's essay in chapter 5.

16. Ibid.

17. *Irish World,* 13 Feb. 1875, 6.

18. Ibid.

19. Ibid.

20. Ibid., 19 Dec. 1874, 3.

21. Ibid., 20 Feb. 1875, 6.

22. Quoted in Lady Gregory, *Our Irish Theater* (Gerrards Cross: Colin Smythe, 1972), 20.

5. Reporting the Stage Irishman: Dion Boucicault in the Irish Press

1. Eileen McMahon, "The Irish-American Press," in *The Ethnic Press in the United States,* ed. Sally M. Miller (Westport, Conn.: Greenwood Press, 1987), 177. My descriptions of ethnic press are indebted to Sally M. Miller, Robert E. Park, and Eileen McMahon.

2. Richard Fawkes, *Dion Boucicault: A Biography* (London: Quartet Bookes, 1979), 21.

3. Ibid., 118.

4. Ibid., 114.

5. The *Celtic Monthly* in Feb. 1880, for example, ran a story called "Brentano and the Actors."

6. David Krause, ed., *The Dolmen Boucicault* (Dublin: Dolmen Press, 1963), 26.

7. Ibid., 115–16.

8. "Dion Bourcicault's [*sic*] Latest," review of *The Colleen Bawn, New York Freeman's Journal and Catholic Register,* 21 Apr. 1860, 1.

9. See McMahon for a fuller discussion of editor Patrick Lynch's affect on the *Irish-American.* Lynch brought the paper to the leading nationalist newspaper by the time of his death in 1857.

10. "The New Irish Drama," review of *The Colleen Bawn, Irish-American,* 21 Apr. 1860, 2.

11. "The Colleen Bawn," review of benefit, *Irish-American,* 19 May 1860, 2.

12. Fawkes, 170.

13. For more on the Fenians, see Patrick J. Quinlivan, "Hunting the Fenians: Problems in the Historiography of a Secret Organization," *The Creative Migrant,* ed. Patrick O'Sullivan (London: Leicester Univ. Press, 1994), 133–54.

14. L. Perry Curtis Jr., *Apes and Angels: The Irishman in Victorian Caricature* (Washington, D.C.: Smithsonian Institution Press, 1971), 45.

15. McMahon, 185.

16. Fawkes, 194.

17. John O'Daily, "Theatrical Misrepresentations of Ireland," *Irish World,* 19 Dec. 1874, 3.

18. E. Lamb, "The Irish Drama," *Irish World,* 9 Jan. 1875, 6.

19. Dion Boucicault, "Boucicault on Irish Caricatures," *Irish World,* 6 Feb. 1875, 6.

20. "Response to Letter of Dion Boucicault," *Irish World,* 6 Feb. 1875, 6. See the parallel discussion of the Boucicault letter in Deirdre McFeely's essay in chapter 4.

21. "Democrat," "Holding the Mirror Up to Nature" *Irish World,* 20 Feb. 1875, 6.

22. Algernon S. Sullivan, "A Testimonial to Dion Boucicault." *Irish World,* 20 Feb. 1875, 6.

23. Townsend Walsh, *The Career of Dion Boucicault* (New York: Dunlap Society, 1915), 139.

24. "Dion Boucicault," *Irish-American,* 13 Mar. 1875, 5.

25. Bronson Howard, "Old and New World Audiences," *Celtic Monthly,* Dec. 1874, 274.

26. M. H. F., "Boucicault's Home," *Celtic Monthly,* Jan. 1879, 73.

27. Editorial, *Celtic Monthly,* Jan. 1879, 93.

28. Notes, *Irish-American,* 15 Feb. 1879, 6.

29. Bartlett, President's Speech, Banquet of the Friendly Sons of St. Patrick. Delmonico's, 17 Mar. 1879. Compiled by Mr. J. Kelly, Stenographer, 3rd Civ. District Court (Archives Irish Historical Society, New York).

30. Editorial, *Celtic Monthly,* Nov. 1879, 375–76.

31. "Dion Boucicault's Death," *New York Freeman's Journal and Catholic Register,* 27 Sept. 1890, 7.

32. Joseph Curran, *Hibernian Green on the Silver Screen: The Irish and American Movies* (Westport, Conn.: Greenwood Press, 1989), 19. Ironically, the only one of Olcott's films to survive is one on the same subject as Boucicault's last failed Irish play—a film called *Bold Emmet*, which centered around a pair of hapless lovers involved in attempts to aid the martyred hero, reminiscent of Shaun and his sweetheart.

6. Kilkenny, Melbourne, New York: George Tallis and the Irish Theatrical Diaspora

1. "Sir George Tallis Looks Back", *Melbourne Herald,* 13 Nov. 1931.

2. For a photograph of the *Argus* offices see Patsy Adam Smith, *Victorian and Edwardian Melbourne from Old Photographs* (Sydney: John Ferguson, 1979), 7, photograph no. 9.

3. Michael Tallis and Joan Tallis, *The Silent Showman: Sir George Tallis, The Man Behind the World's Largest Entertainment Organization of the 1920s* (Kent Town, South Australia: Wakefield Press, 1999), 14.

4. Note, however, that the bulk of the J. C. Williamson papers, which are held at the National Library of Australia in Canberra, have yet to be catalogued.

5. For an ebullient but well-documented and well-illustrated account of the effects of the gold fields on the material culture of Melbourne, see Michael Cannon, *Melbourne after the Gold Rush* (Melbourne: Loch Haven Books, 1993).

6. "Sir George Tallis Looks Back." Unfortunately, George Tallis's contribution to *The J. C. Williamson Memorial: With Valedictory Notices from Partners or Associates, Portraits and Addenda* (ed. A. G. Stephens [Sydney: The Bookfellow, 1913], 41) does not contain any recollection of their first meeting.

7. For Williamson's own account of his acquisition and development of the play, see Stephens, 18ff.

8. Extract from the *Sydney Morning Herald,* 27 Nov. 1880 quoted in Harold Love, *The Australian Stage: A Documentary History* (Sydney: New South Wales Press in association with Australian Theater Studies Centre, School of Drama, Univ. of New South Wales, 1984), 97–100.

9. See Love, 100–101, for extract from Nellie Stewart, *My Life's Story* (1923), 45–47, 65.

10. For a photograph taken in 1901 of the Princess Theatre, see Smith, 165, photograph 165.

11. Quoted in Tallis and Tallis, 25.

12. Love, 94.

13. Ibid., 104.

14. J. C. Williamson in Stephenson, 16, 20–21, gives an interesting account of working with Boucicault in California, staging *Arrah-na-Pogue* in London and the disputes over staging *The Shaughraun* at the Adelphi.

15. Cited as "Unsourced cutting from scrapbook owned by Mr Warren Mann, Melbourne" and quoted in Love, 102–6.

16. Ibid., 105: "The Theatre Royal in Melbourne will fairly accommodate £225. We opened on Saturday, 11th of July, to £280. Where the odd £55 was packed away is no concern of ours. We played seven weeks in this city, taking, gross, £8070, of which, of course, the lion's share went to the management. Mine, after paying salaries and travelling, was £2470. From all the sources we heard that this was the largest ever played to date in the colonies. It greatly

exceeded my expectations. Our best week was the first, in which the receipts were £1331. Our worst week was the second week of *The Colleen Bawn,* and the fifth of our engagement, when we encountered very wet weather. The receipts were £960."

17. Anonymous, *Leader,* 1874, quoted in Love, 95.

18. Cited as "Unsourced cutting from scrapbook owned by Mr Warren Mann, Melbourne" and quoted in Love, 104.

19. Ibid., 105.

20. Unsigned review in the *Australasian,* 21 Sept. 1889 quoted in Love, 107–8.

21. For Tallis's recollections of the Bernhardt tour, see the *Melbourne Herald,* 13 Nov. 1931. Tallis "supervised some of the arrangements for touring the great Sarah Bernhardt" (Tallis and Tallis, 38), but see also "Tallis was involved with the Bernhardt tour" (ibid., 43), which does not specify the nature or the extent of that involvement.

22. Henry Gyles Turner, *A History of the Colony of Victoria: From Its Discovery to Its Absorption into the Commonwealth of Australia in Two Volumes* (1904; reprint, Melbourne: Heritage Publications, 1973), vol. 2, 291–326.

23. Charles S. Cheltnam, ed., *The Dramatic Year Book for the Year Ending December 31st 1891* (London 1892), 614–16, in Love, 109–11.

24. Tallis and Tallis, 43.

25. Ibid., 59, 316–19.

26. Ibid., 67.

27. Tallis Manuscripts MS 9522 National Library of Australia Manuscript Collection, Sir George Tallis, Box 5.

28. Particularly valuable for staging Boucicault's *The Fires of New York.*

29. Tallis and Tallis, 111.

30. Ibid., 148.

31. Ibid., 103.

32. Ibid., 103.

33. *Punch* (Melbourne), 1913, quoted in Tallis and Tallis, 111.

34. Tallis and Tallis, 148.

35. *Sydney Mail,* Sept. 1926, cited in Tallis and Tallis, 192.

36. *Adelaide Advertiser,* 31 July 1929; Melbourne *Age,* 6 Aug. 1929. Quoted in Tallis and Tallis, 243.

7. The Abbey, Its "Helpers," and the Field of Cultural Production in 1913

1. W. B. Yeats, "The Pot of Broth," in *The Collected Plays of W. B. Yeats* (1934; reprint, London: Macmillan, 1972), 95, 96. The play was written by Gregory and Yeats together and is included in *Collaborative One-Act Plays, 1901–1903,* edited by James Pethica (Ithaca: Cornell Univ. Press, 2007). For all the citations to the Quinn Papers, thanks must be given to the Manuscripts and Archives Division of the New York Public Library.

2. R. F. Foster, *W. B. Yeats: A Life,* vol. 1, *The Apprentice Mage, 1865–1914* (New York: Oxford Univ. Press, 1997), 497–98, 620–21n14.

3. For the story of the gallery controversy, see Lucy McDiarmid, "Hugh Lane and the Decoration of Dublin, 1908–," *The Irish Art of Controversy* (Ithaca: Cornell Univ. Press, 2005), 10–49.

4. "The Abbey Players and the Dublin Art Gallery Fund. Opinion of the Solicitor General," typed copy (Jan. 1914) in Quinn Papers, New York Public Library. Lady Gregory sent Quinn all the documents related to the argument over the guarantee fund, and he had them typed and filed along with copies of his letters to her. The dispute over the funds raised in the United States by de Valera (1919) and Irish American committees (1919–1921) in order to support the Dáil Éireann government was similar in some respects: an Irish celebrity, political in the one case, cultural in the other, toured the United States and raised money from Irish Americans to support an Irish cause that at a later point did not have unanimous support in the home country. But the results of the later case were different: according to Francis M. Carroll, "The story of what happened to the money raised through the Bond-Certificates has never been fully told. Roughly half of the funds were sent to Ireland, and a proportion of that was spent by the Dáil; the remainder stayed in New York banks. After the Civil War started in Ireland in 1922, the Free State government instituted lawsuits in Ireland and the United States in order to obtain possession of the money. In Ireland the courts awarded the money to the government, but the New York courts held that neither the Free State government nor the Republicans qualified for the money, and in 1927 it was ordered that the money be given back to the Bond-Certificate holders." Francis M. Carroll, "Eamon de Valera and the Irish Bond-Certificate Drive, 1919–1921," in *James Joyce and His Contemporaries,* ed. Diana A. Ben-Merre and Maureen Murphy (Westport, Conn,: Greenwood Press, 1989), 168n20.

5. Adrian Frazier, *Behind the Scenes: Yeats, Horniman, and the Struggle for the Abbey Theatre* (Berkeley: Univ. of California Press, 1990).

6. Pierre Bourdieu, *The Field of Cultural Production,* ed. and intro. Randal Johnson (New York: Columbia Univ. Press, 1993), 37.

7. Ibid., 37.

8. Ibid.

9. Lady Augusta Gregory, *Our Irish Theatre* (1913; reprint, New York: Oxford Univ. Press, 1972).

10. AG to WBY, 22 Jan. 1914. Typed copy, Quinn Papers, NYPL.

11. AG, "Enclosure in WBY's of December 10." Typed copy, Quinn Papers, NYPL.

12. Ibid.

13. Baker was later the mentor of Eugene O'Neill. One of two founders of Harvard's theater collection, he taught in the English Department from 1888 to 1924 and started a playwriting workshop in 1906. Unable to persuade Harvard to offer a degree in playwriting, he moved to Yale University in 1925, where he helped found the Yale School of Drama.

14. Ibid.

15. *Chicago Tribune,* 30 Jan. 1912, 9; 31 Jan. 1912, 14; 3 Feb. 1912, 6; 12 Feb. 1912, 8.

16. Ibid., 22 Jan. 1913, 9.

17. Ibid., 15 Jan. 2002, 15.

18. See http://www.college.harvard.edu/student/houses/histories/index.html.

19. See *Chicago Tribune,* 19 Aug. 1908, 13. Thus Mrs. Judge Kavanagh was already part of the field of production of Irish diasporic culture before she became one of the "helpers."

20. Ibid., 22 Jan. 1913, 9.

21. See http://www.poetrymagazine.org/magazine/1210/1210_notes.html.

22. Carol Duncan, *Civilizing Rituals: Inside Public Art Museums* (London: Routledge, 1995).

23. *Chicago Tribune,* 5 Jan. 1913, A2; 5 Jan. 1913.

24. Ibid., 9 Jan. 1913, 6.

25. Abbey Players to AG, 7 Nov. 1913. Typed copy, Quinn Papers, NYPL.

26. AG to Abbey Players, 15 Nov. 1913. Typed copy, Quinn Papers, NYPL.

27. Abbey Players to AG, 18 Nov. 1913. Typed copy, Quinn Papers, NYPL.

28. Abbey Players to AG, 4 Dec. 1913. Typed copy, Quinn Papers, NYPL.

29. WBY to AG, 21 Jan. 1913. Typed copy, Quinn Papers, NYPL.

30. AG to WBY, 22 Jan. 1913. Typed copy, Quinn Papers, NYPL.

31. See note 4.

32. *Times Literary Supplement,* AG to Sydney Pawling, 5 Jan. 1914. Berg Collection, NYPL; AG to JQ, 20 Jan. 1914. Typed copy, Quinn Papers, NYPL. Adrian Frazier, *George Moore, 1852–1933* (London: Yale Univ. Press, 2000), 369.

33. See Lucy McDiarmid, "A Box for Wilfrid Blunt," *PMLA* 120, no. 1 (Jan. 2005), 163–80.

34. WBY to AG, ALS, postmarked 12 Jan. 1914, Berg Collection, NYPL.

8. Mac Liammóir's *The Importance of Being Oscar* in America

1. Eric Bentley, "Irish Theater: Splendeurs et Misères," *Poetry* 53 (Jan. 1952): 217.

2. See Phyllis Ryan, *The Company I Kept* (Dublin: Town House, 1996).

3. Micheál Mac Liammóir, *Theater in Ireland,* rev. ed. (Dublin: At the Sign of the Three Candles, 1964), 55.

4. Hilton Edwards to Micheál Mac Liammóir, 30 Aug. 1957, Gate Theatre Archive, Northwestern Univ.

5. Ibid.

6. Christopher Fitz-Simon, *The Boys: A Biography of Micheál MacLíammóir and Hilton Edwards* (London: Nick Hern, 1994), 215.

7. Micheál Ó hAodha, *The Importance of Being Micheál: A Portrait of Mac Liammóir* (Dingle, Kerry: Brandon, 1990), 159.

8. Hilton Edwards to Samuel Beckett, 9 Oct. 1956. Gate Theater Archive, Northwestern Univ. Correspondence box 4, folder 1. Beckett offered Edwards *All That Fall.* After plans for this production fell through, he wrote to Hilton Edward's secretary: "I greatly regret this, but hope I may have the honour at some future time, with this piece or with another, of a Hilton Edwards production" (Samuel Beckett to Miss [Pam] Pyer, Jan. 7, 1956 [*sic,* 1957]; Gate Theater Archive, correspondence, box 4, folder 1a.

9. Hilton Edwards, introduction to *The Importance of Being Oscar* (Dublin: Dolmen, 1963), 8. Subsequent references in the text refer to this edition.

10. St. John Ervine, *Oscar Wilde: A Present Time Appraisal* (London: Allen and Unwin, 1951), 285. Mac Liammóir would surely have been aware of the existence of this biography since he immersed himself in studying Wilde. In 1930, the Gate paired the Irish premiere of Ervine's *The Lady of Belmont* with a production of *The Merchant of Venice.*

11. Fitz-Simon, 217–18.

12. Mac Liammóir's performance was recorded in 1961 and released as an LP by CBS.

13. Owen Dudley Edwards, "Impressions of an Irish Sphinx," *Wilde the Irishman,* ed. Jerusha McCormack (New Haven: Yale, 1998), 56.

14. *All for Hecuba: An Exhibition to Mark the Golden Jubilee of the Edwards–Mac Liammóir Partnership and of the Gate Theater, 1928–1978* (Dublin: Hugh Lane, 1978).

15. In his introduction, Hilton Edwards writes that Mac Liammóir realized "what a distinguished dramatic critic has best described as: 'a new form: oral biography'" (5).

16. Ibid., 10.

17. Unless otherwise cited, all of the reviews quoted, provided by a clipping service, are collected in the scrapbooks in the Gate Theater Archive.

18. John McCarten, "Turbid Aquarium," *New Yorker,* 25 Mar. 1961, 114.

19. Éibhear Walshe, "Sodom and Begorrah, or Game to the Last," *Sex, Nation and Dissent,* ed. Éibhear Walshe (Cork: Cork Univ. Press, 1997), 153.

20. Noel Coward, *Bitter Sweet in Play Parade* (Garden City, N.Y.: Garden City Publishing, 1924), 341.

21. Hellman's play premiered on Broadway at the Maxine Elliott Theater on 20 Nov. 1934 and ran for 691 performances, more than eighteen months. In 1936, William Wyler, who also directed the 1961 film, released *These Three,* a sanitized adaptation of *The Children's Hour* that erased any suggestion of homosexuality and instead used a heterosexual romance as the object of rumor. Drury's novel was adapted for the stage by Loring Mandel and ran from 17 Nov. 1960 until 20 June 1961 at the Cort Theater. Gore Vidal's *The Best Man* also began as a successful Broadway play, opening on 30 Mar. 1960 and running until 8 July 1961.

22. See G. Tom Poe, "Secrets, Lies and Cold War Politics: 'Making Sense' of Otto Preminger's *Advise and Consent,*" *Film History* 8 (1996): 332–45.

23. *An Oscar of No Importance* (London: Heinemann, 1968), 125. Subsequent references given in the text.

24. Ó hAodha, 164.

25. Richard Ellmann, *Oscar Wilde* (New York: Knopf, 1984), 589.

26. See, for instance, Peter Ackroyd, *The Last Testament of Oscar Wilde* (London: Hamish Hamilton, 1983) and Alan Sinfield, *The Wilde Century* (London: Cassell, 1994).

9. Beckett and America

1. Associated Press. "Coconut Grove Theater That Ushered in 'Godot' Designated Landmark," *Gainesville Sun,* 6 Oct. 2005.

2. Dirk van Hulle, *Beckett the European* (Tallahassee: Journal of Beckett Studies Books, 2005), 2.

3. James Knowlson, *Damned to Fame: The Life of Samuel Beckett* (New York: Simon and Schuster, 1996), 467.

4. Pascale Casanova, *The World Republic of Letters.* Trans. M. B. DeBeuoise (Cambridge, Mass., Harvard Univ. Press, 2004), 109, 110.

5. Alan Schneider, *Entrances: An American Director's Journey* (New York: Limelight Editions, 1987), 229.

6. Arthur Gelb, "Wanted: 70,000 Playgoing Intellectuals," *New York Times*, 15 Apr. 1956, sec. 2, pp. 1, 3.

7. Harold Clurman, "Theatre," *Nation*, 5 May 1956, 390.

8. Patricia O'Haire, "Beckett Still Writing, Still Waiting," *New York Daily News*, 3 Nov. 1988. Clippings, Billy Rose Theater Collection, New York Public Library.

9. Michael Feingold, "Funny about Samuel Beckett," *Village Voice*, 23 July 1996, 31.

10. Kenneth Rexroth, "Samuel Beckett and the Importance of Waiting," in *Bird in the Bush: Obvious Essays* (New York: New Directions, 1959); reprint, http://www.bopsecrets. org/research.

11. Mel Gussow, "Beckett, as a Beckettian, Isn't Always the Purist," *New York Times*, 16 Nov. 1988, C21, C26.

12. Ryan Plocher, "In Godot, Existential Despair Can Be Hilarious," *Emory Wheel*, 31 Jan. 2006. http://www.emorywheel.com/detail.php?n=18532.

13. Knowlson, 354.

14. Ibid., 608.

15. Frederick Neumann, interview, in *Beckett Remembering Beckett: A Centenary Celebration*, ed. James Knowlson and Elizabeth Knowlson (New York: Arcade Publishing, 2006), 242, 246.

16. Schneider, 357, 358.

17. Ibid., 363, 356.

18. Knowlson, 556.

19. Howard Skempton, "Beckett as Librettist," *Music and Musicians* (May 1977); reprint, http://www.cnvill.demon.co.uk/mfskmptn.htm.

20. Morton Feldman, *Morton Feldman Says: Selected Interviews and Lectures, 1964–1987*, ed. Chris Villars (London: Hyphen Press, 2006), 94.

21. Everett C. Frost, "Last Words on Music: An Interview," liner notes, *Words and Music*, Montage MO782145, 2001, 8–9.

22. Ibid., 11.

23. Peter Hall, "Godot Almighty," *Guardian*, 24 Aug. 2005; Conor McPherson, "Chronicles of the Human Heart," *Guardian* 1 Mar. 2005.

24. Kenneth S. Brecher, "Samuel Beckett: Private in Public," *New York Times* 12 June 1988, B18.

10. Another Look at Those "Three Bollocks in a Cell":
Someone Who'll Watch Over Me and the Shackles of History

1. In the early 1990s McGuinness was already widely celebrated in Ireland and Britain, having received the *London Evening Standard*'s Most Promising Playwright Award (among other prestigious awards) for his 1985 play, *Observe the Sons of Ulster Marching Towards the Somme*.

2. Frank Rich, *"Someone Who'll Watch Over Me:* Coping with Incarceration, or The Lighter Side of Beirut," *New York Times*, 26 Nov. 1992.

3. Linda Winer, "A Look at Hostages, Very Neat and Tidy," *Newsday*, 24 Nov. 1992, 39.

4. Helen Lojek, "Watching Over Frank McGuinness's Stereotypes," *Modern Drama* 38 (1995): 352–53.

5. Frank McGuinness, *Someone Who'll Watch Over Me* (London: Faber and Faber, 1992), 27. All citations to *Someone Who'll Watch Over Me* are from this edition.

6. In the Wimbledon scene, Edward even casts the now dead Adam in the role of the "umpire," whose job is to neutrally arbitrate disputes between the opposing players (43).

7. Circle Theater Press Release, http://www.circletheater.com/someone.htm.

8. Jim Kershner, "Capturing Hostages' Psychological Make-up," *Spokesman Review,* 8 Sept. 2005.

11. *Faith Healer* in New York and Dublin

1. Brian Friel papers, National Library of Ireland, NLI MS 37,080/4, letter from BF to Warren Brown, 30 Oct. 1975. Much of the information in this essay is gleaned from this outstandingly rich archive.

2. Ibid., letter from Michael Barnes to BF of 9 Mar. 1976.

3. Ibid., letter to Barnes from BF, 29 Sept. 1976.

4. NLI MS 37,075/8 contains a typescript of "The Game."

5. NLI MS 37,080/4, letter of Oscar Lewenstein to Sheila Lennon, 10 Mar. 1976.

6. Ibid., letter of Sheila Lennon to Oscar Lewenstein, 3 Mar. 1976.

7. See NLI MS 37,077/3 for these reviews of the Baltimore production.

8. See NLI MS 37,077/4 for all New York reviews cited here.

9. This account is based on two sources: a personal interview with Brian Friel, 30 Mar. 2006, and notes kept by the playwright at the time of the production, Brian Friel, *"Faith Healer* Comes to New York", *Princeton University Library Chronicle,* 68, no. 1–2 (Autumn 2006-Winter 2007), 516–18. I am most grateful to Mr. Friel for his generosity in sharing his memories of the production with me.

10. See NL MS 37,077/4 for both Boston and New York reviews cited here.

11. NLI MS 37,077/13.

12. NLI MS 37,077/4.

13. See NLI MS 37,077/5 for all material on the 1980 Abbey production cited here.

14. See NL MS 37,078/4 for a transcript of the radio interview with Richard Pine as well as other reviews of this Abbey revival.

15. Ulf Dantanus, *Brian Friel: A Study* (London: Faber, 1988), 172.

16. NLI MS 37,080/8.

17. Ibid., letter of BF to Michael Colgan, 14 Dec. 14, 1998.

18. Ibid., fax of Noel Pearson to BF, 24 Nov. 24 1999.

19. See http://www.imdb.com/name/nm0443420/.

12. "Dancing on a One-Way Street": Irish Reactions to *Dancing at Lughnasa* in New York

1. Karen Fricker, "Dancing Like It's 1990 in Eire," *Variety,* July 1999, 43.

2. Brian Friel, *Plays 2* (London: Faber and Faber, 1999), 68.

3. Comments about the productions of *Dancing at Lughnasa* arise from my attendance at performances of the Abbey production in 1991, 1993, 1999, and 2000 and from

viewing of videotaped performances of the 1990 and 2000 productions at the Abbey Theater Archive.

4. Central Statistics Office, Ireland (CSO). "Online Statistics": http://www.cso.ie.

5. Tony Coult, *About Friel: The Playwright and His Work* (London: Faber and Faber, 2003), 195–96.

6. Victoria White, "Towards a Post-Feminism?" *Theatre Ireland* 18 (Apr.-June 1989): 33–34.

7. Coult, 57.

8. Friel, *Plays 2,* 88.

9. Coult, 199.

10. Friel, *Plays 2,* 36–37.

11. Patrick Burke, "'As If Language No Longer Existed": Non-Verbal Theatricality in the Plays of Friel," in *Brian Friel: A Casebook,* ed. William Kerwin (New York: Garland Publishing, 1992), 19.

12. Coult, 149.

13. Anthony Roche, "Contemporary Drama in English, 1940–2000," in *The Cambridge History of Irish Literature,* vol. 2, ed. Margaret Kelleher and Philip O'Leary, (Cambridge: Cambridge Univ. Press, 2006), 645.

14. Alex Witchell, "Life May be a Madness, But It's Also a Poem," *New York Times,* 17 Oct. 1993, sec. 2, p. 5.

15. Photographs of the new building appeared on the front pages of both the *Irish Independent,* 13 Mar. 1990, 1, and the *Irish Times,* 13 Mar., 1.

16. Brian Friel, *Essays, Diaries, Interviews: 1964–1999,* ed. Christopher Murray (London: Faber and Faber, 1999), 104–5.

17. *Evening Press,* 25 Apr. 1990, 5. *Irish Independent,* 25 Apr. 1990, 11. *Guardian,* 1 May 1990, 22.

18. Fintan O'Toole, *Critical Moments* (Dublin: Carysfort Press, 2003), 95.

19. "The Abbey Stuns South Bank," *Sunday Independent,* 21 Oct. 1990; "Raves for Friel Play," *Irish Times,* 20 Oct. 1990; Julie Kavanagh, "Friel at Last," *Vanity Fair,* 21 Oct. 1991. The *Sunday Business Post* article appeared on 3 Nov. 1991. The figure quoted was inaccurate— the actual amount predicted was $75,000. The *Irish Times* readers' competition was held in Nov. 1991.

20. See, for example, *Irish Times,* 24 Nov. 1991, 1.

21. Princess Grace Irish Library PGIL-Eirdata, "Brian Friel", http://www.pgil-eirdata .org/html/pgil_datasets/authors/f/Friel,Brian/life.htm.

22. Brian Friel, *Molly Sweeney* (Oldcastle: Gallery Press, 1994), 31–32.

23. Christopher Murray (1997) and Fintan O'Toole (1997) both remark on the similarities between *The Glass Menagerie* and *Dancing at Lughnasa.*

24. Tennessee Williams, *The Glass Menagerie* (New York: New Directions, 1970), 23.

13. "The Irish Play": Beyond the Generic?

1. Nicholas Grene, *The Politics of Irish Drama: Plays in Context from Boucicault to Friel* (Cambridge: Cambridge Univ. Press, 1999), 261–81, and Anthony Roche, "Contemporary Irish Drama in English, 1940–2000" in *The Cambridge History of Irish Literature,* vol. 2,

1890–2000, ed. Margaret Kelleher and Philip O'Leary (Cambridge: Cambridge Univ. Press, 2006), 519–27.

2. Fintan O'Toole, "The Death of the Playwright," *Irish Times,* 21 Oct. 2005, and "Playing to a New World Order," *Irish Times,* 12 Dec. 2005, http://www.ireland.com.

3. O'Toole, "Playing to a New World Order."

Bibliography

Ackroyd, Peter. *The Last Testament of Oscar Wilde*. London: Hamish Hamilton, 1983.

Alfred, William. *Hogan's Goat*. New York: Farrar, Straus and Giroux, 1966.

All for Hecuba: An Exhibition to Mark the Golden Jubilee of the Edwards–Mac Liammóir Partnership and of the Gate Theater, 1928–1978. Dublin: Hugh Lane, 1978.

Associated Press. "Coconut Grove Theater That Ushered in 'Godot' Designated Landmark." *Gainesville Sun*, 6 Oct. 2005.

Bartlett. President's Speech. Banquet of the Friendly Sons of St. Patrick. Delmonico's, 17 Mar. 1879. Compiled by Mr. J. Kelly, Stenographer, 3rd Civ. District Court. Archives Irish Historical Society, New York.

Bartley, J. O. *Teague, Shinkin and Sawney*. Cork: Cork Univ. Press, 1954.

Bentley, Eric. "Irish Theater: Splendeurs et Misères," *Poetry* 53 (Jan. 1952): 216–32.

Boucicault, Dion. "Arragh-na-Pogue." *The Dolmen Boucicault*. Ed. David Krause. Dublin: Dolmen Press, 1964, 111–72.

———. "Boucicault on Irish Caricatures." *Irish World*, 6 Feb. 1875, 6.

———. *Plays by Dion Boucicault*. Ed. Peter Thompson. Cambridge: Cambridge Univ. Press, 1984, 133–69.

Bourdieu, Pierre. *The Field of Cultural Production*. Ed. and intro. Randal Johnson. New York: Columbia Univ. Press, 1993.

Bourgeois, Maurice. *John Millington Synge and the Irish Theater*. London: Constable, 1913.

Brecher, Kenneth S. "Samuel Beckett: Private in Public." *New York Times* 12 June 1988, B18.

"Brian Friel" PGIL-Eirdata (Princess Grace Irish Library), http://www.pgil-eirdata .org/html/pgil_datasets/authors/f/Friel,Brian/life.htm.

Bronson, Howard. "Old and New World Audiences." *Celtic Monthly*, Dec. 1874, 273–76.

Brougham, John. "Po-co-hon-tas, or the Gentle Savage," *Drama from the American Theater (1762–1909)*. Ed. Richard Moody. Cleveland: World, 1966, 397–421.

Burke, Patrick. "'As if Language no Longer Existed': Non-Verbal Theatricality in the Plays of Friel." In *Brian Friel: A Casebook*. Ed. William Kerwin. New York: Garland Publishing, 1992, 13–23.

Campbell, Marie. "Survival of Old Folk Drama in the Kentucky Mountains." In *Buying the Wind*. Ed. R. M. Dorson. Chicago: Univ. of Chicago Press, 1964, 215–33.

Cannon, Michael. *Melbourne after the Gold Rush*. Melbourne: Loch Haven Books, 1993.

Carroll, Francis M. *American Opinion and the Irish Question 1910–1923*. Dublin: Gill and Macmillan, 1978.

———. "Eamon de Valera and the Irish Bond-Certificate Drive, 1919–1921." In *James Joyce and His Contemporaries*. Ed. Diana A. Ben-Merre and Maureen Murphy. Westport, Conn.: Greenwood Press, 1989, 161–68.

Carson, William. *The Theater on the Frontier*. New York: Benjamin Blom, 1932.

Casanova, Pascale. *The World Republic of Letters*. Trans. M. B. DeBeoise. Cambridge, Mass.: Harvard Univ. Press, 2004.

Cheltnam, Charles S., ed. *The Dramatic Year Book for the Year Ending December 31st 1891*. London, 1892.

Clark, William Smith. *The Early Irish Stage: The Beginnings to 1720*. Oxford: Clarendon Press, 1955.

Clurman, Harold. "Theatre." *Nation*, 5 May 1956, 390.

Cohen, Roger. "Vive La Dolce Vita," *New York Times*, 16 Apr. 2006, 1, 4.

"The Colleen Bawn." Review of benefit. *Irish-American*, 19 May 1860, 2.

Coppa, Frank J., and Thomas J. Curran, eds. *The Immigrant Experience in America*. Boston: Twayne Publishers, 1976.

Coult, Tony. *About Friel: The Playwright and His Work*. London: Faber and Faber, 2003.

Coward, Noel. *Bitter Sweet in Play Parade*. Garden City, N.Y.: Garden City Publishing, 1924.

Crowley, Alice Lewisohn. *The Neighborhood Playhouse*. New York: Theater Arts Books, 1959.

Cullingford, Elizabeth Butler. *Ireland's Others: Ethnicity and Gender in Irish Literature and Popular Culture*. Cork: Cork Univ. Press, 2001.

Curran, Joseph. *Hibernian Green on the Silver Screen: The Irish and American Movies*. Westport, Conn.: Greenwood Press, 1989.

Curtis, L. Perry, Jr. *Apes and Angels: The Irishman in Victorian Caricature*. Washington, D.C.: Smithsonian Institution Press, 1971.

Dantanus, Ulf. *Brian Friel: A Study*. London: Faber and Faber, 1988.

Deane, Seamus, Introduction to *Selected Plays of Brian Friel*. Washington, D.C.: Catholic Univ. of America Press, 1984, 11–22.

Delanty, Greg. "To President Mary Robinson." *American Wake*. Belfast: Blackstaff Press, 1995.

"Democrat." "Holding the Mirror Up to Nature." *Irish World*, 20 Feb. 1875, 6.

"Dion Boucicault." *Irish-American*, 13 Mar. 1875, 5.

"Dion Boucicault's Death." *New York Freeman's Journal and Catholic Register*, 27 Sept. 1890, 7.

"Dion Boucicault's Latest." Review of *The Colleen Bawn*. *New York Freeman's Journal and Catholic Register*, 21 Apr. 1860, 2–3.

Dorson, Richard. "Mose the Far-Famed and World Renown." *American Literature* 15 (Mar. 1943-Jan. 1944), 288–300.

Duggan, George C. *The Stage Irishman: A History of the Irish Play and Stage Characters from the Earliest Times*. London: Longmans, Green and Co, 1937.

Duncan, Carol. *Civilizing Rituals: Inside Public Art Museums*. London: Routledge, 1995.

Dunne, Finley Peter. "The Popularity of Fireman." In *Mr. Dooley and the Chicago Irish: An Anthology*. Ed. Charles Fanning. New York: Arno Press, 1976, 161–65.

Editorial. *Celtic Monthly*, Jan. 1879, 93.

Editorial. *Celtic Monthly*, Nov. 1879, 375–76.

Edwards, Hilton. Introduction to *The Importance of Being Oscar*. Dublin: Dolmen, 1963, 5–12.

Edwards, Owen Dudley. "Impressions of an Irish Sphinx." *Wilde the Irishman*. Ed. Jerusha McCormack. New Haven: Yale, 1998, 47–70.

———. "The Stage Irish." *The Creative Migrant*. Ed. Patrick O'Sullivan. London: Leicester Univ. Press, 1994, 83–115.

———. "The Stage Irish." *The Creative Migrant*. Ed. Patrick O'Sullivan. London: Leicester Univ. Press, 1994, 83–115.

Ellmann, Richard. *Oscar Wilde*. New York: Knopf, 1984.

Ervine, St. John. *Oscar Wilde: A Present Time Appraisal*. London: Allen and Unwin, 1951.

Fawkes, Richard. *Dion Boucicault: A Biography*. London: Quartet Books, 1979.

Feingold, Michael. "Funny About Samuel Beckett." *Village Voice*, 23 July 1996, 31.

Feldman, Morton. *Morton Feldman Says: Selected Interviews and Lectures, 1964–1987*. Ed. Chris Villars. London: Hyphen Press, 2006.

Finson, Jon W., ed. *Edward Harrigan and David Braham: Collected Songs, 1873–1882*. Recent Researches in American Music. Madison: American Musicological Society, 1997.

Fitz-Simon, Christopher. *The Boys: A Biography of Micheál MacLíammóir and Hilton Edwards.* London: Nick Hern, 1994.

Foner, Eric. *Politics and Ideology in the Age of the Civil War.* Oxford: Oxford Univ. Press, 1980.

Foster, R. F. *W. B. Yeats: A Life.* Vol. 1, *The Apprentice Mage, 1865–1914.* New York: Oxford Univ. Press, 1997.

Franceschina, John. *David Braham: The American Offenbach.* New York: Routledge, 2002.

Frazier, Adrian. *Behind the Scenes: Yeats, Horniman, and the Struggle for the Abbey Theatre.* Berkeley: Univ. of California Press, 1990.

———. *George Moore, 1852–1933.* London: Yale Univ. Press, 2000.

Fricker, Karen. "Dancing Like It's 1990 in Eire." *Variety,* 12–18 July 1999, 5.

Friel, Brian. *Essays, Diaries, Interviews: 1964–1999.* Ed. Christopher Murray. London: Faber and Faber, 1999.

———. "*Faith Healer* Comes to New York." *Princeton University Library Chronicle* 68, no. 1–2 (Autumn 2006-Winter 2007): 516–18.

———. *Molly Sweeney.* Oldcastle: Gallery Press, 1994.

———. *Plays 2.* London: Faber and Faber, 1999.

Frost, Everett C. "Last Words on Music: An Interview." Liner notes, Words and Music, Montage MO782145, 2001.

Gaer, Joseph, ed. *The Theater of the Gold Rush Decade in San Francisco.* New York: Burt Franklin, 1970.

Gailey, Alan. *Irish Folk Drama.* Cork: Mercier Press, 1969.

Gelb, Arthur. "Wanted: 70,000 Playgoing Intellectuals." *New York Times,* 15 Apr. 1956, sec. 2, pp. 1, 3.

Gilroy, Frank. *The Subject Was Roses.* New York: Random House, 1965.

Gregory, Lady Augusta. *Our Irish Theatre.* 1913. Reprint, New York: Oxford Univ. Press; Gerrards Cross: Colin Smythe, 1972.

Grene, Nicholas. *The Politics of Irish Drama: Plays in Context from Boucicault to Friel.* Cambridge: Cambridge Univ. Press, 1999.

Grene, Nicholas, and Chris Morash, eds. "Introduction: Theatre and Diaspora." *Irish Theatre on Tour.* Dublin: Carysfort Press, 2005.

Gussow, Mel. "Beckett, as a Beckettian, Isn't Always the Purist." *New York Times,* 16 Nov. 1988, C21, C26.

Hall, Peter. "Godot Almighty." *Guardian,* 24 Aug. 2005.

Harrington, John P. "Irish Theater." In *An Encyclopedia of the Irish in America.* Ed. Michael Glazier. South Bend, Ind.: Notre Dame Univ. Press, 1990, 900.

———. "The Abbey in America: The Real Thing." *Irish Theatre on Tour.* Ed. Nicholas Grene and Chris Morash. Dublin: Carysfort Press, 2005, 35–50.

Hogan, Robert. *Dion Boucicault.* New York: Twayne Publishers, 1969.

Howard, Bronson. "Old and New World Audiences." *Celtic Monthly*, Dec. 1874, 273–76.

Howells, William Dean. "Editor's Study." *Harper's*, July 1886, 315–16.

Hughes, Declan. "Who the Hell Do We Think We Still Are? Reflections on Irish Theater and Identity." In *Theater Stuff: Critical Essays on Contemporary Irish Theater*. Ed. Eamonn Jordan. Dublin: Carysfort Press, 2000, 8–15.

"Irish Historic Pageant in New York." *Outlook* 104 (1913): 258–59.

J. B. "Representation or Misrepresentation." *Irish World*, 9 Jan. 1875, 6.

Jefferson, Joseph. *Autobiography of Joseph Jefferson*. Ed. Alan S. Downer. 1890. Reprint, Cambridge, Mass.: Harvard Univ. Press, 1964.

Kahn, E. J. *The Merry Partners: The Age and Stage of Harrigan and Hart*. New York: Random House, 1955.

Kershner, Jim. "Capturing Hostages' Psychological Make-up." *Spokesman Review*, 8 Sept. 2005.

Knowlson, James. *Damned to Fame: The Life of Samuel Beckett*. New York: Simon and Schuster, 1996.

Kosok, Heinz. "The Image of Ireland in Nineteenth-Century Drama." *Perspectives of Irish Drama and Theater*. Ed. Jaqueline Genet and Richard Allen Cave. Irish Literary Studies 33. Maryland: Barnes and Noble Books, 1991, 50–67.

Krause, David, ed. *The Dolmen Boucicault*. Dublin: Dolmen Press, 1963.

———. *The Profane Book of Irish Comedy*. Ithaca, N.Y.: Cornell Univ. Press, 1982.

Krieg, Joann. *Whitman and the Irish*. Iowa City: Univ. of Iowa Press, 2000.

Lamb, E. "The Irish Drama." *Irish World*, 9 Jan. 1875, 6.

Lojek, Helen. "Watching Over Frank McGuinness's Stereotypes." *Modern Drama* 38 (1995): 348–61.

Love, Harold, ed. *The Australian Stage: A Documentary History*. Sydney: New South Wales Press in association with Australian Theater Studies Centre, School of Drama, Univ. of New South Wales, 1984.

Mac Liammóir, Micheál. *An Oscar of No Importance*. London: Heinemann, 1968.

———. *Theater in Ireland*. Rev. ed. Dublin: At the Sign of the Three Candles, 1964.

MacNeill, Máire. *The Festival of Lughnasa*. London: Oxford Univ. Press, 1962.

Maryoga, Margaret G. *A Short History of the American Drama*. New York: Dodd, Mead and Co., 1943.

McCarten, John. "Turbid Aquarium." *New Yorker*, 25 Mar. 1961, 114.

McDiarmid, Lucy. "A Box for Wilfrid Blunt." *PMLA* 120, no. 1 (Jan. 2005): 163–80.

———. *The Irish Art of Controversy*. Ithaca: Cornell Univ. Press, 2005.

McGuinness, Frank. *Someone Who'll Watch Over Me*. London: Faber and Faber, 1992.

McMahon, Eileen. "The Irish-American Press." *The Ethnic Press in the United States.* Ed. Sally M. Miller. Westport, Conn.: Greenwood Press, 1987, 177–90.

McPherson, Conor. "Chronicles of the Human Heart." *Guardian,* 1 Mar. 2005.

M. H. F. "Boucicault's Home." *Celtic Monthly,* Jan. 1879, 73.

Miller, Kerby A. *Emigrants and Exiles: Ireland and the Irish Exodus to North America.* New York: Oxford Univ. Press, 1985.

Miller, Sally M., ed. *The Ethnic Press in the United States.* Westport, Conn.: Greenwood Press, 1987.

Molin, Sven Eric, and Robin Goodfellowe. "Nationalism on the Dublin Stage." *Éire-Ireland* 21, no. 3 (1986): 135–38.

Moloney, Mick. *McNally's Row of Flats: Irish American Songs of Old New York by Harrigan and Braham.* Nashville, Tenn.: Compass Records, 2006.

Moody, Richard. *Ned Harrigan: From Corlears Hook to Herald Square.* New York: Nelson Hall, 1980.

Murphy, Maureen. "Irish-American Theater." *Ethnic Theater in the United States.* Ed. Maxine Schwartz Seller. Westport, Conn.: Greenwood Press, 1983, 221–37.

Murray, Christopher. "'Recording Tremors': Friel's *Dancing at Lughnasa* and the Uses of Tradition." Ed. William Kerwin. *Brian Friel: A Casebook.* New York: Garland Publishing, 1997.

Neumann, Frederick. Interview. *Beckett Remembering Beckett: A Centenary Celebration.* Ed. James Knowlson and Elizabeth Knowlson. New York: Arcade Publishing, 2006, 241–54.

"New Irish Drama, The." Review of *The Colleen Bawn. Irish-American,* 21 Apr. 1860, 2.

Nicholson, Asenath. *Ireland's Welcome to the Stranger, or Excursions Through Ireland in 1844.* Ed. Maureen Murphy. Dublin: Lilliput Press, 2004.

Niehaus, Earl F. *The Irish in New Orleans, 1800–1860.* Baton Rouge: Louisiana State Univ. Press, 1965.

Notes. *Irish-American,* 15 Feb. 1879, 6.

O'Daily, John. "Theatrical Misrepresentations of Ireland." *Irish World,* 19 Dec. 1874, 3.

Odell, George C. D. *Annals of the New York Stage,* vol. 9 (1870–1875). New York: Columbia Univ. Press, 1937.

O'Flatharta, Antoine. *Grásta I Meiriceá.* Indreabhán: Cló Iar-Chonnachta, 1990.

O'Haire, Patricia. "Beckett Still Writing, Still Waiting." *New York Daily News,* 3 Nov. 1988.

Ó Danachair, Caoimhín. *A Bibliography of Irish Ethnology and Folk Tradition.* Dublin: Mercier Press, 1977.

Ó hAodha, Micheál. *The Importance of Being Micheál: A Portrait of Mac Liammóir.* Dingle, Kerry: Brandon, 1990).

O'Neill, Eugene. *Long Day's Journey Into Night*. New Haven: Yale Univ. Press, 1956.

O'Súilleabháin, Amhlaoibh. *Cín Lae Amhlaiobh*. Baile Átha Cliath: An Clómhar, 1970.

O'Súilleabháin, Seán. *Irish Wake Amusements*. Cork: Mercier Press, 1967.

O'Toole, Fintan. *Critical Moments*. Dublin: Carysfort Press, 2003.

———. "Irish Theater: The State of the Art." *Theater Stuff: Critical Essays on Contemporary Irish Theater*. Ed. Eamonn Jordan. Dublin: Carysfort Press, 2000, 47–58.

———. "Marking Time: From Making History to Dancing at Lughnasa." Alan J. Peacock, ed. *The Achievement of Brian Friel*. Gerrards Cross: Colin Smythe, 1997, 202–14.

———. "Playing to a New World Order." *Irish Times,* 12 Dec. 2005. http://www.irishtimes.com.

———. "The Death of the Playwright." *Irish Times,* 21 Oct. 2005. http://www.irishtimes.com.

———. *The Ex-Isle of Ireland*. Dublin: New Island Books, 1997.

Park, Robert E. *The Immigrant Press and Its Control*. New York: Harper and Brother, 1922.

Pethica, James, ed. *Collaborative One-Act Plays, 1901–1903*. Ithaca: Cornell Univ. Press, 2007.

Plocher, Ryan. "In Godot, Existential Despair Can Be Hilarious." *Emory Wheel,* 31 Jan. 2006. http://www.emorywheel.com/detail.php?n=18532.

Poe, Tom G. "Secrets, Lies and Cold War Politics: 'Making Sense' of Otto Preminger's *Advise and Consent*." *Film History* 8 (1996): 332–45.

Portaniere, Michael, and Matthew Murray. "Second to Nun: *Doubt* Wins Pulitzer Prize." *Theatre News,* 4 Apr. 2005. http://www.theatermania.com/content/news.cfm/story/5867.

Preston, Katherine K., ed. *Irish American Theatre:* The Mulligan Guard Ball *and* Reilly and the Four Hundred. New York: Garland Publishing, 1994.

Quinlivan, Patrick J. "Hunting the Fenians: Problems in the Historiography of a Secret Organization." *The Creative Migrant*. Ed. Patrick O'Sullivan. London: Leicester Univ. Press, 1994, 133–54.

Raleigh, John Henry. "O'Neill's *Long Day's Journey into Night* and New England Irish-Catholicism." *O'Neill: A Collection of Critical Essays*. Ed. John Gassner. Englewood Cliffs: Prentice Hall, 1964, 124–41.

"Response to Letter of Dion Boucicault." *Irish World,* 6 Feb. 1875, 6.

Rexroth, Kenneth. "Samuel Beckett and the Importance of Waiting." *Bird in the Bush: Obvious Essays*. New York: New Directions, 1959. Reprint, http://www.bopsecrets.org/rexroth/essays/beckett.htm.

Rich, Frank. *"Someone Who'll Watch Over Me:* Coping with Incarceration, or The Lighter Side of Beirut." *New York Times,* 26 Nov. 1992, C13.

Richardson, Gary A. "The Greening of America: The Cultural Business of Dion Boucicault's *The Shaughraun." American Drama,* Spring 1994, 1.

Roche, Anthony. "Against Nostalgia: The Year in Irish Theater, 1989." *Éire-Ireland* 24, no. 4 (1989): 114.

———. "Contemporary Irish Drama in English, 1940–2000." In *The Cambridge History of Irish Literature,* vol. 2. Ed. Margaret Kelleher and Philip O'Leary. Cambridge: Cambridge Univ. Press, 2006, 478–530.

Rodechko, James Paul. *A Case Study of Irish-American Journalism, 1870 1913.* New York: Arno Press, 1976.

Ryan, Phyllis. *The Company I Kept.* Dublin: Town House, 1996.

Schneider, Alan. *Entrances: An American Director's Journey.* New York: Limelight Editions, 1987.

Sharp, William. *A History of the Diocese of Brooklyn, 1853–1953.* New York: Fordham Univ. Press, 1954.

Sinfield, Alan. *The Wilde Century.* London: Cassell, 1994.

"Sir George Tallis Looks Back." *Melbourne Herald,* 13 Nov. 1931.

Skempton, Howard. "Beckett as Librettist." *Music and Musicians,* May 1977; http://www.cnvill.net/mfskmptn.htm.

Smith, Patsy Adam. *Victorian and Edwardian Melbourne from Old Photographs.* Sydney: John Ferguson, 1979.

Stephens, A. G., ed. *The J.C. Williamson Memorial: With Valedictory Notices from Partners or Associates, Portraits and Addenda.* Sydney: The Bookfellow, 1913.

Sullivan, Algernon S. "A Testimonial to Dion Boucicault." *Irish World,* 20 Feb. 1875: 6.

Tallis, Michael, and Joan Tallis. *The Silent Showman: Sir George Tallis, The Man Behind the World's Largest Entertainment Organization of the 1920s.* Kent Town, South Australia: Wakefield Press, 1999.

Turner, Henry Gyles. *A History of the Colony of Victoria: From Its Discovery to Its Absorption into the Commonwealth of Australia in Two Volumes.* 1904. Reprint. Melbourne: Heritage Publications, 1973.

Van Hulle, Dirk. *Beckett the European.* Tallahassee: Journal of Beckett Studies Books, 2005, 1–9.

Walsh, Townsend. *The Career of Dion Boucicault.* New York: Dunlap Society, 1915.

Walshe, Éibhear. "Sodom and Begorrah, or Game to the Last." *Sex, Nation and Dissent.* Ed. Éibhear Walshe. Cork: Cork Univ. Press, 1997.

Watt, Stephen M. "Boucicault and Whitbread: The Dublin Stage at the End of the Nineteenth Century." *Éire-Ireland* 18, no. 3 (1983): 23–53.

———. "Nationalism on the Dublin Stage: A Postscript." *Éire-Ireland* 21, no. 4 (1986): 137–41.

Welch, Robert. *The Abbey Theatre, 1899–1999.* Oxford: Oxford Univ. Press, 1999.

White, Victoria. "Towards a Post-Feminism?" *Theatre Ireland* 18 (Apr. June 1989): 33–35.

Whitman, Walt. "Song of Myself." *Leaves of Grass: Inclusive Edition.* New York: Doubleday, Doran, 1928.

Williams, Tennessee. *The Glass Menagerie.* New York: New Directions, 1970.

Winer, Linda. "A Look at Hostages, Very Neat and Tidy." *Newsday,* 24 Nov. 1992, 39.

Witchell, Alex. "Life May be a Madness, But It's Also a Poem." *New York Times,* 17 Oct. 1993, sec. 2, p. 5.

Yeats, W. B. *The Collected Plays of W. B. Yeats.* 1934. Reprint, New York: Macmillan, 1976.

Index